W9-CFZ-191

FLORIDA STATE
UNIVERSITY LIBRARIES

OCT 10 1994

TALLAHASSEE, FLORIDA

THE SERVICE/QUALITY SOLUTION

Using Service Management to
Gain Competitive Advantage

Catch a fish for a man and
he is fed for a day;

Teach him to fish and
he is fed for life.

Unknown

THE SERVICE/QUALITY SOLUTION

Using Service Management to Gain Competitive Advantage

David A. Collier

ASQC Quality Press
Milwaukee, Wisconsin

IRWIN
Professional Publishing

Burr Ridge, Illinois
New York, New York

*To Cindy, Christopher, and Thomas
and Dot and Ham*

© RICHARD D. IRWIN, INC., 1994

All rights reserved. No part of this publication may be
reproduced, stored in a retrieval system, or transmitted,
in any form or by any means, electronic, mechanical,
photocopying, recording, or otherwise, without the prior
written permission of the publisher.

This publication is designed to provide accurate and
authoritative information in regard to the subject matter
covered. It is sold with the understanding that neither the
author or the publisher is engaged in rendering legal, accounting,
or other professional service. If legal advice or other expert
assistance is required, the services of a competent professional
person should be sought.

*From a Declaration of Principles jointly adopted by a Committee
of the American Bar Association and a Committee of Publishers.*

Sponsoring editor: Jean Marie Geracie
Project editor: Karen M. Smith
Production manager: Jon Christopher
Designer: Mercedes Santos
Art manager: Kim Meriwether
Art studio: Arcata Graphics
Compositor: Alexander Graphics
Typeface: 10.5/12 Times Roman
Printer: Book Press, Inc.

ASQC Quality Press
   Acquisitions editor: Susan Westergard
   Marketing administrator: Mark Olson
   Production editor: Annette Wall

Library of Congress Cataloging-in-Publication Data

Collier, David A.
   The service/quality solution : using service management to gain
competitive advantage / David A. Collier.
       p.   cm.
   Includes bibliographical references and index.
   ISBN 1-55623-753-7
   1. Customer service—United States—Management.   2. Service
industries—United States—Quality control.   I. Title.
HF5415.5.C62   1994
658.8'12—dc20   93–41421

Printed in the United States of America
1 2 3 4 5 6 7 8 9 0 BP 1 0 9 8 7 6 5 4

 ASQC
Quality Press
611 East Wisconsin Avenue
Milwaukee, WI 53202

Preface

The Service/Quality Solution is about a philosophy and style of management and the challenges that organizations face in using service/quality to gain competitive advantage. The solution requires new paradigms, terms, visions, ways of ·organizing and doing work, and ways of thinking and acting. For example, a product-producing perspective doesn't work well in an information- and service-providing business. Services are unique performances between a customer (buyer) and a service provider (seller). Services are acted out, usually with the customer participating; they are not built in the traditional sense. After a service encounter is completed, it vanishes forever. Bundling and unbundling services with goods create new challenges for humankind.

Every major shift in human orientation is based first on a new set of paradigms and innovative ways of thinking. Do we hunt, fish, farm, build, perform, informate, or servomate? Each paradigm shift has been a key challenge for humankind over the millennium. Paradigm pioneers keep presenting their ideas. At first no one listens, but eventually people restructure their thinking and their work. Service management, and its approach to service/quality performance, is part of this restructuring.

This book presents many service management examples from many sources. They are all important—even the ones you disagree with—and they challenge obsolete business thinking. The implications of some of these simple service management truths are far reaching. Service management can help humankind move away from a goods-producing perspective and the industrial revolutions of the past to a service-providing perspective and the Servomation Age. The Servomation Age is a combination of the service revolution and the information age.

The Service/Quality Solution has three general objectives. The first is to help people make the transition from a product-perspective to a service management- and consumer benefit package-perspective. A second objective is to define and present a service management approach to building quality and competitive advantage. The third objective is to publicize service/quality challenges and solutions. The focus here is on the service/quality solution in the United States, but organizations worldwide can apply the ideas in this book to their businesses.

The challenge for American companies is to sustain and extend their leadership in using service/quality as a competitive weapon in the marketplace. Or will American companies, especially service-providing companies, lose their lead as has happened in some U.S. goods-producing industries? This is a key message of the Service/Quality Solution.

By the time the reader reaches the sections of the book on service/quality management, interlinking, and service encounters, he or she should be thinking service management, not service marketing or service operations or some other narrow view of designing, creating, and completing service encounters. The service management way of thinking is how the customer views the goods and/or service bundle. This way of thinking should also be a top management viewpoint that should permeate the organization to reach all managers, supervisors, and employees. Thus, everyone should be exposed to a service management approach to service/quality, regardless of where they reside within the organization.

The book uses vignettes and diagrams to help highlight key points. At the same time, it conveys—and expands on—important ideas, approaches, and a philosophy of management. Therefore, it is a hybrid type of book—part professional book and part textbook. The book uses a service management approach and also provides a glimpse of the future.

Above all, we must not lose sight of the overall game we are in—the incredibly tough game of global economic competition. Service management and service/quality are serious business. They are key contributors to your standard of living, the availability of good jobs, trade and financial performance, and national well-being.

Welcome to the exciting management challenge of the 1990s and beyond: How to use services and a service management approach to gain competitive advantage.

David A. Collier

Acknowledgments

To the many students, faculty, and managers who helped me understand service management and service/quality, its implications, and how to apply it to build quality and competitive advantage—thank you. Several anonymous book reviewers were also helpful in improving earlier drafts of this book. Their insights and suggestions are appreciated.

Finally, I want to thank my wife, Cindy, and my two young sons, Christopher and Thomas. Many long hours of work were involved in researching and writing this book and seeing it to completion. Meanwhile, little Christopher and Thomas interrupted me frequently to remind me of the secondary importance of this book compared to the twinkle in their eyes.

D. A. C.

Contents

Prologue

Lessons from the Past

"They think safety is first and quality is second. If they achieve perfection on these two, then they say productivity increases, costs decrease, and profits go up," commented a 30-year veteran manager of quality. He had worked for a once-proud American Fortune 500 company his entire career. His physical appearance showed the wear and tear of those years—the hair was almost gone, dark sagging circles under his eyes, and a big six-foot three-inch frame that seemed tired. His mannerisms included a shrug, usually coinciding with whenever he said the word "they."

He began his presentation with how the company and its management viewed quality in the 1960s and how those views had changed over the years. He often noted during his talk that most of his ideas were wrong. By 1980, his company had closed 12 major facilities and fired over 50,000 American workers. He related to the audience a story in which American management was so desperate that its focus was "how to cut material and value out of the product and customer service, without the customer knowing it or without having to reduce the price. "But," he said, "the company was saved."

In the 1980s, "they" bought his entire company. He stated that "it was only when 'they' redefined the business, provided a new sense of direction, and defined the role of product and service quality that the answers seemed so simple and correct."

This manager and his company had fought in the global marketplace and lost. His comments, mannerisms, and physical appearance all seemed so sad. Likewise, his American audience seemed uncomfortable. His stated message to the audience was that safety and quality are the number one and number two priorities, yet the subliminal, and much more powerful, message was that this once-decisive and once-proud American manager had lost his confidence and sense of direction, and now sought directions from "them."

The identity of this former American corporation, or who "they" are, is not important. There will be other American companies that forget how to produce world-class products and services, and thus, repeat this experience. Likewise, "they" will change over time.

Who will be next?[1] Sears? Mellon Bank? Humana? ITT? Travelers? Steinway? Columbia Pictures? Eastern Airlines? Holiday Inns? Texas Instruments?

1

Safeway Stores? Bank of America? Hyatt Hotels? Burger King? General Motors? New York Stock Exchange?

Can American managers respond to the challenges of the 21st century? In the Servomation Age—a combination of the service revolution and the information age—will American organizations rise to the occasion and maintain their lead in service/quality performance or lose their current competitive advantage in providing world class services?

I

INTRODUCTION

Do not follow where the path may lead. Go instead where there is no path and leave a trail.

Unknown

Chapter One

Service/Quality Challenges

T he champion of capitalism, the United States of America, must now compete against its former students, and some energetic new ones. The stage is set for intense global economic competition.

What will be the focus of economic competition in the new world order? My answer is service/quality performance. The term *service/quality* means excelling at services and quality, and any combination of the two.

This book begins with the big picture. Chapter 1 defines three premises and eight challenges about service/quality. These premises and challenges outline the environment in which solutions must be found. Chapters 2 to 16 define service management and its approach to solutions.

The book ends with a service encounter between a buyer (customer) and seller (service provider). A *service encounter* is defined as one or more moments of truth. A *moment of truth*, as first defined by Mr. Jan Carlzon, CEO of Scandinavian Airlines Systems, is any episode, transaction, or experience in which a customer comes into contact with any aspect of the service delivery system, however remote, and thereby has an opportunity to form an impression.[1] All the activities and resources of a company exist to create and deliver service encounters better than do competitors.

In their article "Will Services Follow Manufacturing into Decline," Quinn and Gagnon conclude that "If service industries are properly nurtured, they will grow and generate much of America's future wealth. If they are misunderstood, disdained, or mismanaged, the same forces that led to the decline of US manufacturing stand ready to cut them to pieces. With some 70 percent of the US economy already in services—not including the three-fourths of all manufacturing costs that represent support services—the stakes are immense. It can happen here."[2]

A 1993 article in *The Wall Street Journal*, titled "US Service Exports Are Growing Rapidly, But Almost Unnoticed," highlighted the economic strength of US services trade.[3] It reported that the US merchandise deficit in 1992 was $96 billion and was over $100 billion in seven of the past nine years. Images of jobs lost and unfair trade practices arise in the minds of many Americans when numbers such as these are widely reported in the press. As the article states,

---

Challenge 1

The Service/Quality Challenge

A challenge for American companies is, Will they sustain and extend their leadership in using service/quality as a competitive weapon in the marketplace? Or will American companies, especially service-providing companies, lose their lead, as happened in some US goods-producing industries?

"But almost unnoticed, US companies that sell services, rather than raw materials or manufactured goods, racked up a $59 billion trade surplus last year, a nearly fivefold increase from 1986. . . . It becomes clear that the United States has an ace-in-the-hole in world trade. . . . Few people know that last year the United States ran a *surplus in services with Japan* totaling $14 billion . . . Some experts believe that the recently reported $167 billion in [total] services exports for 1992 may be understated by at least 20 percent."[4]

So, how well prepared and positioned is America to meet the service/quality challenge in the 21st century? The debate on this question is spirited. Example reforms mentioned to improve chances of the United States maintaining its lead in service-related businesses include: (1) more government–private enterprise cooperation, (2) reducing American's defense budget and reallocating the peace dividend, (3) removing or reducing worldwide trade barriers, (4) reducing the federal budget deficit, (5) emphasizing real productivity improvements in creating goods and services with less emphasis on financial gimmicks such as leveraged buyouts, and (6) improving a weak US educational system.

Solutions to these challenges will improve US international competitiveness. But the underlying challenge is one of producing goods and providing services to worldwide markets better than do all competitors. Service/quality is America's ace-in-the-hole. The question is whether American organizations can maintain their lead in service/quality expertise? Or will Japan and other international competitors do it again, and leave many American workers out of a job and bewildered as to what to do next.

Some American businesses are standards of service/quality excellence around the world. American Airlines, American Express, AT&T, Federal Express, Marriott, McDonald's, Wal-Mart, and Xerox exemplify excellent service/quality performance. But American companies have no greater inherent advantage in providing services such as those in banking, airlines, or hotels than they once had in producing televisions, VCRs, or automobiles. America can lose the service/quality challenge, much like it lost some manufacturing challenges. A fragmented or half-hearted approach has the same inherent disadvantages for US service-providing organizations that it had for some US goods-producing firms.

And even though American nameplate service companies are embracing service/quality improvement, the overall effort in service industries is low. For example, the Gunneson Group International, Inc., a quality consulting company reports that only 10 percent of American service companies have any kind of quality program. The Gunneson Group predicts that by the year 2000, perhaps 70 percent of those with more than 500 employees will adopt a formal quality improvement initiative.[5]

There is no organization of human endeavor that is untouched by this service/quality challenge. For example, government, corporations, farms, unions, churches, associations, hospitals, and the military—all have a stake in the Service/Quality Challenge. This challenge is also more complicated than previous economic challenges because (1) service, information, entertainment, time, and people play greater roles, while products are relatively less important, and (2) powerful global competitors add a new dimension to economic competition.

The Service/Quality Solution shows how to compete in a variety of domestic and global markets, using service/quality performance to differentiate one's goods and services from competitors' and thereby gain competitive advantage. It is the next economic phase beyond that of improving product quality, and it includes the information-, entertainment-, and service-content of what customers value, experience, and buy. Services are slowly replacing goods as the centerpiece of what is valued in the marketplace.

Customers eventually figure out the best value in the marketplace. Value is some combination of customer satisfaction and price. Customer satisfaction is really measuring the intent to purchase again and the high probability the satisfied customer will recommend the good or service to other potential customers.

Before we examine some of the issues surrounding service/quality challenges, let's briefly review where are the world markets and who are the international competitors.

THE MARKETPLACE

A good market is one where the population or a major segment of the population is large and growing. Also, for a good market opportunity to exist, customers must possess the ability to pay for goods and services. Table 1–1 shows the 32 most populous countries in the world and estimates of their gross domestic product per capita.

Many market opportunities stand out in Table 1–1. First, Australia, Canada, France, Germany, Italy, Japan, New Zealand, Spain, the United Kingdom, and the United States all show high average gross domestic product (GDP) per capita. Algeria, Brazil, Mexico, South Africa, Turkey, the former USSR, and Venezuela also are shown to be promising market opportunities. Other good market opportunities that do not have enough total population to be listed in Table 1–1

TABLE 1–1
Where Are the Markets?

Country	1989 GDP ($ millions)	1989 Per Capita ($)	2010 Population (thousands)
Africa			
Nigeria	$ 72,434	$ 711	213,363
Ethiopia	4,638	106	96,385
S. Africa	86,557	2,622	66,369
Zaire	7,014	214	64,467
South America			
Brazil	289,119	2,044	213,916
Colombia	41,386	1,382	44,119
Argentina	59,828	1,921	39,885
Peru	19,458	939	30,885
Venezuela	59,229	3,242	29,697
North America			
United States	3,292,724	13,526	282,037
Mexico	207,944	2,504	131,092
Canada	324,623	12,548	29,423
Asia			
China	554,676	519	1,398,189
India	246,307	307	1,166,146
Indonesia	96,611	561	261,035
Japan	1,369,685	11,235	132,517
Pakistan	44,188	398	188,961
			continued

include Hong Kong, South Korea, Taiwan, and Singapore (the Four Tigers of Far East Asia), plus Czechoslovakia and Hungary.

Of course, even in countries with low average per capita income, such as India and China, there may be segments of the population that have the ability to pay. The data in Table 1–1 are for illustration purposes only. Obviously, much more detailed market analysis is necessary to explore potential market opportunities. The point is that a global view of markets is essential in today's economic competition.

Many country-specific political and economic uncertainties also are evident today. For example, the former Soviet Union and Eastern European countries are beginning an economic renaissance. China may follow in their path. A unified European market with few import/export trade regulations and restrictions is a mega-attractive market opportunity.

Today, a traditional mass market is often fragmented into many market niches. Markets are now consumer driven, not company driven. Technology is

TABLE 1–1 *(concluded)*

Country	1989 GDP ($ millions)	1989 Per Capita ($)	2010 Population (thousands)
Europe			
West Germany	$ 901,920	$14,831	58,799
Italy	523,304	9,142	58,124
United Kingdom	629,807	11,061	57,379
France	746,918	13,435	58,131
Spain	245,109	6,299	42,394
Poland	58,237	1,543	41,392
Near East and North Africa			
Turkey	82,116	1,564	80,481
Egypt	38,436	766	84,129
Morocco	19,316	829	40,816
Algeria	56,023	2,425	41,615
Iraq	30,194	1,770	38,047
Ocenania			
Australia	195,941	12,123	20,032
New Guinea	3,043	822	5,805
New Zealand	26,630	8,062	3,802
Former USSR	1,132,635	4,024	334,004
World (totals)	$13.4 trillion		7,255 million

Sources: 1989 gross domestic product (GDP) and per capita data from *Industry and Development, Global Report 1989/90*, United Nations Industrial Development Organization (UNIDO), Vienna, 1990. GDP values originate from national account statistics in 1980 constant prices. 2010 population data from *World Population Profile: 1989*, U.S. Department of Commerce, Bureau of the Census (issued September 1989).

also providing the capability to customize goods and services to individuals—the so-called *mass customized market* where each market is a small group or even a single customer.

One hotel chain at the high quality end of the lodging industry, for example, keeps guest profiles on over 250,000 hotel guests. Each guest profile documents the guest's preferences for everything from chocolate chip cookies to seating preferences in the dining room. The hotel chain is following a service strategy of mass customization by individual.

The US cable television industry is another example of mass customization. When US customers are offered hundreds of television channels, we leave the age of broadcasting and enter the age of narrowcasting. Small niche markets and targeted advertising become the way to do business. With a few satellites, each niche market can be worldwide.

Challenge 2

Find or Create Market Opportunities Using Service/Quality as a Key Differentiator

Where are the best market opportunities worldwide? What role should service/quality play in becoming a leader in each market?

The rapid exchange of technology and information also provides companies with many market opportunities that open and close quickly. Some markets are born, grow, and die all within a year. This technical and logistical capability will allow companies to segment markets across nations and launch new goods and services in several global markets simultaneously. Global market segmentation with product life cycles of several weeks or months is where global economic competition is headed. In Chapter 6, we examine how services can be used as a part of such a time-based competitive strategy.

What are the implications of these new market opportunities and system capabilities? Never in modern history have so many market opportunities become accessible to free enterprise companies. Never has technology been so fast and far-reaching. Never has American service/quality and information technology expertise been better positioned to take advantage of this opportunity.

Services that complement a primary good can lead to competitive advantage for world-class manufacturing firms. Supporting services that complement a primary service can lead to competitive advantage for world-class service firms. Many global competitors are both world-class manufacturers and service firms. Understanding the role of service/quality, and how it can be bundled to goods is critical to long-term marketplace success.

Although this book focuses on the service/quality aspects of consumer benefit packages (to be defined shortly), product features and performance are obviously important for marketplace success. How Reebok shoes, Revco pharmaceuticals, Benetton sweaters, or Apple computers are packaged and sold all depends on world-class product features and quality. But product quality and features frequently become the qualifier to be in the market.

When technical/product parity exists in the customer's mind or the customer simply doesn't have the opportunity or expertise to evaluate technical/product quality, service/quality performance leaps to center stage. Service/quality becomes the order winner—the primary differentiator in the customer's mind. Goods are becoming of secondary importance relative to services! That's right, think services first, then goods. Not vice versa. Service's dominance over goods is a difficult idea for product-mentality people to embrace. This book tries to help people make the transition, to service dominant paradigms of management.

How to define and configure goods and services into world class consumer benefit packages (CBPs) is the subject of Chapter 4. Chapters 5 and 6 offer alternative paradigms of service strategy that provide a service management framework for management decision making. Those three chapters, Part II of this book, define *consumer benefit package management*, which is a combination of consumer benefit package definition, design, and service strategy.

THE COMPETITORS

The world's 50 largest publicly held companies, based on *Business Week's* 1993 Global 1,000 are summarized as follows. The United States has 23 companies in the top 50, Britain has 4, Germany has 1, the Netherlands/Britain 2, Switzerland has 2, and Japan has the remaining 18.[6] The rankings are based on market value and include both goods-producing and service-providing companies. Nippon Telegraph & Telephone of Japan leads the list with a market value of $140.5 billion. American Telephone & Telegraph is ranked second with a market value of $82.4 billion. Minnesota Mining & Manufacturing is ranked 48th with a market value of $24.7 billion and Bell Atlantic 51st with a market value of $23.3 billion.

Table 1–2 lists the top 10 companies by major service industry group ranked by sales or assets in *Fortune's 1993 Global Service 500*. Here are companies that will shape global service industries. For example, no US commercial bank is in the top 10, as Table 1–2 shows. Citicorp is the largest US commercial bank, with $214 billion in assets, and ranked 27th by *Fortune*. BankAmerica Corporation is the next largest US commercial bank with $180 billion in assets and ranked 32nd. The service/quality challenge in global commercial banking is going on now.

The United States leads the *1993 Global Service 500* with 135 companies, Japan has 128; Germany, 45; Britain, 42; France, 33; Canada, 18; Spain, 16; Italy, 15; Sweden, 9; Switzerland. 15; Netherlands, 11; and Australia 6. Table 1–3 shows the largest US service firms by number of employees. Some of these US jobs, and other service-related jobs, are at risk one way or another.

These large companies are shaping markets, alliances, industries, and global economic competition. How well or poorly they use service/quality to gain competitive advantage is critical to their marketplace success. Each target market and industry requires different definitions and uses of service/quality to gain competitive advantage. The race for service/quality supremacy has begun.

As pointed out in an article in *Fortune* entitled "America Still Reigns in Services":

> Whatever international whipping it has endured in manufacturing, the US is still out front in services. Last year American companies peddled an estimated $160 billion of ads, auto insurance, and other services to foreigners. Some $70 billion

TABLE 1–2
Who Are the Competitors?

	The Top 10 Ten Diversified Service Companies				The Top 10 Commercial Banking Companies		
1992	*Companies Ranked by Sales*		*Sales ($ millions)*	*1992*	*Companies Ranked by Assets*		*Assets ($ millions)*
1	Itochu (trading)	Japan	156,323	1	Dai-Ichi Kangyo Bank	Japan	493,434.0
2	Sumitomo (trading)	Japan	145,362	2	Fuji Bank	Japan	493,363.0
3	Mitsubishi (trading)	Japan	142,716	3	Sumitomo Bank	Japan	490,934.0
4	Marubeni (trading)	Japan	138,880	4	Sanwa Bank	Japan	485,032.1
5	Mitsui (trading)	Japan	137,555	5	Sakura Bank	Japan	470,814.9
6	Nissho (trading)	Japan	86,239	6	Mitsubishi Bank	Japan	460,820.6
7	AT&T (telecomm.)	U.S.	65,101	7	Norinchukin Bank	Japan	379,060.0
8	Tomen (trading)	Japan	61,847	8	Industrial Bank of Japan	Japan	370,026.4
9	Nippon T&T (telecomm.)	Japan	52,237	9	Credit Lyonnais	France	350,675.8
10	Nichimen (trading)	Japan	51,655	10	Deutsche Bank	Germany	306,586.1

	The Top 10 Retailers				The Top 10 Transportation Companies		
1992	*Companies Ranked by Sales*		*Sales ($ millions)*	*1992*	*Companies Ranked by Revenues*		*Revenues ($ millions)*
1	Sears Roebuck	U.S.	59,101.1	1	East Japan Railway	Japan	18,806.5
2	Wal-Mart Stores	U.S.	55,483.8	2	SNCF	France	17,346.7
3	Kmart	U.S.	37,724.0	3	United Parcel Service	U.S.	16,541.1
4	Tengelmann	Germany	26,744.6	4	AMR	U.S.	14,495.0
5	Ito-Yokado	Japan	24,175.3	5	Nippon Express	Japan	13,745.3
6	Rewe-Handelsgruppe	Germany	22,922.2	6	UAL	U.S.	12,889.7
7	Kroger	U.S.	22,144.6	7	Deutsche Bundesbahn	German	12,403.4
8	Carrefour	France	22,119.1	8	Air France	France	12,299.6
9	DAIEI	Japan	20,020.8	9	Lufthansa	Germany	11,074.6
10	E. Leclerc	France	19,260.4	10	Delta Air Lines	U.S.	10,836.8

	The Top 10 Diversified Financial Companies				The Top 10 Utilities		
1992	*Companies Ranked by Assets*		*Assets ($ millions)*	*1992*	*Companies Ranked by Assets*		*Assets ($ millions)*
1	AXA	France	189,976.5	1	Electricite de France	France	117,658.5
2	Federal Natl. Mortgage Assn.	U.S.	180,978.0	2	Tokyo Electric Power	Japan	107,746.2
3	ING Group	Netherlands	177,980.8	3	Deutsche Bundespost Telekom	Germany	92,609.7
4	American Express	U.S.	175,752.0	4	STET	Italy	78,107.1
5	Salomon	U.S.	159,459.0	5	Kansai Electric Power	Japan	53,091.0
6	Cie de Suez	France	145,341.1	6	France Telecom	France	48,561.6
7	Allianz Holding	Germany	126,566.6	7	Ontario Hydro	Canada	46,671.0
8	GAN	France	126,009.7	8	Chubu Electric Power.	Japan	45,805.4
9	Union Des Assurances de Paris	France	123,667.3	9	British Gas	Britain	44,014.7
10	Merrill Lynch	U.S.	107,024.2	10	GTE	U.S.	42,144.0

continued

TABLE 1–2 *(concluded)*

1992	The Top 10 Life Insurance Companies Companies Ranked by Assets		Assets ($ millions)	1992	The Top 10 Savings Institutions Companies Ranked by Assets		Assets ($ millions)
1	Nippon Life	Japan	280,939.4	1	Abbey National	Britain	108,651.6
2	Dai-Ichi Mutual Life	Japan	198,053.0	2	Halifax Building Society	Britain	93,252.9
3	Sumitomo Life	Japan	173,636.3	3	La Caixa	Spain	61,338.5
4	Prudential of America	U.S.	154,779.4	4	Nationwide Anglia Building Soc.	Britain	52,809.0
5	Meiji Mutual Life	Japan	119,037.7	5	H.F. Ahmanson	U.S.	48,140.5
6	Metropolitan Life	U.S.	118,178.3	6	Confederation Desjardins	Canada	42,291.2
7	Asahi Mutual Life	Japan	90,666.4	7	Great Western Financial Corp.	U.S.	38,439.2
8	Mitsui Mutual Life	Japan	74,510.6	8	Woolwich Buiding Society	Britain	35,197.1
9	Prudential	Britain	72,802.5	9	CT Financial Services	Canada	34,815.6
10	Yasuda Mutual Life	Japan	65,087.1	10	Caixa Geral de Depositos	Portugal	33,000.9

Source: "Fortune Guide to the Global Service 500," *FORTUNE*, August 23, 1993, pp. 159–196. © 1993 Times Inc. All rights reserved. Reprinted with permission.

was in the form of service exports, in which the US enjoys a trade surplus. While service companies as a whole took in roughly 5 percent of their revenues overseas, versus 10 percent for the manufacturing sector, many were much more outgoing. Foreign sales ranged from about 10 to 40 percent of total sales for such service stalwarts as Toys'R'Us, Fluor Corp., Electronic Data Systems, American International Group, Citicorp, and Arthur Andersen . . . More often than not, US retail bankers, hotel chains, hospitals, and mass merchandisers set the standards for efficiency and quality that foreign rivals strive to match. On the theory that the best defense is to carry the war into the enemy homeland, foreigners are attacking US service companies in their own markets. Since 1980 they have almost quadrupled their investment in service enterprises on US soil. Measured by book value, in fact, their $125 billion stake in the American service economy now exceeds US direct investment in services abroad.[7]

Some foreign competitors take a long-term view of winning in the global marketplace. For example, a Japanese firm bought several major resort hotels for a price that averages about $300,000 per hotel room. Hotel economics are terrible at this price. The Japanese firm studied the best hotel management systems in the world. It decided to hire a US firm that originally owned the hotel to run the hotel on a 10-year contract. Many Japanese managers are being trained by this American hotel management company. What will happen when the contract expires? Who will own the assets? Who will have the management expertise? Who has a long-term versus short-term viewpoint? Who will be the dominant hotel company in 10 to 20 years?

TABLE 1-3
The Biggest U.S. Service Firm Employers

Rank		1992 Number of Employees	Rank		1992 Number of Employees	Rank		1992 Number of Employees
1	Wal-Mart Stores	425,000	18	American Express	114,352	35	Federated Dept. Stores	73,000
2	Sears Roebuck	403,000	19	May Department Stores	111,000	36	Bell Atlantc	71,400
3	Kmart	356,000	20	ITT	106,000	37	Ameritech	71,300
4	American Tel. & Tel.	312,700	21	Safeway	104,900	38	Albertson's	71,000
5	United Parcel Service	267,000	22	Winn-Dixie Stores	102,000	39	Electronic Data Systems	71,000
6	Marriott	195,000	23	Prudential of America	101,600	40	Halliburton	69,200
7	J.C. Penney	192,000	24	Limited	100,700	41	Waste Management	67,275
8	Kroger	190,000	25	BellSouth	97,112	42	Hospital Corp. of Amer.	66,000
9	Dayton Hudson	170,000	26	Great Atl. & Pacific Tea	94,600	43	Humana	65,800
10	McDonald's	166,000	27	Beverly Enterprises	93,000	44	US West	63,707
11	Woolworth	143,000	28	UAL	86,100	45	Pacific Telesis Group	61,346
12	American Stores	132,712	29	Federal Express	84,162	46	Borg-Warner Security	60,400
13	GTE	131,000	30	Bankamerica Corp.	83,235	47	Walt Disney	60,000
14	ARA Group	124,000	31	Nynex	81,860	48	R. H. Macy	60,000
15	AMR	119,300	32	Citicorp	81,000	49	Southwestern Bell	59,500
16	Melville	116,000	33	Delta Air Lines	73,533	50	Walgreen	53,500
17	TW Holdings	116,000	34	Publix Super Markets	73,000		The 500 Median	8,613

Source: "Fortune's Service 500 Ranked by Performance," *FORTUNE*, May 31, 1993, pp. 242. © 1993 Times Inc. All rights reserved. Reprinted with permission.

14

COMPETING IN NEW AND GLOBAL MARKETS

How do you gain competitive advantage in each market? To help answer that question, we must understand three key premises.

Premise 1

Service/Quality Performance Is the Best Competitive Weapon

A key premise of this book is that the best way to build quality and competitive advantage in global markets, and to grow profits, is by being better than competitors in providing service/quality. Excellent service/quality performance, tailored to local markets and cultures, and even individual customers, is the best way to differentiate one's consumer benefit package(s) from those of competitors. The old adage *Think globally but act locally* is even more true for using services as a strategic weapon. *Excelling at service/quality is also the toughest competitive strategy to implement and the most difficult for your competitors to duplicate.*

One term that must be understood early in this book is *consumer benefit package*. Chapter 4 will define consumer benefit package (CBP) and employee benefit package (EBP) in detail. For now we shall rely on the following definition of a CBP:

> A *consumer (or customer) benefit package (CBP)* is a clearly defined set of tangible (goods-content) and intangible (service-content) attributes the customer recognizes, pays for, uses, and/or experiences. The term *benefit package* is broader than either *product package* or *service package*. A CBP is some combination of goods and services configured in a certain way. It includes the purchase of a primary good with supporting goods and/or services, or of a primary service with supporting goods and/or services.

For example, a primary good complemented by supporting services might be the purchase of a particular automobile partly because of a superior repair service, a good warranty, and a friendly, trustworthy salesperson. The services are wrapped around the good.

Conversely, personal checkbook service is a primary service supported by facilitating goods (a monthly account statement, the checkbook itself) and services (e.g., customer service hotline). Here, supporting services are wrapped around a primary service. Also, a CBP can be a bundle of services (travel agency, credit cards, hotel, restaurants, airlines, entertainment, etc.) as for a vacation. Many other CBP configurations are possible.

A consumer benefit package (CBP) is different from an employee benefit package (EBP) only in terms of who is the ultimate recipient or customer of the benefit package. Employees have benefit packages, so why not consumers? Customers buy CBPs, while employees produce or provide CBPs.

In this book, *product* always means goods-content (physical or tangible) attributes only. A *service* is any primary or complementary activity that does not directly produce a physical product—that is, the nongoods part of the transaction between buyer (customer) and seller (provider). Services are typically performances. Goods are consumed, while services are experienced. All of these basic service management ideas will be more fully explained in Chapters 2 and 4. A first step toward adopting a service management approach to building quality and competitive advantage is to understand its terminology.

Premise 2

Service/Quality Performance Is More Difficult to Manage Than Product/ Quality Performance

Service/quality performance is more difficult to define, measure, and consistently execute than product/quality performance.

The main reasons Premise 2 is so are:

1. Human behavior is involved in all aspects of experiencing or providing services. Products don't exhibit personalities, expectations, or cultural values, but service encounter design must consider human behavior.

2. Each service encounter is unique, never to be repeated exactly, while most products are identical.

3. A pure service package is more complicated to design, deliver, and manage than a pure product package.

4. Forecasting human behavior in a service setting is more difficult than forecasting product demand in a manufacturing setting.

5. Managing high-contact service providers requires service management skills (marketing, operations, and personal) while goods-producing jobs require a narrower range of skills or the jobs are more departmentalized.

6. Service capacity, such as available staff hours, is your inventory in a service-providing business, whereas physical inventory helps buffer all

manufacturing and materials management functions in a goods-producing business.

7. Standards of performance include more qualitative and human factors in performing a service than in producing a product.

If you believe Premise 2, then those who excel at service/quality performance develop a unique capability. Few competitors can quickly copy this capability. And, therefore, you gain and maintain competitive advantage.

Premise 3

To Truly Understand Service/Quality, One Must Truly Understand Service Management

The third and final premise of this book is that to truly understand service/quality as a competitive weapon, one must truly understand service management. Service management is the bedrock of ideals, principles, and philosophy of management upon which to base an effective service/quality improvement effort. This book is about a new way of thinking, managing, and taking action called *service management*. We should be teaching service management to all students and employees. Service management, and its approach to service/quality, is one competitive advantage US companies still enjoy.

People frequently say they understand the philosophy of service management. But in the classroom or a company setting, it often is obvious they don't. Once they begin to define the consumer benefit package and accompanying strategy or to design the service delivery process and associated service encounters or to empower frontline service providers, it's easy to identify a narrow perspective. This narrow perspective is usually a product- or functional-perspective. For example, a product-perspective follows the physical product through the process. The product's presence and movement dominates all thinking and analysis viewpoints. However, if *product parity* roughly exists "in the customer's mind," then information, entertainment, service, and the customer's perspective is what should be followed through the process.

Why do some people have such a difficult time shedding a product- or functional-perspective? There are many reasons but let's focus on just two.

First, people have been trained and educated that way. Goods-producing examples dominate teaching materials. And the majority of management techniques were founded in a product-dominated world. (Yet, four of five jobs in the

United States are in service industries.) Any shift to the service management paradigm must modify and overcome decades of product-perspective and industrial-based training. Scuba divers often say they see red beyond a depth of 50 feet of seawater but the fact is red light is absorbed very fast after passing through only 15 to 20 feet of water. What you think you see and what is there is a problem that can only be overcome by education and training.

Second, the age of management specialization encourages people to take many courses in a narrow field of study such as marketing research or purchasing or finance. This specialization supposedly is the key to a good entry level job. But later in the person's career, this same emphasis on specialization hinders their transition to practicing service management.

Challenge 3

Think Service Management

How can management and worker thinking, style, and action shift from a product- or functional-perspective to a service-management-perspective? Can this change be made quickly enough in your organization to compete in the Service and Information (Servomation) Age?

A product mentality shows up in all kinds of ways in US society and business practices. Many examples are given throughout this book of the disadvantages of thinking from a product-perspective while doing business in a service economy. Even the US government is a victim of the product-mentality disease. For example, the accuracy of US government services trade statistics is suspect. Many argue that it is more difficult to track the economic activity of consulting, waste management, accounting, medical, and banking services, for example, than that of products. Therefore, service trade statistics are viewed by many as inaccurate. As Mr. Sinai, a Boston Company economist, notes, "Information is as much a product as an automobile. But this is not the way people look at it. We are conditioned by the goods economy of yesteryear."[8]

New competitors may have an advantage here by not having to carry the excess baggage of the Second Industrial Revolution (1950s–1970s). They can simply skip several old models and styles of management founded after World War II, step over the carcass of a product-perspective, and avoid many of the barriers to thinking and practicing service management. Truly learning to think and practice service management is a paradigm shift of the highest order for many people.

TIME-BASED STRATEGIES AND INSTANTANEOUS SERVICES

All parts of a traditional organization hoard time. In fact, slow decision cycles and processes are designed into traditional organizational structures. Mechanisms such as safety lead time, extra layers of approval and vertical management, functional silos with protective barriers that inhibit coordination and speed, large consumer benefit package setup and changeover times, and annual decision, review and audit cycles are all part of the business world.

Challenge 4

Use Time-Based Competitive Strategies to Improve CBP, Process, and Service Encounter Performance

Service- and information-based processes consume the vast majority of the time it takes to get something done. Something (i.e., people, information, paper, equipment) is always waiting. Primary and supporting service- and information-based processes and service encounters offer the greatest opportunities for executing a successful time-based competitive strategy. A *time-based competitive strategy is not complete until it reaches the service encounter level.*

Time-compression and service/quality will increasingly dominate product quality as keys to competitive advantage. How you package time, information, entertainment, and service with tangible attributes (i.e., a CBP configuration) is the key to gaining competitive advantage.

No wonder actual or value-added work occurs less than five percent of the total time the consumer benefit package is in the system. The remaining time somebody or something is waiting.

Historically, this happens because time has not been used as a competitive weapon. Breaking the management paradigm concerning time will continue to cause much economic upheaval. As discussed in Chapters 6 and 7, time-compression is an immensely powerful competitive weapon that exploits the inherent weakness of traditional management models and practices. For example, the power of first-to-market and of short product life cycles for growing profits are only beginning to be understood and used.

Time is so important that it is a separate competitive priority, along with price, innovation, flexibility, product/quality, and service/quality in Chapter 5.

In the past, time and all its surrogates, such as convenience and responsiveness, could be considered a subset of other competitive priority categories. But today, the timing of service encounters and service processes are so important that time must be carefully analyzed on its own.

The challenge for management is to design flexible consumer benefit packages and delivery systems that can change quickly in response to new or revised customer requirements. The life cycle of most consumer benefit packages will be measured in hours, days, weeks or months, not years. The term *instantaneous service* reflects this change and/or increase in customer expectations for a given CBP. For example, today, people can't wait to fax almost everything—even their lunch orders. Information movement is now measured in seconds.

Personal telephones the size of a small calculator represent a new service/quality performance plateau in the telecommunications industry. This personal communication network (PCN) allows you to call a person, not a place such as an office or automobile. LiTel is testing these pocket phones and digital radio-wave-based networks. These smart systems will tie into existing local and long-distance telephone networks. Just as in *Star Trek* stories, a person-to-person communication network is expected to be in full operation in the continental United States by 2010.

The key driving forces behind rising customer expectations are technology and better process designs. Charles Schwab & Co., Inc., the world's largest discount broker, uses lower prices, convenience, speed, and customer control as centerpieces of its competitive strategy. The telephone book is full of companies with names that contain words such as instant, speedy, fast, prompt, quick, and rapid. Electronic financial services and all other information-based industries are continuing their march down the electronic learning (experience) curve or shifting to a new curve or service/quality plateau. Each step or shift sets new customer expectations and company standards of performance. Time and service/quality are two of the remaining variables in the businessperson's tool kit that have not been fully exploited.

INTERLINKING TO GAIN
COMPETITIVE ADVANTAGE

In Part V of this book, two chapters are devoted to a new competitive weapon called *interlinking*. Chapter 14 defines interlinking and the basic issues surrounding it. Chapter 15 explains the idea and methods for developing a *service/quality process map*. Also, Chapter 11 defines 16 tools of service/quality measurement and data analysis. For now, let's define interlinking.

Interlinking defines quantitatively the causal (cause and effect) relationships between external and internal performance criteria. Simple interlinking models define the relationships between two performance variables. Complex interlinking models define the relationships between more than two performance variables, sometimes in very complex ways.

External performance criteria are outside the boundaries of the organizational unit. *Internal performance criteria* are defined and measured within the organizational unit. The organizational unit can be a department or company or even an entire industry, that is, any entity that has customers. A customer is the next entity (person/department/firm) that receives, pays for, uses, or experiences the output of the service-providing or goods-producing delivery system.

Measures of internal performance focus mainly on in-house or backroom operating and marketing criteria that are hidden or decoupled from the customer or external environment. Example internal measures are the average waiting time, hours to process an application, cost per transaction, and errors per thousand transactions. Measurement can be more objective against numerical specifications. Performance indicators are typically interval measures.

Measures of external performance focus on a company's financial performance, third-party ratings of performance, and the customer's perceptions of a company's goods and services. It includes financial performance data available to the public and investors, ratings of the company or its products or services by a third party (such as Standard & Poor's bond ratings or *Consumer Reports'* product ratings), and the customer's perceptions of the company or their goods and services via marketing surveys, interviews, and the like. Measurement is often more dependent on human judgment. Performance indicators use interval, ordinal, or nominal measurement scales.

Interlinking uses this knowledge about the relationships among performance measures to formulate strategic plans, differentiate one's consumer benefit package from that of competitors', allocate resources wisely, and grow profits. In general, interlinked and information-driven companies gain competitive advantage by being systematically smarter than their competitors. They *see and predict* changes in customer satisfaction faster than competitors do. They know how internal, operational performance relates to customer satisfaction, and they act quickly to take advantage of their new insights as conditions change in the marketplace. Interlinking uses the capabilities of information technology to analyze causal relationships with the goal of winning in the marketplace. It tries to improve management decision making and intuition with smart data analysis. Interlinking is part of a quality and a time-based competitive strategy.

Figure 1–1 is a simple example of how an internal operational measure of service/quality performance is related to the customer's perception of that same service. The horizontal axis is the average hours to isolate and repair a case of customer-reported telephone line (circuit) trouble. The vertical axis of Figure 1–1 measures (as a percentage of satisfied customers) the customer's perception of service after the problem is fixed. This interlinked data indicates about a 70 percent correlation between these two (internal versus external) performance variables. Thus, as telephone repair time decreases (improves), customer satisfaction of process performance increases.

FIGURE 1-1
Interlinking Process/Internal Performance to Customer Satisfaction/External Performance

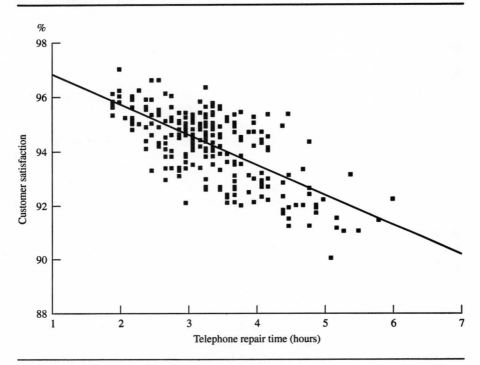

How much would it cost to gain a one-hour improvement in telephone repair processing time? How much would the customer's perception of service improve? Interlinking models have answered questions such as these.

One advantage of interlinking is to know which variables provide a good basis for decision making and which do not. For example, telephone repair time is very well correlated with the customer's perception of service. Thus, telephone repair time is a good internal performance measure for management decision making. This is a valuable insight into what process performance measure(s) drive customer satisfaction.

Other internal/process performance indicators are unrelated or not strongly related to customer satisfaction or financial performance. Some internal measures of performance can be very misleading. Many poor strategic and tactical management decisions can be traced to using the wrong criteria and measures.

Today's competitive environment no longer will tolerate inconsistent or poor management decisions based on nonexistent, inaccurate, or misleading information. Data must be scrutinized and mined for every insight that helps the organization to build quality and competitive advantage. Smart data analysis or interlinking is a necessity to compete in the Servomation Age. It is an organizational capability whose time has come.

Challenge 5

Use Interlinking to Excel at Service/Quality Performance and Gain Competitive Advantage

Data analysis paradigms and methods applicable to services must be developed that help companies build quality and competitive advantage. Interlinking can help managers design CBPs, service encounters, reward and recognition systems, and service processes better and quicker than competitors do and with less risk of marketplace failure. Interlinking can help managers segment markets and allocate process resources better. Interlinking can help reduce the organization's learning cycle and, therefore, is a form of time-based competition. Management by fact can replace management by opinion, and strengthen management and employee intuition and decision-making powers. Data analysis capabilities and information intelligence become the dominant asset in the Service and Information (Servomation) Age.

Companies spend millions of dollars on hardware and software to collect, transmit, and store vast amounts of performance data. Yet, similar amounts of money are not spent on improving people's data analysis skills and knowledge at all levels of the company. If people don't understand it, they won't use it. Basic-to-complex data analysis methods all have their place at different levels and areas of the organization. Information and information analysis are the life-blood of world-class organizations, and interlinking is a part of this data analysis effort. Emerging techniques most applicable to service processes are discussed in Chapters 11, 14, and 15.

THE ROLE OF SERVICE IN NEW AND FOREIGN MARKETS

Global service styles and customers' expectations differ greatly. For example, what are the attributes of the American, Japanese, and French service styles? How are they changing? How fast are they changing? What are the standards of performance? What, for example, does *convenience* mean in different cultures?

Which consumer benefit package attributes does each group or culture value the most and the least? How should we segment markets in different countries and cultures?

Other questions that focus on tailoring the consumer benefit package and service delivery process to the group culture and value system include:

How does the customer view and value time?

When is self-service appropriate in different cultures?

Is the consumer benefit package a necessity, a luxury, or taboo?

Which cultures are risk-seeking versus risk-averse?

What human behaviors can insult the customer during a service encounter?

When is it the cultural norm to ignore first-come-first-serve waiting line logic and behavior?

What service encounter protocols enhance personal relationships and business transactions?

What should be the pace of the service encounter in each culture?

How does each culture view and value trust? What are the consumer benefit package, process, and service encounter implications of this and other basic cultural values?

When is group identity more important than individual identity?

Designing the service encounter is a supreme challenge. Good answers to these types of questions are becoming more and more important as the global economy develops. Answers to such questions are a key input into consumer benefit package design and strategy (Part II of this book) and service delivery system design (Part III).

There are remarkably few public studies, and regrettably little documentation, of varying service styles and customer expectations for the cultures in the world today. The studies that have been done are normally proprietary in nature. Yet, Tables 1–1 and 1–2 showed the extent of global markets and companies where these issues are extremely important.

If enough commonalties exist among cultures, or technology allows it, universal consumer benefit packages can be designed, produced, and marketed worldwide. Here, the mass market is the world. Cable News Network and VISA credit cards are two examples of universal consumer benefit packages being marketed globally.

However, many say that the days of mass markets are over. Technology and other capabilities have contributed to the decline of mass market strategies and plans. The day of highly specialized niche markets and individually customized consumer benefit packages scattered around the world has arrived. Focused consumer benefit packages are the wave of the future, some with very short life cycles.

MBNA America's focused consumer benefit packages are examples of this ever-increasing degree of customization. MBNA America's primary business is providing credit card services to affinity groups. MBNA America customizes its consumer benefit packages to over 1,400 associations and organizations, each with unique goals, culture, and CBP attributes. MBNA knows what attributes of the consumer benefit package encourage group retention of their services by *affinity group*. Information analysis plays a major role is defining, designing, and managing over 1,400 focused consumer benefit packages. This same expertise in US domestic markets can be used to segment global markets.

Challenge 6

Excel at Understanding Personal Relationships and Different Cultures

Providing services, whether they be primary or supporting services, usually involves a relationship between the customer or customer's group and the service provider. Subtle differences in consumer benefit package (CBP) design, service process design, and service encounter execution are all dependent on understanding group culture, values, norms, behaviors, and service styles. The success of service process performance not only depends on what CBP attributes are provided but also how they are provided. Take advantage of national or group differences to increase market share and profits.

Another idea—related to Challenge 6 and *how* services are provided—is important to understand early in this book. That is, why do customers find it easier to evaluate service content compared to goods or technical content for most CBPs they purchase? The answer helps us see why services are frequently more important than the technical or goods content of a CBP, at least in the customer's mind.

Recognize that the customer frequently cannot distinguish between the goods (i.e., the physical product) or technical content (i.e., technical core) of competing CBPs. Here, the primary good is the central thing being purchased. Consumers either (1) don't have a true opportunity to make a technical/physical comparison or (2) don't have the expertise or equipment to test the goods content of competing CBPs. Therefore, they evaluate these competing CBPs based on things they *can* evaluate, such as services.

For example, customers can seldom correctly evaluate whether their hospital operation was 68, 78, or 98 percent good. But they can evaluate the friendliness of hospital service providers or the accuracy of the hospital bill or the quality of hospital food and food delivery and pickup.

QUALITY IMPROVEMENT AND PERFORMANCE

Quality should be equal in status to revenues and costs. If you believe this statement then company resources and efforts should be allocated equally among functional areas or, better yet, eliminate functional areas. The effect of this reallocation of resources and focus is to elevate the power and status of the operations or service management function(s) and of the processes in the organization.

Challenge 7

Integrate Quality Improvement into All Organizational Strategies, Systems, Decisions, and Performance Reports

How quickly can the organization truly integrate quality improvement into all organizational systems and management decisions? Here, quality includes all product and service features of the consumer or employee benefit package as well as the time to develop them, get them fully deployed, and modify them for local conditions. Quality improvement becomes an integral part of the firm's strategy and decision cycles as to how to generate revenues, lower costs, and grow profits.

To implement this statement of corporate philosophy and strategy, many initiatives must be taken. Example initiatives are as follows:

Quality performance becomes an input to every employee performance evaluation, including the CEO's. Company annual reports should include a report on quality improvement and customer satisfaction performance, tracking trends and comparing against standards, just as they do for revenues, costs, and profits.

Quality benefits and costs become an integral part of all financial and accounting documents, reports, budgets, and the organization's decision cycles.

Quality performance, both product and service related, becomes quantified and relationships defined between quality, revenue, cost, time, customer satisfaction, and profit performance.

Quality performance is evaluated by employees and stockholders who have easy access to performance information. These stakeholders hold management accountable for quality performance and have the power to make management changes.

When management actions such as these are taken, we can begin to talk about quality as an integral part of a firm's strategic and tactical plans. Business has a long way to go in this regard, as recently reported by an Ernst & Young and American Quality Foundation study.[9] They asked businesses from Canada, Germany, Japan, and the United States the following question: "How often does senior management evaluate information regarding the business consequences of quality performance; that is, gains in market share or profit resulting from quality improvements?"

The survey results show that the following percentage of businesses look at quality performance less than annually: Canada (14 percent), Germany (9 percent), Japan (2 percent) and United States (18 percent). The authors of the survey conclude that "In many businesses, senior management does not review quality performance even monthly. In contrast, most financial reviews occur more frequently, and 10-day sales reports are not uncommon. Until the reporting of quality results achieves parity with traditional financial and operating reporting, the link between quality, performance, and profit cannot be fully realized."[10] Interlinking is the way to determine these linkages!

Wendy's International is taking some of these actions concerning the reporting of quality performance. Their annual shareholder's report, for example, shows trends in employee turnover rates. All trends are decreasing and better than industry averages. Implied in these data and their discussion is that employee turnover reflects employee satisfaction and that, in turn, influences customer satisfaction.

Wendy's in the 1991 Shareholder Report also candidly states, "Customers give Wendy's high marks for quality, variety, and atmosphere. They do not rank Wendy's as high on price/value, operational consistency, and convenience. So in addition to building on its current strengths, Wendy's has aimed its strategies at improving customers' perceptions of the latter three, as well. All six characteristics together—quality, variety, atmosphere, price/value, operational consistency, and convenience—are referred to as the "total quality equation."[11]

Marriott's 1991 Annual Report does not report quality and customer satisfaction trends per major business group, but quality improvement initiatives are in their annual report. For example, "At 14 hotels, we are delivering a prototype service called "The First 10," which eliminates the "handing off" of customers during their arrival at the hotel, and facilitates a rapid, smooth check-in. Guests are preregistered, met at the front door with a key, and taken to their rooms by the same person who greeted them. This ensures that the first 10 minutes at the hotel—which help form a lasting impression of their stay—will be pleasant ones."[12]

In general, goods-producing firms are ahead of service-providing firms on implementing quality initiatives. One reason for this is that goods-producing firms have had to respond to foreign competitors. Many service-providing firms have not had to respond to foreign firms invading their markets. But those days are over. Service/quality challenges are being played out now.

THE MOST POWERFUL AMERICAN
STRATEGIC ALLIANCE

The ability of the United States to educate and retrain all of its people is suspect.[13] I could overload you with statistics but that is not necessary. Regardless of what numbers are used, strategic alliances should be formed between educational institutions and businesses. These alliances can be a powerful economic weapon. All of the preceding seven service/quality challenges depend on a highly educated, skilled, and adaptable workforce. Bricks and mortar don't execute the vast majority of service encounters—people do.

There is evidence that the lack of skilled American workers is limiting what American companies can accomplish. A study by the National Association of Manufacturers found that "30 percent of association members could not reorganize their factories because their employees were unable to learn new jobs, and 25 percent said they could not improve product quality because their workers were unable to understand new quality-control techniques."[14]

Challenge 8

Strengthen the Strategic Alliance between American Education and American Business

The most powerful American strategic alliance has yet to be fully established and deployed. It is an alliance between American education and American business—big and small. Such an alliance could be the economic knockout punch for world competitors in the Service and Information (Servomation) Age. The Servomation Age requires not only people with creative skills but also others with the capability to execute great CBP ideas. The masters of execution ultimately win in the marketplace.

To establish these Education–Business Strategic Alliances (EBSAs), American business must view and evaluate US educational systems as their top priority *vendor*. They must get involved, define what people skills they want, and help US educators excel at it. It must become a partnership of the highest national priority.

Implementing such strategic alliances demands much from both business and educators. For example, businesses must work more with educational systems to help them design curriculum, train master teachers, sponsor plant tours and student recognition and award programs, fund class projects and research programs, sponsor scholarships, establish permanent executive-on-loan teacher positions, and keep track of and hire the graduates. All school boards should be required to have business representatives on the board at all times. EBSAs must also include businesses with fewer than 500 employees, since they provide 57 percent of the U.S. jobs.

Companies and educational institutions must communicate closely, *not only on what the company thinks they need, but also in terms of what is possible*. For example, interlinking needs people at all levels of the organization to do smart data analysis. Educators can help practicing managers understand what is possible.

Also, service encounters depend greatly on frontroom and high-contact service management skills. These skills are mostly mental and behavioral service management skills—not physical, goods-producing skills. These skills can be taught if employees, managers, and educators work together.

And the US federal government is trying to tap the continuous improvement expertise used by US companies. If this alliance works, it can have great benefits. Vice President Al Gore, for example, is spending one-half of his time trying to champion the quality movement in US federal government offices. If it works, "some quality consultants say Uncle Sam could save up to 25 percent of what it spends each year by adopting total quality management concepts. If the federal government could do that, it would save $600 billion over five years."[15] As we see, a service/quality solution can be a key player in reducing the US government deficit, and providing more effective and efficient government services.

CONCLUSION

Quality professionals have seen the failures, the half-hearted support of top management, the inadequate facility, process, and organizational infrastructure; the long duration of consumer benefit package development and design, underskilled and trained employees trying to do a job, and the disappointed look of employees when they know management decisions or actions are not right. The *Service/Quality Solution* provides a blueprint to help people overcome these problems and disappointments. Good solutions to service/quality challenges can help maintain US international competitiveness, create jobs, raise standards of living worldwide, and improve the quality of life for everyone.

These eight challenges and three premises are interrelated and provide a big picture for studying service management's approach to building quality and competitive advantage. It is just as important for the service providers who create and deliver millions of service encounters daily to understand the big picture as it is for management and government officials. Table 1–4 outlines some big-picture questions every organization—big and small, public and private, goods-producing and service-providing—should be evaluating. The service/quality solution begins in your organization by answering these questions.

TABLE 1–4
Service Management Action Starter Questions

1. Do the people in your organization rely too much on a product or functional perspective for decision making? Develop an action plan to shift organizational thinking and practice toward service management.

2. What is your organization's plan of action for using service/quality as a competitive weapon in domestic and mutlicountry markets? Are you building service management, process, and interlinking capabilities? (Examine Table 1–2 closely.)

3. Where in your organization can interlinking help you gain competitive advantage? What types of relationships between performance criteria would you like to have defined? How would you use this smart information to gain competitive advantage? What actions can you take to improve the organization's interlinking capabilities?

4. Is instantaneous service a reality in some areas of your organization's business and industry? What are the implications? How is your organization planning and preparing for time-based competition at the CBP, process, and service encounter levels?

5. How well is quality improvement and performance integrated into your organization's strategy, systems, decision cycles, and internal and external performance reports? Should you develop a plan to report quality performance and improvement in your annual report before stakeholders ask for it?

Chapter Two

Basic Service Management

T he service/quality challenge is won or lost at the line of scrimmage—that is—
during many service encounters over an extended period. This chapter
reviews a few (but not all) basic ideas of service management. Other key ideas are
introduced as needed in later chapters. Its difficult to win at the line of scrimmage
if you don't master these basics—the theory and precepts of service management.

Customers take an integrative view of the service encounter. At points of contact with the service delivery process, providing the service often includes the
simultaneous execution of marketing, operations, and human resource management tasks. The customer does not care which functional department is responsible for what part of the service encounter. The marketing department must
design advertising programs that help set customers' expectations at levels
attainable by the service delivery process. The operations functions must design
a service delivery process that executes the service encounter well and meets all
the technical and procedural needs of the service encounter. The personnel function must hire the right people for the job, train them properly, and motivate
them to treat each customer and service encounter as a special event. No functional area is really a support function. Each functional area is an equal player in
delivering excellent service encounters.

Backroom (backstage) operations also is increasingly being viewed and managed just like the frontroom (frontstage). Sometimes the backroom is connected
directly to the customer through telephone lines. At other times, backroom capability is so critical to frontroom service encounter success that they are both
defined and managed as frontroom activities. One senior executive of a $4 bil-
lion service company that does corporate relocations and vehicle fleet management said, "There are no more backroom operations. Everything is frontline."[1]

DEFINING SERVICE MANAGEMENT

Definitions of service management are varied but the following definitions are
representative:

Service management is the study of how marketing and operations come together
through technology and people to plan, create, and deliver consumer benefit

packages and their associated service encounters. It is the fusion of many disciplines and, therefore, service management is extremely interdisciplinary. Service management tries to match the art it intends to serve, that is, the realities of managing a service at points of contact with customers.

Service management is also the ability to conceive and design consumer benefit packages and strategies, and associated service delivery processes and service encounters. A corporate culture must be created through knowledge and leadership that fulfills certain customer needs and wants; and manages the growth and daily activities of the organization as effectively and efficiently as possible.

The general objectives of service management may include one or all of the following: maximizing profit, maximizing customer satisfaction, minimizing costs, and/or maximizing productivity—subject to limited resources. For-profit service firms may attempt to attain all objectives, while not-for-profit service organizations focus on the last three objectives.[2]

TECHNICAL (OUTCOME) AND FUNCTIONAL (PROCESS) QUALITY

The customer evaluates service encounter performance in at least two ways. Gronroos defines these two ways as *technical* quality and *functional* quality.[3] Both of these ideas contribute to the body of knowledge called service management.

Technical quality is *what* the customer gets via a service encounter or transaction. It is the *outcome* of the service encounter. Functional quality is *how* the customer gets the service encounter or transaction. Here the *process* of how the consumer benefit package and/or service encounter is delivered is important. As we shall discuss in future chapters, the customer is almost always able to evaluate functional (process) quality whereas technical (outcome) quality may not be easy to evaluate.

For telephone repair service, the technical or outcome quality may be that the customer's telephone now works—they can communicate with other people or machines. An automatic system test or a repair person may have to fix the telephone. The customer judges the technical outcome—it works or it does not, the dial tone is loud and clear, the call goes through fast, there is no static on the line, etc.

Process or functional quality is *how* the customer receives, pays for, experiences, or uses the service. This includes all aspects of how the service was delivered to the customer. It includes procedural steps and the style of service. This notion recognizes the service delivery process is at least as important as the service outcome.

For telephone repair service, process quality includes: how knowledgeable and polite the customer service representative was to the customer when the customer reported a problem, not missing a scheduled repair visit to the customer's site, steps in the service delivery process, polite and skilled repair persons, and the like. Process quality includes how the process worked and how the people in the process interact. Deficiencies in process quality can negate excellent technical (outcome) quality.

Also, the customer doesn't care what functional areas created and delivered the service encounter(s) or what functional areas were responsible for technical or functional quality performance. That is a manager's responsibility, not the customer's.

Service management recognizes these simple facts and discards the idea of functional areas as we get closer to points of contact with the customer. This service management view takes an integrative, customer's view of designing and managing service encounters and service delivery processes. The organizational structure necessary to enhance service encounter performance must be carefully designed. In Chapter 8 we investigate a service management approach to organizational design.

Let's continue in this chapter to understand some basic ideas and terms of service management. As you read this book, if you have trouble clearly identifying and separating the marketing, operations, or human resource management ideas—good! You are beginning to *think service management*.

THE CUSTOMER EVALUATION PROCESS

How do customers evaluate goods and services? Zeithaml synthesized past research on this question with one result being the paradigm shown in Figure 2–1.

Search qualities are attributes which a customer can determine prior to purchasing the consumer benefit package (CBP). They include CBP attributes such as color, price, freshness, style, fit, feel, hardness, and smell. As Figure 2–1 shows, goods such as supermarket food, furniture, clothing, and houses are high in search qualities.

Experience qualities are attributes of the CBP that can only be discerned after purchase or during consumption. Examples of these attributes are friendliness, taste, wearability, safety, and customer satisfaction. These evaluation criteria fit the idea that services are experienced while goods are consumed.

Credence qualities are characteristics of the CBP which the consumer may find impossible to evaluate even after purchase and consumption. CBPs high in credence qualities include hospital operations, a new set of brake linings, and execution of your will.

These three evaluation criteria form a continuum, as shown in Figure 2–1, from easy to difficult to evaluate. One premise is that goods are easier to evalu-

FIGURE 2–1
How Customers Evaluate Goods and Services

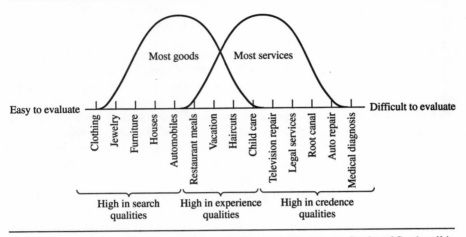

Source: V A Zeithaml, "How Consumer Evaluation Processes Differ between Goods and Services," in *Marketing in Services*, ed. J H Donnelly and W R George (Chicago: American Marketing Association, 1981), p. 186. Reprinted with permission.

ate than services. A second premise is that goods are high in search qualities while services are high in experience and credence qualities.

Of course, CBPs are usually some combination and configuration of goods and services. This makes for a more complex customer evaluation process than is shown by Figure 2–1. But the paradigm in Figure 2–1 provides a good baseline for designing CBPs and the processes that deliver them. Chapter 4 will explore various CBP configurations and their implications and Chapter 7 will examine process design.

Another contribution by Zeithaml are 11 hypotheses that provide insight into the nature of a service encounter.[4] Here are several of those hypotheses:

1. Consumers seek and rely more on information from personal sources than from nonpersonal sources when evaluating services prior to purchase.

2. Consumers use price and physical facilities as the major cues to service quality.

3. The consumer's evoked set of alternatives is smaller with services than with products.

4. Consumers adopt innovations in services more slowly than they adopt innovation in goods.

5. Consumers perceive greater risks when buying services than when buying products.

6. Brand switching is less frequent with services than with products.

7. Consumers attribute some of their dissatisfaction with services to their own inability to specify or perform their part of the service.

Zeithaml concludes that if research confirms these hypotheses about services, service providers may need to alter their marketing mixes to recognize different consumer evaluation processes.

The four traditional P's of the marketing mix (product, price, place, and promotion) are expanded in Chapter 6 to help managers accommodate many of these ideas. Three additional P's—physical evidence, process, and participants—are added to the traditional four P's. The total are called the seven P's of service management and are a new paradigm of management that accommodates service much better than the traditional four-P model.

DEFINING A SERVICE ENCOUNTER

A service encounter, as defined by Solomon et al., is "face-to-face interactions between a buyer and a seller in a service setting."[5] They call this a "personal service encounter" and point out that "Any encounter is assumed to contain learned and consistent behavior patterns; each participant should enact certain behaviors in order for the transaction to proceed smoothly. It will be argued that the degree of congruence with this learned pattern or 'script' by both the service provider and customer is an important determinant of satisfaction with the encounter. Thus, the focus is on the interdependence of both individuals."

Their definition of a service encounter relies upon the interpersonal face-to-face interaction between the service provider and the customer. They also suggest that *service encounters are role performances.*

Shostack's view of the service encounter expanded the definition to include "a period of time during which the consumer directly interacts with a service."[6] This broader definition recognizes that human interaction, either face-to-face or decoupled by a contact technology such as a telephone line, is not required to complete a service encounter. This view includes any interaction the customer might have with any other physical evidence such as buildings, equipment, employees' uniforms, advertisements, and the like. How physical evidence affects the service encounter and consumer benefit package is investigated in Chapter 6.

A related service management concept first noted by Mr. Jan Carlzon is called a moment of truth or trust.[7] Carlzon defines a moment of truth as "an episode in which a customer comes into contact with any aspect of the company, however remote, and thereby has an opportunity to form an impression.'' By managing these moments of truth we manage the customer's perception of service.

Each of these definitions of the service encounter ignores "how the service provider and customer interact.'' For example, the interaction between customers and service providers (often called customer service representatives) is frequently through a telephone line. Is a service encounter (transaction) performed through a telephone line, direct human contact? Under Solomon's definition—no. Under Shostack's definition—maybe. Under Carlzon's definition—yes. Thus, the evolution of a good definition of a service encounter is the work of many contributors.

CONTACT TECHNOLOGIES

How does the method of contact affect the definition of a service encounter? The work by Chase and Bowen helps to answer this question on the role of contact technologies in a service encounter.[8] Six types of contact technologies and how they relate to production efficiency, sales opportunity, and service-provider skills are shown in Figure 2–2.

Mail contact, as shown in Figure 2–2, has low face-to-face interaction and hence low sales opportunity, but it can be initiated in the customer's absence, and is therefore potentially highly efficient. *On-site technology* refers to devices such as automatic teller machines. *Face-to-face tight specifications* describes those situations where there is little variation in the service process—neither customer nor server have much discretion in creating the service. Fast-food restaurants and automated rides in family amusement parks are two examples.

Face-to-face loose specifications in Figure 2–2 describes a situation in which there is a general understanding of what the service process is to be, but there are options in the way it will be done. Full-service restaurants and car sales agencies have such characteristics. Finally, *face-to-face total customization* refers to service encounters where specifications of the encounter must be developed through some interaction between the customer and server. Legal, medical, and consulting services belong to this type.

Contact technologies decouple the customer from the service provider. One conclusion from the previous discussion is that contact technologies represent direct contact with the customer. The customer enters your service delivery process regardless of which contact technology he or she chooses. This is especially true if we use Carlzon's definition of a moment of trust to define a service encounter.

L L Bean implicitly recognizes alternative contact technologies in one of its many customer-oriented statements. One statement says, "A customer is the most important person ever in this office—in person or by mail or by phone.'' To L L Bean, the customer should expect and receive outstanding customer service regardless of the contact technology used.

FIGURE 2–2
Different Types of Contact Technologies

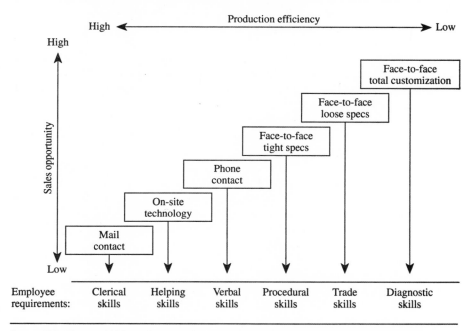

Source: R B Chase and N J Aquilano, *Production and Operations Management—A Life Cycle Approach*, 6th ed. (Burr Ridge, IL: Richard D. Irwin, 1992), p. 123. Reprinted with permission.

This book defines a service encounter as one or more moments of trust. For example, a service encounter can be a subliminal clue such as there are no cars in the parking lot or a bundle of moments of trust such as all the steps and interactions necessary (i.e., the service process) to renew one's driver's license. The field of proxemics, a combination of psychology and sociology, adds to our understanding of subliminal clues such as body language, nonverbal communication, and social or spatial distance. Service encounters are complex mainly because they are acted out between human beings.

SERVICE ENCOUNTERS AS SOCIAL PROCESSES

Normann contributes to our understanding of service encounters by noting that "services consist of acts and performances, and that service encounters are typically social events. The control and management of social events calls for special skills and techniques."[9]

Norman goes on to point out that "effective service companies are often based on social innovation. Inventing the appropriate roles and role constellations, diagnosing and finding ways to use human capacity and energy, designing ways to make people and groups of people learn skills quickly and to maintain the skills while keeping alive the enthusiasm and the thrill of personal development—all typical examples of social innovation."

One way to view a service encounter is as a social process. One extreme example told to me by a bank manager helps illustrate the point. A bank manager told the story of a customer who always paid his bills in person. This customer would travel to the bank, telephone company, utility company, and government offices during an all-day bill-paying process. One day when the bank manager saw him standing in a long line at the teller window, the bank manager politely asked him to come into his office.

"Why do you wait in line? You could pay by mail or place your payment in the drop-off box, and never have to wait," asked the bank manager. "Well," answered the customer, "this is my one day to socialize and catch up on the local news. Everyone is so friendly." On further discussion with this customer, the bank manager commented that "every customer is unique and this one has special needs. I do hope the tellers recognize this."

The top priority is social interaction, for customers like this banking customer. They may not care to minimize waiting time or travel costs. They also may want to talk at length to the bank teller and that can bottleneck the service delivery process and quickly increase waiting times for the other customers.

The service/quality challenge for the service provider and service delivery system is to meet or exceed this customer's expectations while not hindering the service encounter for other customers. Each service encounter is a unique event, never to be repeated exactly. In this banking example, successive service encounter performance is interdependent, not independent. This illustrates the difficulty of designing, managing, and training service providers to execute service encounters well.

By the way, this customer had over $200,000 deposited at this bank but the tellers usually did not know it. So, what is the cost of poor service for this banking customer? What is the value of this loyal customer to the bank? What type of teller training program ensures this customer receives excellent service? How do you evaluate bank tellers when the service encounters they execute are viewed as social processes?

LOSING YOUR IDENTITY BY DESIGN

Almost all of us have visited the hospital where the service encounter requires you to lose your individual identity as you go through the service delivery process. So let's see how doctors, nurses, and hospital management design this not-so-pleasant series of service encounters.

You enter the hospital with your wallet, unique clothes, family or friends, and an important sense of who you are. You perceive a great amount of risk prior to, during, and after this visit to the hospital. You may be sick but you retain your pride and fighting spirit. You fill out the admittance and insurance forms, you give them numbers and they give you numbers. You are asked to take off your clothes, place them in the closet, and put on a hospital gown. You are cold, scared, a stranger among strangers, and the hospital room is *functional*. By now, you have progressively lost your identity and become a *patient*. The service delivery process was *designed* to do this to you!

You complete your set of service encounters by allowing them to examine, analyze, and talk about *you*. The strain of being a patient even if they find you to be healthy is great. The *post service encounter* includes waiting on test results, resolving bill inaccuracies with doctors, hospitals, and insurance companies, and so on. Why does this CBP (and associated process and service encounters) have to be designed by doctors, nurses, and management this way? It doesn't!

Fortunately, some hospital managers have begun to redesign the hospital service encounter processes. Examples of ways to improve the hospital's service encounter include: patient escorts, electronic check-in and check-out, attractive and colorful hospital gowns with your nameplate, electronic insurance claims processing, patient liaisons, homey hospital rooms, patients' bills of rights, staff training programs that emphasize knowing the patient's name and situation, assigning the same caregiver (doctors, nurses, etc.) every day to the patient, a list of telephone numbers of key doctors and nurses after you get home (i.e., for after-service encounter or post sales support), etc.

The set of service encounters described here highlights the fact that to many patients the *process* (i.e., functional quality) of health care delivery is as important as the *outcome* (i.e, technical quality). Moreover, the patient and family must rely mostly on experience and credence qualities to evaluate the CBP and the processes that delivered it. Service management also recognizes that service encounters and CBPs consist of social and technical processes. Hence, the service delivery process should be carefully examined to identify all key moments of truth and make sure these activities are performed from a service management perspective.

HIGH– VERSUS LOW–CONTACT SERVICE DELIVERY SYSTEMS

The idea of high- versus low-contact service providers and service delivery systems is an important service management paradigm. The basic question is, "how much contact does a service provider have with a customer during a service encounter?"

Chase defined a classification system for service delivery systems on a high-to low-contact continuum.[10] His customer contact model "holds that a service system's potential operating efficiency is a function of the degree to which the customer is in direct contact with the service facility relative to a total service creation time for the customer."[11]

According to Chase, "service facilities characterized by high customer contact (HC) are inherently limited in their production efficiency because of the uncertainty that people (the customers) introduce into the service creation process. Low customer contact (LC) is essentially free of this type of uncertainty and therefore is capable of operating at high levels of production efficiency."[12]

High-contact service delivery systems may not have great opportunities for production efficiency but sales opportunities can increase. Low-contact systems have fewer sales opportunities but more opportunity to design and manage an efficient operating system.

FRONTROOM, BACKROOM, AND INSTANTANEOUS MOMENTS OF TRUST

A related set of ideas provides more insight into the nature of service provider and customer interaction. Like the definition of a service encounter, moments of truth (trust) are part of these three types of *process moments of trust*.[13]

Frontroom process moments of trust (FPMT) include only those planned and expected activities that are executed while in contact with the customer or are visible to the customer. FPMT include any activity performed in the direct presence of the customer, such as face-to-face interaction, or indirect presence of the customer, such as through a telephone line.

FPMT have an immediate and nonretractable impact on perceived customer service and quality levels. Poor execution of FPMT can have grave consequences for the service firm, such as lost sales (revenue), less repeat business, and negative word-of-mouth advertising.

Backroom process moments of trust (BPMT) are planned and expected activities hidden (or transparent) from (to) the customer that are necessary to support the frontroom and provide the service. Poor execution of BPMT are at least temporarily internal to the organization. Therefore, the service providers have a chance to catch and correct mistakes before they affect the customer or escape to downstream departments.

Instantaneous process moments of trust (IPMT) are unplanned but expected activities of very short duration that affect customer service and quality levels. Front- and backroom employees create and deliver these moments of trust. IPMT are an important subset of FPMT.

For example, a telephone customer service representative may work with a customer an average of 30 minutes when a customer wants to order new telephone service. The customer service representative is executing FPMT. The telephone line decouples the customer from the service provider but it is still a high-contact service encounter.

Yet, a telephone installation person might talk to the customer in the home for only two minutes while spending one hour installing the telephone throughout the house. The two minutes of conversation with the customer are of short duration compared to the total duration of the job but represent an instantaneous moment of trust. IPMT are just as important as moments of trust of longer duration, and should not be left to chance. IPMT are often overlooked by service-providing companies.

One major hotel chain recognizes the importance of IPMT by requiring housekeeping (maids) and engineering (building maintenance) personnel "to know the customer's name before entering the room." These service providers are also given mandatory refresher training on how to greet the customer. Even hotel security guards spend much of their time providing hotel guests with directions and information in very short "IPMT conversations." Script dialogues can be used to train service providers on how to handle IPMT conversations with customers.

BASIC TENETS OF SERVICE MANAGEMENT

There are many basic tenets of service management. A sample of these service management tenets are given briefly in this section.

Four distinct characteristics that make the management of service-providing organizations different from goods-producing organizations were first defined by Sasser, Olsen, and Wyckoff.[14] The four descriptions that follow are based on their work. Fitzsimmons and Sullivan also contributed to these ideas.[15]

Services are *intangible*. Thus, they are difficult to describe, demonstrate to the buying public, and illustrate in promotional material. Design of the service package and control of the design require a greater understanding of consumer psychology than for a manufactured good because of the intangible and, often, nonexplicit nature of the product.

Intangibility poses new problems for service firm managers as well as for their customers. As Johnson noted, "Buyers are usually unable to judge quality and value prior to a purchase. Consequently, the service company's reputation and the reputation of its salespeople are far more essential to services marketing than to goods marketing."[16]

Services are *perishable*; they cannot be inventoried. Three very perishable commodities are an airline seat, a hotel room, and an hour of a lawyer's day. In essence, the service manager is without an important "shock absorber" called inventory that is available to managers in goods-producing firms to absorb fluctuations in demand.

Services provide *heterogeneous output*. In fact, there is a great deal of variability in the output of a single firm and even a single service employee. The heterogeneity characteristic means that it is difficult to establish standards for the output of a service firm and even harder to ensure that standards are met each time the service is delivered.

Services *require simultaneous production and consumption*, which compounds the problems caused by intangibility, perishability, and heterogeneity. Unlike a manufacturing system, the consumer interacts with and participates in the service delivery system.

Further consideration of these four unique characteristics of service firms, plus other key differences, is documented in Table 2–1. The nine distinguishing characteristics between goods-producing and service-providing organizations are briefly described in the following text.

Consumer benefit package (CBP) is a more appropriate term than product for the things people buy today. A CBP includes the tangible (goods-content) and intangible (service-content) attributes of an economic transaction. Thus, all things people buy fit within the CBP framework. Chapter 1 briefly defined CBPs. Chapter 4 will address CBP configurations and analysis frameworks. Chapters 5 and 6 discuss the strategies necessary to support CBP success in the marketplace. The detailed attributes of each CBP also are the basis for designing the service delivery processes, Part III of this book, and the service quality management system, Part IV of this book.

Customer participation, as noted in Table 2–1, recognizes the customer is frequently engaged in the service process/activity/transaction. That is, the customer is in your factory. When a customer, for example, checks into your hotel or calls the credit card processing center to resolve a dispute, the customer "enters your factory."

Some service firms try to take advantage of the customer being in their service delivery system by encouraging self-service (supermarkets, cafeterias, libraries) and self-cleanup (fast-food restaurants, campgrounds, vacation home rentals). This active participation of the customer in the service delivery process introduces a substantial amount of uncertainty with respect to service time, service-provider capacity, service quality performance, and operating cost. Market segmentation and cultural norms and behaviors also affect how much self-service to use.

The characteristic of *time-dependent demand* recognizes that the demand for services is more difficult to predict than the demand for products over equal planning horizons. Inventory cannot be used to store the service encounter. Therefore, the nature of demand for services, especially over the short term (say, by hour or day), places great pressures on service firm managers and service pro-

TABLE 2–1
Managing a Service Business

Distinguishing Characteristics of a Service Firm and Its Operating Conditions	Examples of Management Issues
Consumer benefit package versus physical product	Clear definition of the consumer benefit package Measure customer service and quality levels Set a standard for service level and quality Build "control" into the service delivery system by: • Intensive training and retraining • Performance evaluation and reward programs for service workers and managers • Audit teams • Increased automation
Customer participation in the service delivery system	Utilize the customers to help provide the service (i.e., employee and customer job design) Design the service facility layout to control customer movement through the facility
Time-dependent demand	Plan capacity based on peak demand Use overlapping workforce schedules (shifts) Plan capacity based on 30-minute intervals by day, by week, by month Increase the degree of automation Provide flexibility or extra capacity for responsive service Influence/shift customer demand Overbook customer demand
Noninventoriable output	Maintain safety capacity Open service facility 24 hours per day Increase the degree of automation Determine the size and number of capacity units Establish the proper capacity balance between stages of the service delivery system
Service provider skills	Ongoing training, motivation, and employee-of-the-month programs Salary incentive programs Simultaneous consumption and production (buyer–seller or marketing–production interface) Employee checklists
Proximity to customer multisite management	Standardize the service facility and its operation Automate and centralize the backroom operation and/or the total service delivery system Add extra layers of management for the "out-in-the-field" part of the organization

continued

ncluded)

Distinguishing Characteristics of a Service Firm and Its Operating Conditions	Examples of Management Issues
No patents on services	Use the judicial system to protect the service package and system Capture market share quickly Erect barriers to entry
Resilience to economic cycles	Degree to which the economic signals must be watched Flexibility of the firm's strategic plans Length of the planning horizons Short- and long-term productivity goals
International transportability	Extent to which a service firm's service package is transportable in the world economy Constraints on exporting the service Implications of going to a multinational service firm

Source: "Managing a Service Firm: A Different Management Game," by D. A. Collier. Reprinted with permission from *National Productivity Review*, V3N1, Winter 1983–84. Copyright © 1984 by Executive Enterprises, Inc., 22 West 21st Street, New York, NY 10010-6990. All rights reserved.

viders. Customer arrival rates and demand patterns for service delivery systems such as those of banks, airlines, supermarkets, telephone service centers, and courts are very difficult to forecast.

For example, the demand for postal service in the United States varies according to annual, monthly, weekly, and daily patterns and involves extremely complex mail mix categories. For emergency fire and ambulance services the ratio of high to low demand (i.e., calls for service) during a given period is as high as eight to one. The arrival and departure patterns of hotel convention guests must be monitored hourly to assure the availability of rooms. As Joseph F. Fredrick, Jr., a senior executive of the Hilton Corporation notes, "We sell time. You can't put a hotel room on the shelf."[17]

The *use of inventory is precluded* by the simultaneous production and consumption of most services. In goods-producing firms, inventory can be used to decouple customer demand from the production process or stages of the production process, or the beginning of the production process from raw material and purchased-part vendors.

For service delivery systems, capacity is the surrogate for inventory. For example, safety capacity for a hospital can take the form of safety beds (equipment) for the purpose of meeting unanticipated patient demand. A float pool of nurse (labor) capacity can alleviate shortfalls in hospital nurse capacity.

Safety capacity for a service system is analogous to safety stock for a goods-producing system. The cost of idle capacity (resources) for a service firm is analogous to inventory-carrying cost for a goods-producing firm.

The usefulness of capacity for a service firm is time dependent. An empty hotel room on Friday evening is lost revenue. There is no way to recapture this lost revenue. If one buys a microcomputer on Friday evening, inventory normally allows the firm to capture the associated revenue. A stockout for a service firm means lack of adequate capacity, whereas for a manufacturing firm it usually means lack of inventory. For this reason, some service firms set their capacity level based on peak demand or close to peak demand or use a high percentage of part-time employees.

Service-provider skills are paramount to a successful service encounter. The customer and service provider (sometimes called buyer–seller) interface is where the service provider is simultaneously doing marketing, human resource management, and operations tasks. The service provider has a significant effect on the perceived value of the service as viewed by the customer. A bank teller or a doctor or a TV repairperson can leave the customer happy or furious.

Close proximity to the customer is essential for service organizations, which typically consist of small units of capacity. For example, post offices, hotels, and branch banks fit these size and proximity requirements. This spatial relationship of service facilities scattered over a wide geographical area is called multisite management. Multisite management complicates the task of managing a service business.

Some service firms can use automation to centralize the low contact (backroom) functions while decentralizing the high contact (frontroom) functions. For example, many major telephone, credit card, and reservation service centers use centralized offices filled with hundreds of customer service representatives, each working with an electronic workstation and a telephone line to create and deliver excellent service encounters. This centralized backroom and decentralized frontroom capability allows companies to gain economies of large scale in the backroom and distribute their services to many individual customers.

In terms of *patent protection,* services are not as well protected as physical products. The chemical formula and patent for fluoride in toothpaste is precise. This set of chemical specifications can be tested in laboratories and presented in court as fact. The intangible nature of a service makes it more difficult to keep a competitor from copying your service process. However, services are protected to some extent by copyrights, trademarks, and by establishing a standard facility design and consumer benefit package.

For example, in *Amstar Corp.* v. *Domino's Pizza* (1980), the central question was whether the use by the defendant of a mark or logo to identify its service was apt to confuse the ordinary customer to the detriment of the plaintiff. The first factor the court cited in evaluating the claim of actual or likely confusion was the public's recognition of a standard service and facility design.

During a recession, for most services, an inventory buildup of service encounters cannot occur. For goods-producing firms, on the other hand, inventories can rapidly build up during a business downturn. Future demand for goods can be filled from these inventories, whereas service output is time-dependent and perishable. These characteristics have led some to argue that the *service sector is more recession-proof* than the goods-producing sector.

For example, during the 1981–83 U.S. recession, *Fortune* magazine noted, "The Service 500 companies came through the economic crunch of 1982 in better shape than the Fortune 500 industrial corporations, whose earnings fell 27 percent."[18] Others suggest that the recession-proof argument for service firms is most realistic for financial, public utility, health care, government, and some professional services. Discretionary services such as leisure, insurance, hotel/motel, restaurant/food, telecommunications, retail trade, and adult education are thought to be affected by the vitality of the economy.

You can transport a Toyota to the United States and sell it. But what about legal services, individual financial services, or medical services, just to name a few? How transportable is a service firm's consumer benefit package in the world economy?

Some services simply cannot be transported between countries because of physical, cultural, or regulatory barriers. For example, the American Express or VISA credit cards are world-class financial services, whereas Blue Cross and Blue Shield finds it difficult to export their insurance services. *In summary, many services today are not as transportable as physical products in the global economy.*

These basic tenets of service management provide additional reasons why you cannot study or manage a service firm without taking a more holistic and integrative view of management. The unique nature of every service encounter also places great demands on service providers and their managers. Service management is not an easy business and the basic ideas of this chapter help explain why.

Several sample questions concerning the ideas of Chapter 2 are summarized in Table 2–2. They are intended to highlight certain service management ideas and how they might apply to your organization.

THE SERVICE ENCOUNTER CONE

The service encounter cone, as shown in Figure 2–3, is a graphical representation of the general steps necessary for the planning and execution of a service encounter. According to *Webster's New Collegiate Dictionary*, a cone is "a solid bounded by a circular or other closed plane base and the surface formed by line segments joining every point of the boundary of the base to a common vertex."[19]

TABLE 2–2
Service Management Action Starter Questions

1. How do customers evaluate each consumer or employee benefit package, and associated process and service encounters provided by your organization? Define outcome, process, search, experience, and credence performance qualities for each consumer and employee benefit package.

2. By making use of service management ideas can you develop a comprehensive customer contact plan for each service process?

3. What role do contact technologies play in your organization's CBP, process, and service encounter designs?

4. How effective and efficient is your organization at frontroom, backroom, and instantaneous moments of truth and execution? Develop an agenda for action to ensure these performances are world class.

5. How can the service management approach depicted in Figures 2–3 and 2–4 be used by your organization to create and deliver world-class service encounters? What steps do you do well and poorly? How can each step be improved?

The framework of this book represents what organizations must do to create and deliver world-class service encounters. This book suggests starting with the big picture (i.e., the base of the cone) and building the capabilities of the organization block by block.

In this cone analogy, the base of the cone is consumer and employee benefit package management that consists of design (Chapter 4) and strategy (Chapters 5 and 6). Here is where top management directs the entire company using a service management approach and management style.

The service delivery system is built upon this base. The delivery system requires job, process, and facility design (Chapter 7), organization and performance design (Chapter 8), and service innovations (Chapter 9). Line segments on the cone (not shown in Figure 2–3) are analogous to valued-added service delivery processes working on a day-to-day basis. Management's job is to combine these resources in such a way as to create and deliver excellent service encounters.

Given the previous management decisions with regard to consumer and employee benefit package management and service delivery system design, the human performance and quality management systems can now be designed. These systems are so integrated in world-class service encounter systems no attempt is made to separate them. Figure 2–4 is another way to view the management steps and actions inherent in Figure 2–3. Chapters most closely related to the service management topic(s) are noted in Figure 2–4. At all levels and activities of the organization, continuous improvement and benchmarking must be an integral part of running the business.

FIGURE 2–3
The Service Encounter Cone Analogy

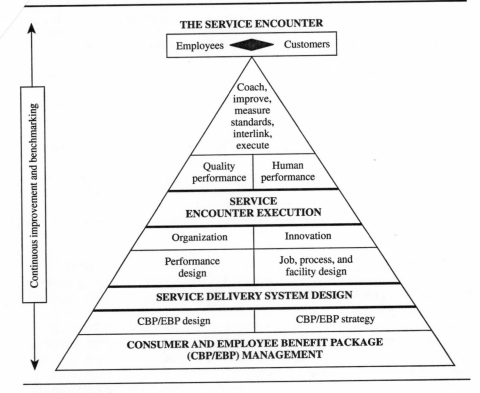

Figures 2–3 and 2–4 outline a service management approach to service encounter management. Both figures identify the following three general steps to planning and decision making: (1) Consumer and Employee Benefit Package Management, (2) Service Delivery System Design, and (3) Service Encounter Management and Execution. This framework and way of thinking outlines my service management approach and how this book is organized. This service management approach can have as few as three organizational levels. It is fast, lean, smart, adapable, empowered, and overlaid with world-class information systems and interlinking capabilities. This organization expands and contracts quickly as conditions change making use of alliances, temporary employees and subcontractors, and network relationships. It is a powerful approach to doing business where executing world-class practices drives results. A service management approach is one way to reinvent the organization.

FIGURE 2–4
A Service Management Approach to Service Encounter Management

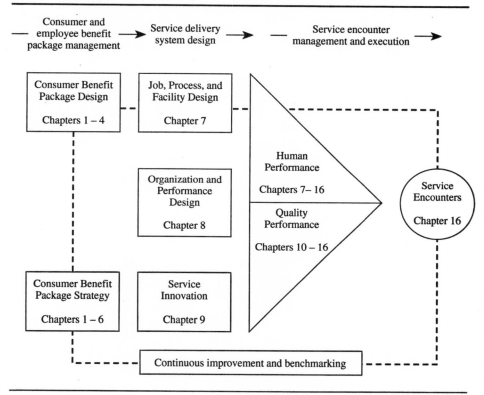

The common vertex of the cone is a service encounter that includes both the service-providing employee(s) and the customer. Here all the strategies, speeches, resource allocation decisions, meetings, training sessions, and so on, converge on the common vertex we call the service encounter.

Millions of service encounters are created and vanish every day, never to be repeated exactly in the same way. Service encounters place new demands on service providers in terms of performance and on-the-spot capability. Chapter 16, the final chapter of this book, addresses some issues surrounding service encounters and summarizes some key points of this book. Service encounters are the reason for the organization's existence and the key to survival and profitability. Service encounters are where the rubber meets the road—its time to perform on-stage.

By the time the reader reaches Part IV of this book on the service/quality management system, she or he should be *thinking service management,* not service marketing or service operations or some other narrow view of designing, creating, and completing service encounters. This way of thinking is an integrative management viewpoint which should permeate the organization—to all managers, supervisors, and employees. Thus, everyone should be exposed to these ideas regardless of their position in the organization.

The centrifugal force of competition can tear the service encounter cone apart quickly. It is also easy to topple the cone, for example, by poorly devised consumer or employee benefit package designs and strategies, poor process design, inadequate data analysis and measurements, and by asymmetrical (marketing versus operations, etc.) policies and actions. It truly is a challenge to all the people working in an organization to keep the organization (cone) intact, strong, and balanced over the long term.

Chapter Three

The Malcolm Baldrige National Quality Award and the Service/Quality Perspective

A s Will Rogers once said, "Thank God We Don't Get All The Government We Pay For!" Seldom do we hear about a successful government program. The Malcolm Baldrige National Quality Award (MBNQA) though is a successful government program—in spite of a few glitches.[1] Our purpose in this chapter is to briefly introduce the MBNQA framework as a guide to continuous improvement for service organizations. The chapter also describes where service organizations have historically been weak performers in the MBNQA scoring scheme, and therefore, identifies opportunities for improvement. Other improvement frameworks such as the International Organization for Standardization (ISO) 9000 series are also growing in importance for services, but space does not permit us to discuss those implications here.

Service processes account for as much as 95 percent of the jobs in the US economy. Eighty percent of US jobs are in the service-providing sector. As much as 75 percent of the remaining 20 percent of the jobs that are in the goods-producing sector are jobs in service processes. Therefore, about 95 percent of the real opportunities for improvement are in service processes. It is also time for federal, state, and local government service processes to do more with less. Improving government service processes must be part of the Service/Quality Solution.

Let's begin with a brief overview of the history of the MBNQA. On August 20, 1987, President Ronald Reagan signed Public Law 100-107, the Malcolm Baldrige National Quality Improvement Act, which established the MBNQA. The award recognizes US firms that excel in quality management and achievement. There are three categories of awards given each year, with up to two awards per category. The three categories are: manufacturing, service, and small business. Table 3–1 lists the previous MBNQA winners.

The US Department of Commerce's National Institute of Standards and Technology (NIST) manages the MBNQA. A consortium that includes the American

TABLE 3–1
Malcolm Baldrige National Quality Award Winners

1988
  Motorola (manufacturing)
  Westinghouse Nuclear Fuels Division (manufacturing)
  Globe Metallurgical (small business)

1989
  Miliken & Company (manufacturing)
  Xerox Business Products Division (manufacturing)

1990
  IBM Rochester, Minnesota Plant (manufacturing)
  Cadillac Division, General Motors (manufacturing)
  Federal Express (service)
  Wallace Company (small business)

1991
  Solectron Corporation (manufacturing)
  Zytec Corporation (manufacturing)
  Marlow Industries Inc. (small business)

1992
  AT&T Network Systems Group/Transmission Systems Business Unit (manufacturing)
  Texas Instruments Defense Systems & Electronics Group (manufacturing)
  AT&T Universal Card Services (service)
  The Ritz-Carlton Hotel Company (service)
  Granite Rock Company (small business)

Productivity and Quality Center and the American Society for Quality Control administers the award.

The MBNQA was established 36 years after the Union of Japanese Scientists and Engineers established the Deming Prize in 1951. Two of the Deming Prize objectives were to: (1) disseminate statistical process control techniques throughout Japanese industry, and (2) increase the public's awareness of quality management goals and techniques. The Deming Prize accomplished those goals and helped transform Japan into a world-class economic power as well.

What are the objectives of the MBNQA? The three stated objectives are: "(1) to increase awareness of quality as an increasingly important element in competitiveness, (2) to share information on successful quality strategies and on the benefits derived from implementation of these strategies, and (3) to promote understanding of the requirements for quality excellence."[2] The MBNQA has accomplished these three objectives. No other US business-related and government-sponsored award has been as successful. Others, such as Garvin[3] and Lopez,[4] concur with this positive assessment of the impact and success of the MBNQA.

THE SEVEN MBNQA EXAMINATION CATEGORIES

The seven 1993 MBNQA examination categories are as follows:

1. Leadership
2. Information and Analysis
3. Strategic Quality Planning
4. Human Resource Development and Management
5. Management of Process Quality
6. Quality and Operational Results
7. Customer Focus and Satisfaction

The titles of the first four MBNQA categories adequately describe the contents of each category. MBNQA Categories 5, 6, and 7 account for 620 of the 1,000 total points, and therefore, we shall focus on these performance areas. The MBNQA also uses three dimensions to score each of these seven performance categories. These dimensions are approach, deployment, and results. We will not examine these ideas here but they are clearly defined in the 1993 Award Criteria brochure.[5]

The 1993 MBNQA Award Criteria defines Category 5 on Management of Process Quality as follows:

> The Management of Process Quality Category examines the systematic processes the company uses to pursue ever-higher quality and company performance. Examined are the key elements of process management, including research and development, design, management of process quality for all work units and suppliers, systematic quality improvement, and quality assessment.[6]

Category 5 is looking for clearly defined and well-documented processes and procedures. These processes and procedures would help people excel even if current employees were replaced by new employees. Excellence must be inherent in the company processes and not just in employee skills. This does not mean that people are of less importance than the process. It means that to do well in the MBNQA scoring process you must excel both in terms of people (Category 4) and process management (Category 5). Also, the focus is on primary, supporting, and supplier processes. All processes are important in the MBNQA scoring system. Part III of this book surveys the topics of process management, organization design and performance, and service technology, all of which relate to MBNQA Category 5.

The 1993 MBNQA Award Criteria defines Category 6 on Quality and Operational Results as follows:

> The Quality and Operational Results Category examines the company's quality levels and improvement trends in quality, company operational performance, and

supplier quality. Also examined are current quality and operational performance levels relative to those of competitors.[7]

The following Note (1) for Item 6.1 of Category 6 is informative. "Key product and service measures are measures relative to the set of all important features of the company's products and services. These measures, taken together, best represent the *most important factors that predict customer satisfaction and quality in customer use.* Examples include measures of accuracy, reliability, timeliness, performance, behavior, delivery, after-sales services, documentation, appearance and effective complaint management."[8]

One key phrase in this paragraph is to *predict customer satisfaction.* This is exactly the subject of Chapters 14 and 15 on interlinking operational (internal) performance to marketing's (external) measures of performance such as customer satisfaction. Note 1 of Item 6.1 also focuses on *internal* measures of performance. Category 6 (Quality and Operational Results) concentrates on internal measures of performance for primary, support, and supplier processes.

The 1993 MBNQA Award Criteria define Category 7 on Customer Focus and Satisfaction as follows:

> The Customer Focus and Satisfaction Category examines the company's relationships with customers and its knowledge of customer requirements and of the key quality factors that drive marketplace competitiveness. Also examined are the company's methods to determine customer satisfaction, current trends and levels of satisfaction and retention, and these results relative to competitors.[9]

Category 7 focuses on results external to the organizational unit. This category is worth 300 points of 1,000 total points and concentrates on the current and future expectations and perceptions of customers. This is the most points allocated to any single MBNQA category. It highlights the importance of customer satisfaction results and service/quality performance.

Interlinking is a way to quantitatively link MBNQA Categories 6 and 7 or any other of the seven MBNQA performance categories. The cause and effect logic of the MBNQA seven performance categories can be supported or refuted using performance data and the interlinking methods outlined in this book. For example, do training expenditures result in improved customer satisfaction?

Two other points should be made concerning the logic of the MBNQA scoring system and interlinking. First, anecdotal responses and answers to the MBNQA issues are scored zero percent. War stories, testimonials, management by opinion, publicity and recognition events with little true content, and the like, are interesting but contribute little to true improvement.

As Chase and Kellogg state:

> First, although there are an increasing number of collections of case studies of successful, quality-oriented service firms, they represent only stage-one knowledge. We recognize that certain service organizations are "good," yet we do not really know why . . . To move to higher levels of understanding, more compare-

and-contrast studies are needed . . . The second way to increase knowledge is by developing measurement models. The SERVQUAL index referred to by Zeithaml and the "service quality process map" discussed by Collier are examples of the types of measurements needed.[10]

Other new approaches and methods, some noted in this book, are on the horizon.

Second, there must be evidence that *results are clearly caused by approach.* What does this statement mean? It means that a company knows their CBPs, processes, and customers so well, they can predict customer satisfaction and company performance as a function of management controlled variables. For example, if a company spent $1 million dollars on process activities A1, A7, and A9, and improved their performance by Y percent, customer satisfaction is predicted to improve by Z percent. Developing this internal and external measurement and interlinking capability is the subject of Chapters 11 to 15.

HOW SERVICE-PROVIDING ORGANIZATIONS CAN IMPROVE THEIR MBNQA PERFORMANCE

If you recall from Chapter 1, Quinn and Gagnon in 1986 conclude, "If service industries are properly nurtured, they will grow and generate much of America's future wealth. If they are misunderstood, disdained, or mismanaged, the same forces that led to the decline of US manufacturing stand ready to cut them to pieces. With some 70 percent of the US economy already in services—not including the three-fourths of all manufacturing costs that represent support services—the stakes are immense. It can happen here."[11]

AT&T Universal Card Services, Federal Express and the Ritz-Carlton Hotel are the service firms that have won the MBNQA as shown in Table 3–1. In the first four years of the awards existence, only Federal Express had won it. Why have service firms had a difficult time winning the MBNQA? The following six reasons help answer this question and also identify opportunities for improvement.

Overcome the Head Start of Goods-Producing Firms

Historically, US service firms have not been under the same intense pressure from foreign competitors as have US goods-producing industries. Therefore, goods-producing firms began their quality journey earlier than most service firms. A collorary to this fact is that it is usually tougher to design and manage a service process than a goods-producing process. For example, following (flowcharting) the product through the manufacturing and distribution systems to improve efficiency and effectiveness are normal tasks of manufacturing design and execution. But when the product is replaced with a human being's unique needs, process- and service-encounter design become much more complicated. It will take time for most service-providing organizations to meet the demanding standards of the MBNQA.

Improve Consumer Benefit Package (CBP) Design and Development

Consumer benefit package design, development, and performance is not well-defined, documented, measured, paced, and tied to compensation in many service businesses. Most US service industries are not as advanced as their US goods-producing counterparts on product research and development, and the processes that support them. Chapters 4 and 9 address the issues of CBP design and innovation.

The MBNQA demands that service firms and service processes improve in CBP design and management. CBP design, the frequency of new CBP designs and modifications, and time to market are competitive weapons in all service industries. Historically, poor CBP design and development processes have hurt service firms in the MBNQA scoring system.

For example, a *Consumer Reports* survey of more than 200,000 magazine readers shows that US cable companies are not performing well in CBP design or support services. The three dominant customer complaints were (1) dissatisfaction with the number, mix, and packaging of cable channels, (2) the inaccuracy of cable bills and associated processes, and (3) difficulties in communicating with cable companies on any issue such as an outage or programming a VCR.[12]

Improve Support Service Process Management

Support service processes are often not flowcharted, documented, measured, evaluated, well managed, or continuously improved. These processes either provide services to internal (employee benefit packages) or external (consumer benefit packages) customers. Both types of customers are the lifeblood of company success. Also, customers sometimes are better at evaluating support services than primary goods-producing or service-providing processes.

Support service processes cost money, influence customer satisfaction, and consume time. Lack of management attention to support service processes occurs both in goods-producing and service-providing organizations. These support services represent 50 to 90 percent of the cost of being in business! This is where the greatest opportunity for productivity improvement and competitive advantage can be found in most organizations. A typical list of support services is shown on the next page.

This long list of support services helps you see the tremendous resources committed to support services and why they constitute such a high percentage of sales. Information, service and people are what's being processed here. Note that many of these services are not really support services. They are essential to providing the external or internal customer with an effective consumer benefit

Union grievance procedures	Customer complaint processes
Travel services	Waste management
Training programs	Company communication systems
Computer software services	Employee counseling
CBP warranty processes	Security and safety systems
Advertising programs	Marketing research
Sales programs	Accounting systems
Supplier programs	Regulatory procedures
Claims processing	Customer-contact procedures
Environmental programs	Health systems and procedures
Franchise systems	Research and development
Repair services	Recognition and reward programs
Financial systems	Refund and recall procedures
Benefits administration	Legal and tax procedures
Strategic planning	Conference/meeting administration

package (CBP) or employee benefit package (EBP). EBPs and their processes should use the same models, procedures and decision making mechanisms as CBPs. The high cost of all EBPs as a percent of sales demands that they be managed with the same intensity and expertise as the organization's primary processes. This is one reason why this book treats CBPs and EBPs the same.

A survey by the Manufacturer's Alliance for Productivity and Innovation (MAPI) asked the following question to 131 firms, 114 of which were manufacturing firms. "Which of the following functions are subject to your company's quality processes?" The answers were as follows: operations, 99 percent said yes; marketing, 64 percent; human resources, 62 percent; administration 59 percent; finance 53 percent; tax, 39 percent; and legal, 31 percent.[13] These data indicate that support service processes require much more management attention.

Support services are of great importance in scoring an MBNQA application. Many MBNQA points, as well as customers, are lost because of support service deficiencies. At least 15 of the 28 MBNQA performance subcategories (items) are related either directly or indirectly to support services. There are no unimportant processes in any organization. Xerox, for example, identifies 67 processes that create its goods and services.

Integrate Support Service Processes with Primary Processes

Service systems and processes, especially support services, lack integration with the organization's primary service-providing, goods-producing, and business processes. The technology and know-how necessary to integrate service processes with the rest of the organization's processes is normally available. The only thing missing is management action to make it happen.

The MBNQA scoring guidelines use the word *integration* to describe the MBNQA performance category called *approach*. The MBNQA Award Criteria consider *approach* to include the following characteristics that relate to integration: (1) the degree to which the approach is systematic, integrated, and consistently applied; (2) the degree to which the approach embodies effective evaluation/improvement cycles; (3) the degree to which the approach is based upon quantitative information that is objective and reliable; and (4) the indicators of unique and innovative approaches including significant and effective new adaptations of tools and techniques used in other applications or types of businesses.[14] Service processes frequently don't meet these integrative and management by fact performance standards.

For example, a *Consumer Reports Travel Letter* surveyed 384 airline frequent-flyer members. It found that one-third of the frequent flyers who tried to redeem their awards didn't get what they wanted one-third of the time. They had to pick other dates, go to different cities, and were delayed in having awards and tickets issued.[15]

The so-called support service (the airline frequent flyer program) was not integrated with the primary service (the routine airline reservation system). Each airline service process was independently designed and operated. Here a supporting service and its lack of integration with the primary service is hurting customer satisfaction of the airline's most valued customers. Integrating and interlinking primary and support processes together can lead to powerful redefinitions of the consumer benefit package. It can restructure the organization and the industry. That is why CBP definition and design—the topic of Chapter 4—is so important.

Improve Management of Customer-Contact Personnel

Management systems for customer- or high-contact personnel are not well designed or managed. Customer- or high-contact jobs are very stressful because service providers must handle customer inquiries, problems, and complaints. Many of these service encounters are handled over the telephone. About 15 percent of the US workforce works in telephone related customer contact jobs.

Examples of service encounters handled over the telephone include making airline, hotel, or rental car reservations; checking on your medical, credit card, or electric bill; ordering merchandise from a mail order business, and reporting a problem with the CBP you purchased. Service encounters that also demand a high degree of customer contact but are not so dependent on the telephone include: hospital nurses, airline flight attendants, dentists, retail store associates, lawyers, teachers, bank trust administrators, and barbers.

The MBNQA criteria expect customer-contact relationships to be well managed. MBNQA Items 7.2 to 7.5 in the 1993 Award Criteria are related to this point. These four items represent 195 of 1,000 maximum points. Some of these points are related to approach while others concentrate on results. One can argue that more than 195 points should be allocated to customer-contact performance, especially for service-providing organizations. The issue here is whether the

MBNQA generic criteria are applicable to education, service, government, and health care organizations.

Federal Express is a world-class leader in customer-contact design, training, and management. In 1990 before Federal Express won the MBNQA, Fred Smith, CEO and founder, stated:

> Probably the most important thing that we have to add to the body of knowledge (for National Quality Month audiences) is what we've learned about the involvement of our employees at the *customer-contact level* of the quality process . . . What I expect out of all employees is that they do their utmost to see that we deliver what we told our customers we would do 100% of the time. Every time a customer has a contact with us, whether it's receiving a bill, talking to us on the telephone, accepting or shipping a package, or processing a claim—heaven forbid!—the customer must be 100 percent satisfied with the way we've handled it. That's what we want our employees to recognize as the first and foremost aspect of each of our jobs.[16]

The second example of a high-performance customer-contact system is Yard-Master, a regional lawn care company. It guarantees beautiful lawns; a typical six-treatment lawn care service costs about $250 per year. Customer-contact relationships are the cornerstone of its competitive strategy. In the summer of 1991, the Midwest experienced a severe drought. Many lawns burned up because of water restrictions or simple neglect. The company called customers who had dead lawns and explained that it would reseed the yard with a seed-slitter machine, free of charge. Did the customer want the reseeding done? The company would guarantee a beautiful lawn no matter who was the party at fault. MBNQA Item 7.3 covers explicit or implicit promises (service guarantees) to the customer. The service guarantee was invoked by the employees who inspect each lawn, not by a customer complaint. The service guarantee and well-trained customer-contact personnel closed the customer service loop. Yard-Master used these capabilities to increase market share and gain competitive advantage.

Select Examiners that Know How to Score Service Firms

Service is a performance. Managing a performance, like the direction of a play, is very different from managing production. Space does not allow us to examine all the differences between designing and managing service-providing processes and goods-producing processes, some of which were described in the previous chapter. Understanding service management can help all MBNQA examiners do a better job, especially for service firms.

Scoring MBNQA applications must match the art it intends to serve. For service firms, the art is designing and managing service encounters—in other words, managing a performance. The 1992 Application for the MBNQA Board of Examiners added a *new* section that asks the examiner to rank his or her ability to evaluate manufacturing, service, small manufacturing business, and small service business. This information will be used to better match examiner expertise to the applicant's type of business.

CONCLUSION

The Malcolm Baldrige National Quality Award has raised the consciousness of the United States about quality performance. It helps explain the vital role quality performance plays in creating the world's standard of living and quality of life. It has accomplished its three objectives, some better than others, during its early years. Despite its critics, the MBNQA was established to achieve long-term national goals, and it is indeed achieving those goals.

Certainly, some MBNQA Winners will fail in the marketplace. The award criteria and audit procedures do not ensure continuous marketplace success. No award system can guarantee success forever. If one did, everyone would sign up! And some MBNQA applicants will divert too much of their resources to the award process, and not enough to taking care of business. These problems are outside the intended bounds of the MBNQA. The award defines a solution space around quality. Meanwhile, many people will study the guidelines, evaluate how they apply to their business, and try to do it their own way.

One telling fact about the MBNQA is that it took the United States until 1987—36 years after Japan's famous Deming Prize was established—to begin the program. That was a long time for the United States to ignore or downplay quality at the national level and underestimate the power of a government-sponsored national award.

A future challenge is using or modifying the MBNQA for service processes such as hospitals, schools, airlines, and government services. Here is where there are great opportunities to improve national competitiveness. Goods-producing processes were easy targets compared to doing the same thing for service processes.

An examination of Chapter 1's Table 1–2 shows that foreign service companies are positioning themselves to go after market share in the top marketplace in the world—the United States. Service firms, big and small, must get serious about the MBNQA, its approach, and all of its implications. The MBNQA framework is one approach that helps people find solutions.

P A R T

II

CONSUMER BENEFIT PACKAGE MANAGEMENT

"How well you integrate service-, entertainment-, and information-content into your consumer and employee benefit package(s) are keys to competitive advantage . . . perfect products are not enough anymore."

The Author

Chapter Four

Consumer Benefit Package Design

C onsumer benefit package (CBP) management, Part II of this book, has two major building blocks—CBP design and CBP strategy. CBP design and strategy are essential steps to designing world-class service encounters. The Service Encounter Cone that was shown in Figure 2–3 highlights these two essential building blocks.

A consumer (or customer) benefit package is a clearly defined set of tangible (goods-content) and intangible (service-content) attributes (features) the customer recognizes, pays for, uses, or experiences. It is some combination of goods and services configured in a certain way. A CBP includes the purchase of a primary (core) good with peripheral goods and/or services or of a primary (core) service with peripheral goods and/or services. The final set of CBP features or attributes fulfills certain customer needs and wants.

Product package and service package could be viewed as two components of a CBP. But these two components of the CBP are intermingled and not independent, especially in the customer's mind. There is great risk in separating the product package from the service package in terms of design, management, and execution. The customer buys a CBP, not a subset of a CBP or a pure product or service package.

A consumer benefit package is different from an employee benefit package (EBP) only in terms of who is the ultimate recipient of the benefit package. Employees have benefit packages, so why not consumers? The term *benefit package* is broader than either *product* or *service* package.

In this book, *product* always means goods-content (physical or tangible) attributes only. Attempts to define *service* have been only partially successful. In an earlier work, I wrote the following: "Is a service an idea, entertainment, information, a change in the customer's appearance or health, a circumstance— being at the right place at the right time, a convenience, a feeling of security, a physical thing, shelter, or what?"[1]

A more complicated definition of a service, defined by Sasser, et al., and refined by Fitzsimmons and Sullivan, is as follows: "A service is a package of explicit and implicit benefits performed with a supporting facility and using facilitating goods."[2]

For example, an individual checkbook service has explicit benefits by documenting and monitoring cash inflows and outflows. The implicit benefits of this service include a sense of security, privacy, flexibility, control, and stability in the individual's financial well-being. The supporting facilities include the main and branch banks and automatic teller machines. The facilitating goods are used or consumed by the individual and include the paper, checkbook, and monthly statements.

In other previous work I defined "a service as any primary or complementary activity that does not directly produce a physical product—that is, the nongoods part of the transaction between buyer (customer) and seller (provider)."[3] Other definitions of service also suggest that output is consumed where it is produced, that services require the presence of the customer, that services cannot be inventoried, and that a service is a deed, a performance, or an effort.

CONSUMER BENEFIT PACKAGE DEFINITION AND CONFIGURATION

The terminology of a consumer or employee benefit package that recognizes *both* product and service attributes is shown in Figure 4–1. The four levels of the CBP terminology are shown in Figure 4–1. The first level is the *consumer benefit package* (CBP) itself. Three elements make up a CBP. The first element of a CBP and the second level in the hierarchy is the *primary* (core) thing or circumstance the customer recognizes, pays for, uses, or experiences. *Primary* customer wants and needs are satisfied by *primary* CBP attributes.

The second element of a CBP and a third-level term is *peripheral*. A *peripheral* good or service is a secondary characteristic of the CBP. *Peripheral* customer wants and needs are satisfied by *peripheral* CBP attributes. The terms *accessory, auxiliary, complementary, facilitating, satellite,* and *supporting* all refer to a product or service attribute (feature) that attaches itself to the primary (core) thing or circumstance the customer is buying. This book uses the term *peripheral* to emphasize it is away from the center or core. A peripheral good or service is also a permanent (standard) part of the CBP design at all delivery sites and points of creation.

A peripheral good or service is often the key to differentiating one's CBP from that of competitors and gaining competitive advantage. For example, Daniel Brock, vice president of marketing at USAir, the last US carrier to start a frequent-flyer program in 1985, commented that "It was pretty clear to us that if you wanted to be in the US air-transportation business, you had to have a frequent-flier program. We could not do business without it."[4]

The third element of a CBP and the fourth level of CBP terminology is a *variant*. A *variant* is some CBP attribute (feature) that departs from the standard CBP. It is related to how the CBP is created and delivered at a particular place or in a certain circumstance. A variant allows for customization of a standard CBP

FIGURE 4–1
The Terminology of Consumer (Employee) Benefit Packages—Configuration A

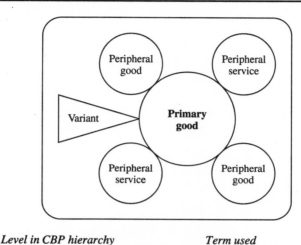

Level in CBP hierarchy	Term used
First (highest)	Consumer or employee benefit package
Second	Primary (core)
Third	Peripheral
Fourth (lowest)	Variant

and is time- or location-dependent. CBP variants allow the CBP design to be flexible and incorporate the innovations of local managers. Once a variant is incorporated into all CBP delivery sites on a continuous basis it becomes a peripheral good or service of the CBP.

Global or universal CBPs (UCBPs) make greater use of variants in their CBP design than domestic or highly standardized CBPs. Universal CBPs are often tailored to local culture, behaviors, regulations, and practices.

A primary good complemented by peripheral services might be the purchase of an automobile partly because of a superior repair service and warranty program. The peripheral service is wrapped or bundled around the primary good. CBP Configuration A in Figure 4–1 is an example of this offering.

An example of a variant for this automotive CBP is at Ricart's Auto Mall in Columbus, Ohio. Here a fishing lake and a car performance test track were added to the auto mall. Why? Ricart views entertainment as a big part of its CBP definition. If customers are having fun they will buy cars too! Fred Ricart, co-owner of the auto mall said, "What do you do with the largest auto complex in the world? We turn it into Disneyland!"[5]

What's next at Ricart's Auto Mall? Day care facilities? An Ohio Division of Motor Vehicles office? He's considering these too! Some of these variants are not appropriate or possible at every auto mall, but they help Ricart stay Number 1 in his industry.

J D Power, an international survey firm, expects that only 5,000 of the current 16,000 US auto dealers will still be in business by early in the coming century.[6] My guess is Ricart will still be the highest-volume automobile dealer in the world.

Ricart offers many things other than cars: convenience, financing, no-hassle guarantees, car selection and variety, friendly employees, an outstanding auto repair service, low prices, free loaner cars, and fun. Adding entertainment and excitement to a CBP design is one way to win the Service/Quality Challenge.

CBP Configuration B in Figure 4–2 shows a primary *service* with peripheral goods and services. Personal checkbook service is an example of a primary service supported by peripheral goods (monthly account statement, checkbook itself) and services (financial record keeping, customer service hotline). Here, peripheral goods and services are wrapped around a primary service. A variant is shown in CBP Configuration B in Figure 4–2 for illustration purposes. But since this CBP is a standardized CBP for all locations and time periods, no variants really exist for this personal checkbook example.

Figure 4–3 shows a group of CBPs bundled together. For example, a bundle of CBPs such as credit cards, a hotel, restaurants, an airline, entertainment, an automobile club, and a travel agency can be combined to create a vacation. Bundled CBP Configuration C in Figure 4–3 shows this possibility. Once you define each part of a vacation CBP in detail, you quickly see how things can go wrong. There are thousands of CBP attributes and millions of opportunities for error. As we shall discuss later in this chapter, the bundle of CBPs provided by hospitals and airlines are probably the most complex, with vacations almost as complex.

The CBP methodology is a quick visual way to discuss a company's goods and services and focus management discussions. Other CBP configurations are possible. The CBP framework provides the paradigms to help formalize CBP design, especially for services and service industries. This is exactly the type of formal framework the Malcolm Baldrige National Quality Award criteria demands.

Management will define and manage the CBP or EBP with clear delineations between primary and peripheral goods and services as shown in Figures 4–1 to 4–3. The internal or external customer may not make such clear distinctions. In fact, the customer may have a peripheral service, such as billing, as the center of his or her CBP with the primary good or service as an aside. Sometimes the customer may ignore or miss a key peripheral good or service or variant, altogether.

Figure 4–4 depicts a CBP or EBP from an individual customer's perspective. Note that the customer views a peripheral good as the center of the CBP configuration. What management defined as the primary (core) good or service is peripheral in this CBP. Also, the question mark in Figure 4–4 depicts a peripheral good or service the customer doesn't recognize or care about. As more information-, entertainment-, and service-content are bundled to the CBP, the more complex and possibly confusing it is to customers. Of course, the idea is to

FIGURE 4–2
Consumer Benefit Package—Configuration B

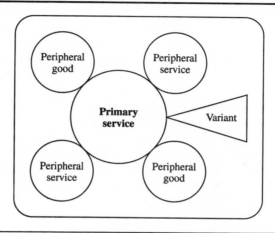

define how the average customer in a given target market views the CBP or customize each CBP to the individual customer. Furthermore, at the service-encounter level these goods and services must be unbundled properly.

One CBP design problem is that management views what the organization sells as it is shown in Figures 4–1 to 4–3, whereas the customer sees it more as in Figure 4–4. This situation creates gaps between what management perceives they are managing and what customers think they are buying. In Chapter 10, we shall introduce a model to help understand these expectation–perception gaps.

The objectives of CBP design are:

1. Make sure the final CBP attributes you are using are the correct ones.
2. Evaluate the relative importance of each attribute in the customer's mind.
3. Evaluate each attribute in terms of process and service encounter capability.
4. Figure out how best to segment the market(s) and position CBPs in each market.
5. Avoid CBP duplication and proliferation.
6. Bring each CBP, and associated process and service encounters, to market as quickly as possible.
7. Use the CBP framework and final attributes to design facilities, processes, equipment, jobs, and service encounters.
8. Maximize customer satisfaction and profits.

FIGURE 4–3
Bundled CBP Configuration C—A Vacation

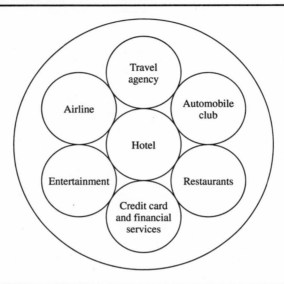

CONSUMER AND EMPLOYEE BENEFIT PACKAGE FAMILIES

A number of related CBPs or EBPs are analogous to traditional product lines. Two points about CBP lines are:

1. The CBP line should have an income statement (revenue minus costs equals profit and contribution margin) and each CBP within the line should also have an income statement. The field of accounting has been only partially successful in meeting these information needs. To manage a CBP line effectively you need clear CBP definitions as shown by Figures 4–1 to 4–7, and the relative economics per CBP line and per CBP within the line. All of these management capabilities and responsibilities fall under the heading of CBP Management.

2. Within each CBP line, the degree of information- and service-content can increase as we go from standardized CBPs for mass markets to customized CBPs for premium markets. Therefore, each CBP has its own unique set of CBP attributes. These final CBP attributes are the basis for facility, process, equipment, job, and service-encounter design. If the degree of information, entertainment, and service content differs greatly within a CBP line, it poses special hazards. For example, management must decide whether to use a common or dedicated service delivery process for each CBP and CBP line. This topic is examined in Chapter 6.

FIGURE 4-4
How a Customer Views the Consumer Benefit Package

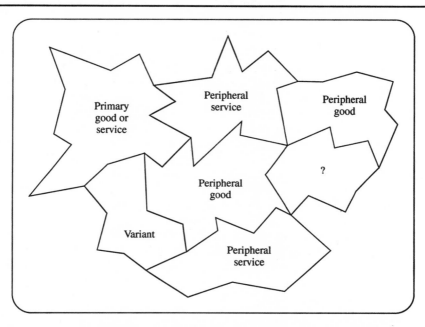

Here we describe CBP definition and design while Chapters 5 and 6 focus on service and CBP strategy. In reality, CBP design and strategy must occur simultaneously. Good management decisions in CBP design and strategy also make it easier to design and manage the service delivery system (Part III of this book), the service/quality management system (Part IV), and service encounters (Part VI).

CBP COMPLEXITY, DUPLICATION, AND PROLIFERATION

The complexity of CBP attributes and configurations is great for many businesses. For example, when checking into the hospital, the patient and the patient's family must interact with a large number of CBPs and respective delivery processes. If you make a flowchart of patient, family, and information movements through the hospital, you see that many service processes affect the total service experience. Example processes of a hospital include: parking lot or transportation service, admissions, insurance, dietary, pharmacy, surgical units, doctors, nurses, janitors, laboratories, imaging units, checkout, home visitations, and billing. Each of these processes has its own set of detailed CBP attributes. It is easy to see why providing excellent service encounters before, during, and after a hospital stay is a difficult job.

Another complex CBP is a pleasant airline flight that is on time with no hassles. The service-delivery processes necessary to accomplish this seemingly simple goal include: airplane routing and scheduling, reservation and booking system, flight attendant scheduling and training, passenger ticketing and boarding, frequent flyer program and administration, airport gate analysis and management, airplane refueling, cabin food service delivery to the plane, pilot scheduling and training, airport and airplane security, baggage service, and airplane maintenance. The output of each of these processes is a CBP. Failure of any of these service processes can ruin the customer's service encounter. Add to this the factors that are beyond the direct control of an airline, such as weather, regulatory actions, other airlines' routes and schedules, and airport and gate capacity, and you see why this is a tough business.

Hospitals and airlines are two of the more complex service delivery systems to manage, and CBP definition helps you see why. Good CBP and process design are essential in these businesses if they are to maximize customer satisfaction and profits.

Duplicate or overlapping CBPs are common in many businesses. Somehow managers are in a hurry to add CBPs but seldom take the time to delete CBPs or integrate CBP processes. CBP proliferation is a major problem that only management can control. Part of the reason for this is management's fear of missing a market opportunity. Another reason for CBP proliferation and duplication is the lack of good performance data for each CBP.

One example of CBP complexity, duplication, and proliferation will illustrate the problems of letting CBP design get out of control. But management caused the problem and management can fix the problem.

One insurance firm found that it had 46 separate forms for initiating CBPs—life and disability insurance, retirement and annuity programs, and so on. The 46 forms caused considerable confusion in the field. The financial planners spent hours filling them out, often did not have the right form at the right time, and frequently had to ask the customer for redundant information if the customers were buying several CBPs. And those 46 different forms had to be processed by the backroom operations people!

Another disadvantage of the 46 CBPs and associated forms was that the forms were not of uniform appearance. Inconsistent forms encouraged a vague corporate identity. These 46 forms were also the communication link among the client, the selling agent, and the backroom processing employees. The forms coupled marketing and operations together.

CBP design and definition was out of control. The customer, the frontroom financial agent, the backroom processing personnel, and management had to deal with this unnecessary complexity. If CBP design is confusing, everything else is confusing. The firm also thought it had 46 different CBPs. What it found out after an extensive CBP analysis was that it actually had only a dozen CBPs. Four forms were then designed to initiate service for these 12 CBPs.

Once the firm completed this CBP redesign and adjusted its service-delivery process, many benefits were gained. These benefits of better CBP design included: improved CBP (and form) processing time, better customer database information, decreased processing costs, improved employee morale and corporate identity, and agents who thought they did a better job of cross-selling their CBPs. The company finally had a set of clearly defined CBPs with which to solicit business. And more importantly, the frontroom CBP requirements were aligned with the backroom process capabilities!

CBP proliferation often strains a single delivery process. The hazard of overloading a single delivery process with too many CBPs or sharing delivery processes can lead to great inefficiencies and CBP ineffectiveness. Job design becomes fuzzy and confusion grows. The decision of when to use shared versus dedicated service processes to provide CBPs is discussed in Chapter 6.

The job of management is to clearly define CBPs and the processes that deliver them. It all begins with CBP design and strategy. Often the problem with CBP proliferation can be traced to functionalism. The battles and mis-communications between functional areas can cause CBP design to be vague and ill-timed. One of the costs of functionalism is CBP proliferation and duplication. Chapter 8 will address how a service management approach to organizational design can help overcome this problem.

How to monitor and control CBP proliferation is a difficult management task. A first step is to establish a CBP executive committee charged with overseeing existing and new CBP design. Interdisciplinary CBP design teams also should be used at the beginning of the CBP development cycle for new CBPs. Then all functional areas have a hand in designing the final CBP, its processes, and service encounters.

Coupled with each CBP design team or executive committee is a colossal demand for good data and smart analysis of the data. Without reliable and timely information, the following example questions are difficult to answer. What are the final CBP attributes? How do we meet or exceed the performance standards for each CBP attribute? How can we best design the facilities, processes, equipment, jobs, and service encounters to create and deliver these world-class CBP attributes? What CBPs should we continue to offer for sale and which ones should we eliminate? What key CBP attribute differentiates us best from competitors and should be the focus of our Comprehensive Customer Contact Plan?

Now that we understand the CBP idea and terminology, let's examine other issues about CBP and EBP definition and design. The chapter will close by describing three methods of CBP attribute analysis and provide examples that illustrate the ideas contained in Figures 4–1 to 4–7.

WHAT IS THE FIRM'S BUSINESS?

People do not always know "What is the firm's business?" They often define it very narrowly or incorrectly. Usually this is to the detriment of services. Why does the customer purchase or not purchase the company's goods and services? What does the customer think he or she is purchasing? A primary or peripheral good? A primary or peripheral service? Both? How are they configured? What attributes (features) of the CBP are most and least attractive to the customer?

In 1972, Ted Levitt, in one of his many landmark articles, warned goods (and service) companies about the dangers of relying solely on a product-producing perspective. He noted that "the problem in so many cases is that customer service is not viewed by manufacturers as an integral part of what the customer buys, but as something peripheral to landing the sale. So many things go wrong because companies fail to adequately define what they sell. What a company "makes" and what a customer "buys" are not always the same."[7]

Levitt goes on to say, "But the distinctions (between goods-producing and service-providing firms) are largely spurious. There are no such things as service industries. There are only industries whose service components are greater or less than those of other industries. Everybody is in service." The CBP framework defined here forces you to think this way—the service management way.

Consider the example of highly profitable Super America, a division of Ashland Oil, which operates over 500 stores that sell gasoline in 16 states. How do you differentiate a product such as plain old gasoline—a necessary commodity today?

First, you bundle several peripheral services (quick self-service food and drink service, fast checkouts, state lottery and automatic teller machines, etc.), and peripheral convenience goods (groceries and merchandise) to the primary good (gasoline), and create a consumer benefit package. You simultaneously strengthen and support this bundle of goods and services with an extraordinary service-delivery-system design and CBP strategy. You take the drudgery out of buying gasoline by skillful CBP and process design.

To support the management and daily execution of this CBP you plan every detail. Your management actions include: the development of a standard facility design to enhance customer movement and transaction processing, keeping the place spotless inside and out, lighting it well, using colorful red, white, and blue signage, using canopies to shield customers from the weather, adding microphones beside each gasoline pump, using multiple cash registers and service attendants to break queues, staying open at least 18 hours a day, and training employees to a high level of competence and sensitivity to friendly customer service.

What is the business of Super America? Selling gasoline to customers? No— many businesses sell gasoline and take a restricted or product view of their business. Super America is a *convenience store that happens to sell gasoline*. (That's right, think service first!) Yes—very few competitors bundle goods and services together as well as does Super America's service-delivery system.

But as discussed in Chapter 2 and highlighted in Table 2–1, competitors can quickly copy the CBP design and delivery system of Super America. There are few, if any, patents on services or service processes. Many convenience stores such as Super America that happen to sell gasoline continue to experiment with peripheral and variant CBP features. Some are adding video rentals, bakeries, and pharmacies to their CBP definition. These CBP innovations and revenue enhancers are part of the CBP research and development effort—the topic of Chapter 9.

Note that from the customer's perspective the purchase is a bundle of goods and services, a CBP, not a product package or a service package. The term *product* is obsolete in today's marketplace for almost everything we buy. The minute you say *product* you have taken too narrow a view of your business. You force yourself, when you say product, to step back in time to when steel mills and refrigerator factories were the pride of the industrialized world. It sets the wrong mindset, philosophy, and strategic attitude. It causes you to define things incorrectly. It provides management with the wrong paradigm to think about its business. A product-mentality places too much importance on the physical product and not enough on the information-, entertainment- and service-content of *what* customers actually buy and *how* they buy it. The CBP framework defined here forces you to always give equal status to the good- and service-content in a CBP.

CUSTOMER (MARKET) WANTS AND NEEDS ANALYSIS

What does the customer want and need? Identifying and defining the true wants and needs of the customer are not easy for many reasons. Two general reasons are as follows.

First, customers may not always know what they want in a CBP until new attributes or features are offered for sale. Kano et al. suggest that customers want or need three types of product (CBP) features.[8] The first they call *one-dimensional quality features*, which are CBP attributes that the customer specifically requests. The customer is happy when these attributes are present. The customer is unhappy when these attributes are absent.

Expected features are CBP attributes the customer expects but may not specifically identify or request. When these attributes are present the customer is satisfied and when they are absent the customer is dissatisfied. *Exciting features* represent features the customers don't ask for because they don't know they exist or could exist. When these attributes are present the customer is excited and very satisfied. When they are absent the customer is not dissatisfied.

Second, as mentioned in Chapter 1 in the discussion of *instantaneous service,* managers are constantly chasing customers' changing wants and needs. Once your company or a competitor reaches a new service plateau and level of performance that attracts customers, either by adding new CBP attributes or improving performance on an existing attribute, everyone in that industry must respond.

To identify correctly the final CBP attributes requires being close to the customer. There are many ways to do this, such as having employees visit and talk to customers, having managers wander around and talk to customers, initiating service/quality measurement systems, and doing good marketing research.

Good marketing research includes using such techniques as focus groups, salesperson- and employee-feedback, warranty performance analysis, on-the-spot interviews with customers, video taping service encounters, mystery shoppers, toll-free telephone hotline customer feedback, and mail, telephone, and comment card surveys. The methods and techniques of marketing research and consumer behavior are critical to developing a good CBP design. Many marketing research books focus on these methods.[9]

Current trends are to segment the market into many niches, often across nations. If the costs of segmenting the market are low, it pays to continue segmenting the market. Some hotel chains, for example, have as many as 14 market segments for business and pleasure travelers.

Marriott has four major market segments, roughly paralleling its major hotel chains. These four chains are Fairfield Inns, Marriott Courtyard, Residence Inns, and Marriott Hotels & Resorts. Marriott is the General Motors of the US hotel industry. Its service/quality challenge is to expand to global markets, maintain high service/quality performance tailored to local cultures, and continue as a world-class competitor in the global lodging business.

If market segmentation costs are high, they can eliminate the benefits of market segmentation. Some airlines have reduced the number of market segments they serve after discovering the incremental cost was greater than the incremental revenue.

Other airlines, most notably American Airlines, have used yield (revenue) management techniques to segment the airline cabin into many market segments, with remarkable success. The SABRE (Semi-Automated Business Research Environment) airline reservation and information system provides the data. Yield management takes these data and analyzes booking and demand patterns, partitions the airline cabin for individual flights into market segments and allocates seats, sets discount-fare policies and rules, and helps manage all this on a real-time basis. The objective is to maximize revenue per flight until take-off time.

The American Airlines Decision Technologies Division is where these yield management models are developed. The division estimates that yield management accounts for about 5 percent, or $500 million, of American Airline's annual revenues per year. Obviously, smart data analysis and market segmentation is profitable at American Airlines.

Other industries are beginning to use yield management to segment their markets on a group and real-time basis. Hotels and automobile rental companies are experimenting with these methods. Telephone and electric utility companies are varying their pricing strategy by time of day or day of the week.

The type and number of CBP features also cost money. It costs money to design the feature and to develop the processes that create and deliver it. Thus, the economics of CBP definition and configuration must be considered in the final CBP design. Qualitative and strategic factors also must be woven into the CBP justification effort.

CONSUMER BENEFIT PACKAGE ATTRIBUTE ANALYSIS

One way to define your CBP is to identify and categorize the attributes in terms of tangible (goods content) and intangible (service content). The essential challenge for management is to ensure that none of the final CBP attributes that might encourage a customer to buy the CBP are misidentified or go unnoticed or underdelivered. Three simple tools can help you do this task. Some of these simple tools are also amenable to more complex data analysis techniques but space does not permit a description here.

The *first tool* is having customers, employees, and managers make independent lists of what attributes they think make up the CBP. The customer-wants-and-needs analysis should be done from the customer's perspective.

Who are the customers for each CBP? Sometimes there is more than one type of customer. For example, hospitals might consider their customers to be the patients, the patients' families, physicians, hospital employees, and third-party insurance payors.

The lists of tangible and intangible attributes should be carefully checked against one another and the information consolidated into a master list. A cross-functional team of managers, customers, and employees should develop the master list.

If the number of attributes is large, it may be necessary to simplify the CBP classification scheme further by using generic subheadings. For example, tangible attributes for a restaurant might be subdivided into food quality, facility, parking lot, equipment, and employee physical appearance. Intangible attributes can be subdivided into convenience, employee service attitude and timeliness, employee technical competence, check accuracy and payment process, and so on.

A *second tool* to help analyze and define final CBP attributes is the *House of Quality*. Hauser and Clausing first defined the house of quality as a matrix where each row represents a customer requirement or want and need.[10] Each column represents a technical requirement of the CBP from the company's viewpoint. Figure 4–5 is a simple example of the house-of-quality format. Customer bene-

FIGURE 4–5
Service Management House-of-Quality Example Format for a Commodity Trading House for Orange Juice, Cocoa, and Coffee

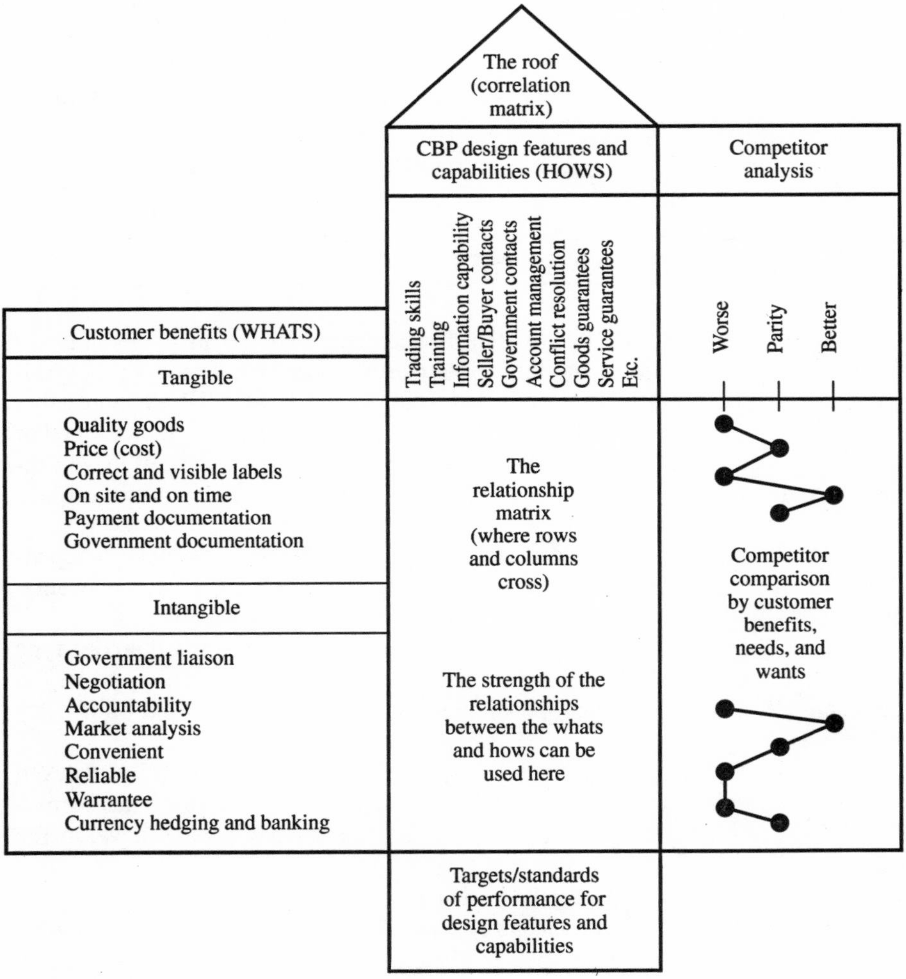

Customer benefits (WHATS)	CBP design features and capabilities (HOWS)		Competitor analysis
	The roof (correlation matrix)		
	Trading skills / Training / Information capability / Seller/Buyer contacts / Government contacts / Account management / Conflict resolution / Goods guarantees / Service guarantees / Etc.	Worse / Parity / Better
Tangible		
Quality goods / Price (cost) / Correct and visible labels / On site and on time / Payment documentation / Government documentation	The relationship matrix (where rows and columns cross)	
Intangible		Competitor comparison by customer benefits, needs, and wants
Government liaison / Negotiation / Accountability / Market analysis / Convenient / Reliable / Warrantee / Currency hedging and banking	The strength of the relationships between the whats and hows can be used here	
	Targets/standards of performance for design features and capabilities	

fits (requirements) can be thought of as *what* the customer requires (wants and needs). CBP design and process capabilities (technical requirements) are *how* the company will meet these wants and needs. Customer wants and needs (the whats) must be determined first and then the final CBP attributes and capabilities (the hows) can be defined to meet these wants and needs.

CBP design can use the house-of-quality format. The house of quality is a bridge between the *whats* and *hows*. Manufacturing firms first used the house of quality for the planning and design of products. But it can be used just as well for CBP design having a high degree of service content.

The relationship matrix (where the rows and columns cross) identifies whether the CBP design features defined by the company have any relationship to specific customer wants and needs. The strength of the relationship is normally shown by various symbols and relative weights. Also, each attribute can be weighted by importance, scores computed, and compared to competitors' CBPs. Many other columns, rows, computations, and matrix areas can be added to the basic house-of-quality format.

In general, the House of Quality is an excellent way to translate customer wants and needs to final CBP features or attributes. The House of Quality helps coordinate the marketing function (whats) with the engineering and operations functions (hows). Urban and Hauser present many ideas and methods to help with House of Quality decisions and information analysis.[11]

The house-of-quality tool is the key method in a broader approach called Quality Function Deployment (QFD). Here, customer wants and needs are systematically collected and organized (the whats) and translated into the organization's technical language and capabilities (the hows). Customer requirements—the voice of the customer—are stated in the customer's own words. Final CBP attributes and capabilities are stated in the technical language of the organization. In QFD the whats and hows are disaggregated into process and service-encounter levels of detail. CBP, process and service-encounter ownership is assigned and measures devised to evaluate performance.[12]

A *third tool* useful for identifying and organizing the attributes of a CBP is an affinity diagram. The only real difference between the affinity diagram and listing CBP tangible and intangible attributes is that the CBP is displayed with its major subheading groups. Within each group, the specific attributes of that group are displayed. Let's illustrate the first tool (CBP attribute lists) and the third (affinity diagram) with an example.

SLIDE-MASTER'S CONSUMER BENEFIT PACKAGE

Slide-Master is a single facility enterprise located near a large downtown metropolitan area. The founders of Slide-Master recognized that many large corporations, consulting and legal firms, and government offices needed a fast, very high quality slide production and delivery service.

The CBP for Slide-Master in Figure 4–6 is formatted in terms of tangible and intangible attributes. This is a list of final CBP attributes. Slide-Master sells a primary good with peripheral goods and services, much like CBP Configuration A in Figure 4–1. The primary good is a multicolored, high-quality slide, made to customer specifications. There are over six million different color combinations.

FIGURE 4–6
Final CBP Attributes for Slide-Master

TANGIBLE (GOODS-CONTENT)

Slides:
Quality, durable, clean, new film and
cardboard
High-resolution pictures and slides
Multiple color combinations (6 million)
Slide properly centered and focused

Equipment/Technology:
Latest computer hardware
State-of-the-art software
High-quality camera
Superior maintenance of all equipment
Well-maintained delivery vehicles with
ads on the sides
Flexible for custom designs

People:
Clean and very well groomed
Attractive uniforms

Packaging:
Heavy, clear, high-quality sleeves
Sequenced and numbered properly
Loaded in attractive boxes or slide
carousels

Facilities:
Ample parking spaces
Secure parking lot
Attractive signs
Clean, attractive building—outside
Up-scale indoor wall pictures and decor
Reception area and service counter—
clean and professional appearance
Soft, relaxing background music
Plush furniture
Bright lighting
Complimentary coffee and soft drinks
Restrooms, soap, etc; clean

INTANGIBLE (SERVICE-CONTENT)

Convenience and timeliness:
Facility close to downtown
Pickup and delivery service
Telephone/fax order capability
Standard 3-day service
Rush 1-day service
Really try to handle last-minute customer
changes
Accurate, itemized billing by 5th working
day of each month

Professionalism:
Absolutely confidential services
Emphasis on telephone courtesy
Refer to client by name
Client order documentation correctly
filled out and processed
Flexible to customer needs

Consulting services:
Artistic expertise
History of previous jobs
Technical knowledge
Nonbusiness hours on-call professional

Service attitude:
User friendliness
Polite, responsive attitude
Do exactly what we promised
Script dialogues for order taking and post-
purchase callbacks
Confident but relaxing behavior

The actual material content of each slide (a piece of cardboard, photographic film, and a plastic sleeve) costs less than a dollar per slide. The slides are then packaged, which includes placing them in the proper sequence, numbering each slide, and placing these in attractive boxes or slide carousels. Each slide goes through quality inspections every step of the way.

Customers pay up to $50 for a single slide. Why would they pay so much for slides? What is the business of Slide-Master?

A review of Figure 4–6 suggests five general categories of tangible attributes. *Slides* and *packaging* are the primary goods customers purchase. The other tangible attributes that support this service transaction are *physical facilities, people,* and *equipment/technology.* These three generic attributes can be thought of as physical evidence that supports the service transaction. We'll study physical evidence—one of the seven P's of service management—in Chapter 6.

The intangible attributes in Figure 4–6 correspond to four generic service attributes, such as *convenience* and *timeliness.* Convenience takes many forms, such as pickup and delivery service by a company representative, the ability to place orders by telephone using a fax machine, accurate monthly billing statements guaranteed to be mailed by the fifth working day of each month, and a facility near its downtown customers.

Professionalism and *consulting services* in Figure 4–6 include a comprehensive consulting service, a professional artist service, absolute confidentiality, post-sale callbacks to clients to see if everything went OK, state-of-the-art software and hardware capability, and the flexibility for last-minute changes. *Service attitude* includes courteous telephone conversations, polite pickup and delivery company representatives, and friendly and flexible consultants and artists.

Slide-Master's CBP performance is evaluated by monthly surveys of employees and customers. The surveys highlight problems, potential new services, and how to handle certain clients. Operating procedures are meticulous to prevent foul-ups in order entry, processing, and delivery. Finally, employee compensation is high since employees must often handle both front- and backroom responsibilities.

Another way to organize and evaluate CBP attributes is an *affinity diagram.* Figure 4–7 shows an affinity diagram for Slide-Master. For simplicity, the detailed attributes of each generic category are not shown. The affinity diagram in the figure graphically depicts subsets of the CBP. Example CBP management questions listed in Table 4–1 (page 84) must be answered for Slide-Master before designing the service delivery system or developing a service/quality management system. And as Figure 4–7 shows, Slide-Master makes successful business presentations—they do more than just make slides (products).

FIGURE 4–7
CBP Affinity Diagram for Slide-Master

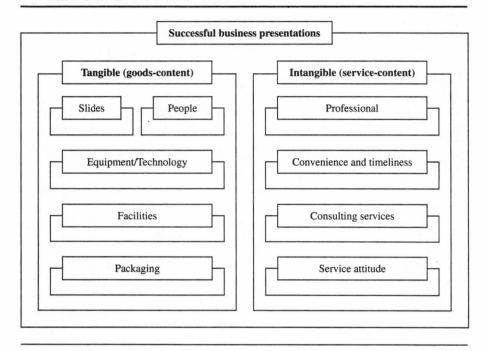

OTHER CBP EXAMPLES

CBP design begins by determining the final attributes of the CBP. Diagrams
such as those shown in Figures 4–1 to 4–7 also help us conceptualize the business and design the CBPs. Customer wants and needs analysis precedes or
occurs simultaneously with CBP design. Let's examine other CBP ideas and try
to gain more insight into the CBP framework.

CBP Configurations A and B in Figures 4–1 and 4–2 depict the way most
goods and services are designed in today's marketplace. CBP Configuration A in
Figure 4–1 is a primary good supported by peripheral goods and services. Many
industries, such as restaurant/food, wholesale/retail, utility, and all goods-producing industries (agriculture, manufacturing, forestry, mining, fishing, and
construction) exhibit this CBP configuration.

CBP Configuration A in Figure 4–1 could be used to describe any of the following companies' goods and services: Grease Monkey/Jiffy Lube (oil change),
McDonald's (fast food), Super America (gasoline), IBM (computers), Borden
(food), Whirlpool (appliances), Caterpillar (tractors), Johnson & Johnson (phar-

maceuticals), the EyeGlass Factory (contact lenses and eyeglasses), Palm Beach (clothes), American Electric Power (electricity), and Sherwin-Williams (paints).

This idea of a primary good with peripheral goods and services can be extended to make another key point. Consider a visit to the hospital for an operation. The objective of the visit is to improve the patient's health, or, if you will, the patient's goods or technical content. This goods or technical-content part of the CBP is the main reason the patient checks into the hospital.

The operation represents the *technical* or *primary core* in the CBP design. The patient usually cannot truly evaluate the quality of the operation. Was the operation 78 percent or 98 percent effective? But there are a host of peripheral goods (hospital food service, accurate bills, etc.) and services (prompt delivery and pickup of hospital meal trays, friendly and respectful hospital staff, etc.) the patient and family can evaluate.

Because the goods content or technical content is difficult for the patient to evaluate, the patient's (customer's) focus shifts to peripheral goods and services. The attributes of the CBP the customer can recognize and evaluate are good candidates for differentiating your CBP from competitors'.

All goods-producing companies can use peripheral goods and services to add value to their CBPs and differentiate them from competitors'. If the customer cannot really evaluate competing primary goods due to inadequate technical knowledge, lack of adequate information or opportunity, lack of time or motivation to do an exhaustive analysis, and so forth, then on what attributes will the customer judge your CBP? Or even if the customer can judge the technical performance of the primary good, say computer chips or riding lawn mowers, the way to gain competitive advantage still is frequently with how you advertise, package, and deliver the peripheral goods and services.

CBP Configuration B in Figure 4–2 is a primary service supported by peripheral goods and services. Marriott's Residence Inn is an example. About 20 percent of the US population moves each year and surveys reveal considerable unhappiness in adjusting to these relocations. It takes an average of 18 months for a family to adjust completely to a major relocation. Residence Inn(s), extended-stay hotels, get about 12 percent of their business from relocated employees. Many of their peripheral goods and services are specifically designed for this market-within-a-market.

Residence Inns do a good job in providing the primary service—a safe, modern, clean, and moderately priced hotel room and bed. Other value-added features coupled to the primary service include peripheral services such as babysitting and local introduction services. Peripheral goods include packages of information on local schools and the community. The core of Residence Inns' CBP is a service. Peripheral goods and services complement the core service.

A pure service configuration represents a primary service complemented by peripheral services. It is difficult to find services with absolutely no peripheral goods but often entertainment services fit into this category. Watching TV or a play or a symphony is close to pure service except for the television, auditoriums, theaters, tickets, and program brochure. Telecommunication services also fit into this category.

A pure good (product) configuration represents a primary good with peripheral goods. Again, pure product CBPs seldom exist in reality. Pure product CBP examples tend to run close to commodity items, such as basic raw materials (coal, coffee, wheat, natural gas, chemicals, soybean, gasoline, orange juice, and so on).

Yet, if you examine these commodities you discover that many peripheral services are attached to the primary good. For example, commodity trading houses make money by selling commodities. But to do an effective selling job, these trading houses must negotiate and write contracts, administer contracts; do market analysis, account receivable management and currency management; warrant the goods; plan logistical requirements; and act as government liaisons.

Consumer goods such as toothpaste, detergent, and shampoo also are close to pure products. However, most have minor peripheral services that enhance the image and purchase of that item—such as shopping-mall product demonstrations or a telephone-hotline service center. What happens to customer satisfaction if the person demonstrating the product or answering the telephone is rude? What if the product demonstration doesn't start on time? What if the telephone hotline always gives the customer a busy signal?

Tom Peters tells an interesting story about how Milliken & Co. turned rags (a pure product) into a multimillion dollar business by introducing the *shop towel*.[13] Milliken differentiated and added value to this so-called mundane commodity—rags—by adding many peripheral services. These services included customer tours of Milliken plants, computer on-line order entry and freight optimization systems, Partners-for-Profit seminars on quality improvement, and the like. The training program for shop towel salespersons is 22 grueling weeks, followed by a one-year on-the-job trial period with small accounts. A similar story is told by Peters about Elgin Corrugated Box Co., which has increased its share of the market since 1970 from 12 to 30 percent by adding value to boxes through peripheral services.

Bundled CBP Configuration C in Figure 4–3 illustrates an aggregation of CBPs to create a vacation. The interdependency of many CBPs and service-providers is illustrated by Figure 4–3. American Express's Travel Related Services is a good example of where a bundled set of CBPs tailored (customized) to individuals is the primary service offered for sale. Supermarkets such as Kroger and Safeway bundle stores within stores to satisfy niche markets and entice higher sales.

Bundled CBPs raise some interesting questions about pricing strategies and strategic alliances. For example, can we charge a premium price for the bundled

CBPs? What is the value of convenience and speed of service for a bundled set of CBPs? What strategic alliance(s) will best bundle CBPs together to gain competitive advantage in the marketplace? What are the risks of using strategic alliances to bundle CBPs?

Another way to think about CBP configuration is to attach a minor, impulse-buy type of good or service to a primary or peripheral good or service. The extra CBP feature is piggybacked onto the CBP. If a *piggybacked CBP feature* is standardized to all delivery points on a continuous basis, it becomes a part of a primary or peripheral good or service. If a piggybacked CBP feature is offered only at selected sites or times, it is a *variant*.

Credit card insurance is a good example of a service piggybacked onto the primary service. Applying for credit card insurance is *so easy*. The insurance application form is a tear-off part of the monthly credit card payment envelope. The fee for this service is charged directly to your credit card account. This peripheral service, revenue enhancer, and CBP innovation, is a way to increase CBP profitability and build competitive advantage.

The five sample questions shown in Table 4–1 focus on CBP design. Where CBP design fits into the total service management analysis framework was shown in Figures 2–3 and 2–4. Answer these questions for your business using service management thinking and the CBP framework.

A CBP executive committee is in the best position to answer these questions. The executive committee should be composed of people who think service-management, who have an interdisciplinary perspective, who are innovative, and who think simultaneously about internal and external issues. These committee members should be your best people and may include your suppliers and customers.

Service management teams (cross-functional) also may be necessary to support the CBP executive committee. These multifunctional teams should be composed of marketing, personnel, engineering, operations, information systems, and strategic planning managers. They should be involved in CBP design and service-process design early in the development of a new CBP. Most of these should be line managers, not division or corporate staff managers. Line managers take these plans and put them into action. You must stay focused and concentrate on achieving measurable results that fundamentally improve your organization's performance. Plans don't pay the bills; bottom-line success is what pays the bills and provides job security.

The risk of independent decisions by one or two functional areas can be great. Example outcomes of inadequate CBP management include: CBP conflict, duplication, and proliferation; poor process capability and marketplace inconsistencies, increased organizational and operational complexity, missed market and innovation opportunities, little or no growth, increased operating costs, and great confusion among employees, managers, and your customers. Any one of these management nightmares can put the firm out of business.

TABLE 4–1
Service Management Action Starter Questions

1. How would you define your organization's consumer benefit packages (CBPs) using the terms, methods, and formats of Figures 4–1 to 4–7? How does the customer evaluate your CBPs before, during, and after purchase? How is the CBP configured? (Repeat these questions for key employee benefit packages.)

2. What is the role of service in each of your CBP configurations? What does the customer purchase? Goods? Services? Both? Primary? Peripheral? Variants? What are the key "differentiators?"

3. Do a CBP attribute analysis for each of your organization's CBPs. How do final CBP attributes meet customer wants and needs? What is the relative importance of each CBP attribute from the customer's perspective? Given these insights, develop a Comprehensive Customer Contact Plan (3C Plan) for each key CBP at the process- and service-encounter level.

4. How does your organization monitor and control CBP complexity, duplication, and proliferation? How well defined and managed are your CBP research and development processes in relation to commercialization processes?

5. What CBPs are profitable, unprofitable, or ill-defined? Which CBPs should be dropped? Do you assign revenues and costs (i.e., income statements) to each CBP and CBP line/family? What other nonfinancial measures of CBP success should you collect, evaluate, and use in performance appraisals?

CBP management is the cornerstone of all subsequent decisions. When CBPs are conflicting, ill-defined, and unstable, it places great strains on facilities, processes, and service-encounter design. Management is ultimately responsible for CBP definition, design, and strategy. If CBP management fails, all else will eventually fail. That is why CBP decisions are of such strategic importance.

Chapter Five

The Service Strategy Whirlpool

S ervice strategy is the structure that supports, protects, and directs the consumer benefit package (CBP). A well-defined consumer benefit package and accompanying service strategy are the basis on which to build quality and competitive advantage. But the whirlpool of decision variables is a dangerous decision-making environment. If CBP management is done well, everything else is easier. Many quality initiatives fail because of lousy CBP management decisions.

Strategic management is a well-documented field of study.[1] Many ideas and methods of strategic management are generic enough that they apply both to goods-producing and service-providing organizations with service-related nuances here and there.

Service strategy is a vision of how the organization defines, designs, and manages consumer benefit packages and their target markets, and the associated service processes and service encounters. It defines the role of service/quality performance. It sets organizational values, performance objectives, priorities and future directions that fulfill customer wants and needs with the objective of growing profits. It provides long-term guidance on three basic strategic questions. What is the organization's business? How do we want to run the business? What is the role of service/quality in our organization to help us gain competitive advantage?

One survey of 250 companies found a whirlpool of quality strategies reported as follows: customer satisfaction (by 88 percent of the companies), employees' involvement (86 percent), total quality management (69 percent), competitive benchmarking (60 percent), supplier partnerships (58 percent), time-based competition (39 percent), and self-managed work teams (35 percent).[2] These strategies must be defined from a service management perspective, not a product- or functional-perspective. Different perspectives result in different answers to the same strategic question(s).

Our discussion of service strategy will not repeat what is found in the previously cited sources. Let's begin our service strategy discussion by examining the nature of the strategic decision maker.

STRATEGIC DECISION MAKERS

To define the best service strategy for a given CBP or CBP line, management must understand each CBP, and its process and service encounters. Strategic decision makers must have the breadth and depth of a service management career path. Such a career path requires detailed knowledge of several functional areas.

Hayes and Wheelwright support these notions, mainly from a manufacturing perspective, by stating the following: "The road to the top formerly threaded up through the corporation (in the 1960s) with stops in several functional areas. This gave potential executives the opportunity to work in various departments and thus learn the details of the business. This approach to executive development had changed drastically by 1970, however . . . Industry expertise gained from in-depth experience acquired a 'nonprogressive' stigma. At the same time, American companies increasingly turned to people with financial, accounting, and legal backgrounds to fill their top positions. By the late 1970s the percentage of newly appointed CEOs with such backgrounds in the largest 100 US corporations was up 50 percent from its level 30 years earlier."[3]

Dr. W. Edward Deming also worries about the quality and training of American management as strategic thinkers and decision makers. In one of his classic speeches, Deming identifies *five deadly diseases* in the American approach to management.[4] These ideas of Dr. Deming do not always endear him to the American management community. Yet, they highlight the importance of, and the issues surrounding, American strategic decision makers.

The *first* deadly disease is *lack of constancy of purpose*, which highlights management having a vague idea of what business they are in, with no firm plan for the future. The *second* deadly disease is an *emphasis on short-term profits*. Here the focus is on how to improve the next quarterly dividend (and stock price) possibly at the sacrifice of long-term growth. These two deadly diseases are probably the cause of most quality improvement failures.

The *third* deadly disease is the *annual rating of performance of salaried employees*, which Deming says is destructive to long-term planning, annihilates teamwork, and demoralizes employees. The *fourth* disease is the *mobility of management*, which encourages no roots in the company, no knowledge of the company, and no understanding of past or present problems of the company. The fourth deadly disease is encouraged by the third.

The *fifth* deadly disease is the *use of only visible figures for management*, which ignores equally important figures that are often unknown or unknowable, such as the value of a happy customer. Deming concludes that "these diseases have weakened American industry, which is now up against the competition of the Japanese who do not have them."[5]

Later, in his book *Out of the Crisis*, Deming adds two other deadly diseases: *excessive medical costs* and *excessive costs of liability, swelled by lawyers that work on contingency fees*.[6] Both of these deadly diseases are *service* components of the price of a CBP. For example, US-owned automobile manufacturers produce most of their cars and trucks at costs comparable to or lower than those of global competitors. But when US health and litigation costs are added, as much as 10 percent of the car's sticker price is added.

The demands on a strategic decision maker are immense, especially in a global economy where services play an increasing role in making and keeping the sale. Service management expertise at the very top of the organization is an essential skill in the Servomation Age. Also, care should be taken to avoid Dr. Deming's seven deadly diseases because they define a hostile environment for making strategic decisions.

COMPETITIVE PRIORITIES

What performance criteria should we use in competing for markets? What is the relative importance (weight) of each criteria per CBP? These are the types of questions the strategic decision maker must address. If the answers to these questions are vague, CBP design and strategy will be vague. If clearly defined and weighted, they are the basis for successful CBP, process- and service-encounter designs.

Competitive priorities can be placed in these general categories:

- Price (cost)
- Flexibility
- Innovation
- Product quality
- Service quality
- Time

Competitive priorities are the performance criteria that management chooses to emphasize when designing and delivering CBPs to customers. Competitive priorities are *not* resources such as equipment or people. Resources achieve performance goals. Resources sometimes become the center of a positioning theme but they represent the means of achievement, not what is achieved.

Figure 5–1 illustrates how the company and the customer view competitive priorities. A world-class company finds the right combination of competitive priorities that gives the customer value while the company makes a profit. Example issues are shown for each competitive priority in Figure 5–1. As we will discuss in Chapter 6, time-based competition has become such an important strategic weapon that it deserves a separate competitive priority category.

Today, time is driving the other competitive priorities. For example, a time-based strategy for product/quality or service/quality has certain implications for each. For product/quality, it might take the form of a multidisciplinary CBP

FIGURE 5–1
Service Strategy and Competitive Priorities

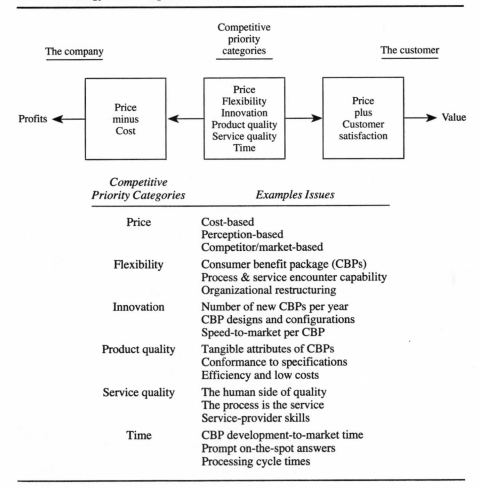

Competitive Priority Categories	Examples Issues
Price	Cost-based Perception-based Competitor/market-based
Flexibility	Consumer benefit package (CBPs) Process & service encounter capability Organizational restructuring
Innovation	Number of new CBPs per year CBP designs and configurations Speed-to-market per CBP
Product quality	Tangible attributes of CBPs Conformance to specifications Efficiency and low costs
Service quality	The human side of quality The process is the service Service-provider skills
Time	CBP development-to-market time Prompt on-the-spot answers Processing cycle times

design team with a six month product design to market target. For service/quality, it might mean empowerment of front-line employees for on-the-spot service recovery. For pricing decisions, time-based strategies may eliminate the maturity (cash cow) phase of the product life cycle, as will be discussed in Chapter 6.

Competitive priorities define the firm's distinctive competencies. If the strategic decision maker assigns equal weight to each of the above performance categories, there are no trade-offs: We should allocate resources equally and try to be all things to all people. This is where the strategy literature offers paradigms to help us organize our thinking and rank order these competitive priorities. For example, Michael Porter's generic strategies of cost leadership and differentiation are popular models for strategic management thinking.[7]

Of the competitive priorities previously noted, service/quality is the best differentiator. It is the most difficult to execute daily, the easiest for the customer to evaluate, and the most challenging for competitors to copy. If you excel at service/quality and maintain parity on all other competitive priorities, you are a leader in your industry. To be world-class you most likely must excel in at least two of the competitive priority categories.

STRATEGIC THEMES AND POSITIONING

Companies position themselves and their consumer benefit packages in the industry and marketplace in many ways. For example, American Express' positioning theme is "Membership Has Its Privileges," or L.L. Bean's theme of "The Sale Is Never Over. 100% Satisfaction in Every Way," or 3M's "New Products. We Hear You." theme.

What image do these positioning themes project to their customers and employees? How do you think each company would rank its competitive priorities? What areas of the organization would you expect to receive special attention and resources? What are the operational implications of these positioning themes? How powerful are these positioning themes in the global marketplace?

Positioning themes must accomplish at least three objectives:

1. Provide strategic direction for the firm both internally and externally.
2. Differentiate the firm's CBPs from those of competitors
3. They must be meaningful to the target market and its customers.

Positioning themes and strategy can also focus on key resource(s). For example, if *people* are the focal point of a strategic plan, then one would expect world-class training, performance evaluation, and profit-sharing programs supported by a corporate culture that encourages innovation, empowerment, and accountability. Delta Airlines, Singapore Airlines, and Mars Candy Company center their strategy around people-power. They begin this process by clearly defining the company's positioning theme and quality values, and then hiring only those people who have similar values.

Marriott has adopted such a strategy, as suggested by the famous quote of the founder, J. Willard Marriott, when he said, "In a service business, you can't make happy guests with unhappy employees." Marriott has an extensive set of people programs that cover all levels in their organization. Marriott's service strategy centers on *employee skills*. Marriott's competitors are physically and technically similar but it is the people dimension that makes Marriott Number 1 in the lodging industry. It is the day-to-day execution of millions of service encounters by employees that differentiates Marriott from competitors.

Other positioning themes can be quality, customer satisfaction, technology, costs, time, and social innovation. For example, one executive search and placement service viewed its business as *facilitating professional (social) interaction between the right employer and right employee.* Talented managers often become trapped in an organization because of limited advancement opportunities. This target population is the reason for the existence of the executive placement firm. Such firms diagnose the situation and find potential employers who can truly use this talented manager. And, the manager feels that his or her personal development is enhanced and growing. The firm's positioning theme was centered on *social interaction*, so they hired and trained for their own staff people who could execute these job requirements well.

When two or more positioning themes are intertwined and they cannot be separated or are of equal importance, then multiple positioning themes are necessary. Federal Express (people and service), CompuServe (technology and service), K mart (price and service), ServiceMaster (technology and people), and Stew Leonard's (product and service/quality) are examples of dual positioning themes. World-class companies usually excel at more than one strategic positioning theme.

A STORY OF FAILURE IN CBP DESIGN AND STRATEGY

Broadway Pizza experienced all five stages of the service firm's life cycle in a relatively short time.[8] The five stages of a service firm's life cycle are:

- Entrepreneurial.
- Multisite rationalization.
- Growth.
- Maturity.
- Decline/regeneration.[9]

One day, the company president, myself, and a handful of Broadway Pizza corporate staff watched the office equipment be repossessed. That experience taught me many lessons, a few of which we shall examine here. Broadway Pizza got caught in the whirlpool of service strategy and CBP definition, and it failed.

Broadway Pizza was founded by a set of entrepreneurs in the early 1980s when the video game craze was going on. The founders defined their consumer benefit package as a combination of robotic entertainment and a pizza food service. A typical store contained computer-controlled animated characters with voice and music synchronized to animated movements. Six colorful animated robots were located in the main dining room singing *Hello Dolly, Summertime,* and *Yankee Doodle Dandy*. Other robots were located in the large animinated character room. Stores typically ranged from 8,000 to 12,000 square feet, depending on building and lot constraints. A new store required an investment of $800,000 to $1 million. The game and ride rooms generally had about 75 video games and rides, such as Pac-Man, Asteroids, Skeeball, and miniature helicopters and rocket ships.

The consumer benefit package of Broadway Pizza was vague, with the risk that the CBPs for pizza food service and robotic entertainment were incompatible. Was Broadway Pizza a pizza parlor, a community gathering place, an entertainment center and amusement park using automation, a fantasy place for kids aged 3 to 12 years old, an arcade, or a place for parties? As noted in Chapter 4, if the CBP is ill-defined or conflicting, then management, the employees, and, ultimately the customer will be confused.

Despite how ill-defined the CBP design and strategy were, the stock initially went public at $15 per share. The entrepreneurial stage for Broadway Pizza had been one of great financial success: a substantial amount of free and positive publicity in newspapers, magazines, and local television and radio, and the financial community had loaned Broadway Pizza considerable monies to finance their growth.

During multisite rationalization, stage 2 of the service firm's life cycle, Broadway Pizza grew to over 100 stores. Some district and region managers were promoted almost immediately to middle management. It was not uncommon for a district or regional manager to be 24 to 30 years old.

Most store managers at first focused their attention on food service and ignored the automation. They left it up to the store maintenance technician to test the robotics and accompanying software, to do preventive maintenance, order parts, and groom the robotic characters. These store managers quickly realized they must manage the *entertainment by automation* side of the business too. If the robotic characters malfunctioned, the manager could quickly have a hundred upset kids and parents.

These first 100 stores were all huge. A typical McDonald's restaurant is 1,800 to 2,000 square feet, yet Broadway Pizza stores were about four to six times this big. Therefore, fixed costs were very high. Besides, many stores were placed in existing shopping center space, and therefore, there was no standard facility design.

By the end of the growth stage, Broadway Pizza had over 250 stores. The stock price at this time reached a high of over $35 per share. What's really alarming is that bankers were still loaning Broadway Pizza huge sums of money! As long as the pro forma balance sheets and income statements looked good, and the banks had the properties for collateral, why not loan Broadway Pizza more money?

Broadway Pizza's sales overall, and for most individual stores, by 1983 were declining. In actuality, the maturity (cash generating) stage of the service firm's life cycle was short lived or nonexistent. They went almost immediately from the growth to the decline stage.

Broadway Pizza by the end of 1983 was in the decline (regeneration) stage of the life cycle. In the fourth quarter of 1983, Broadway Pizza reported losses totaling $16 million. Many turnaround actions were taken, such as selling any stores not constrained by a long-term lease, promoting special events such as *Teenage Ladies Night Out* and *Lunch Specials*, cutting the store square footage as much as possible and renting the remaining space, and raising prices. Young managers who had just bought new houses were fired. On one Friday afternoon, over 800 part-time employees were notified they were no longer needed as of that day. In early 1984, one bank demanded that Broadway Pizza immediately pay a $50 million convertible debenture. Later in 1984, Broadway Pizza filed for Chapter 11 bankruptcy with debts of over $100 million.

Today, if you visit stores such as Broadway Pizza in the United States, you will find these stores to be scaled down with one to three robotic characters, simpler and less frequently changed skits, and the store size reduced to 3,000 to 4,000 square feet. If the store is much bigger than this, you are visiting one of the remaining Broadway Pizza mega stores of an earlier time.

Three lessons from the Broadway Pizza saga are as follows. *First*, if a CBP definition and design contain conflicting (pizza versus entertainment by automation) characteristics, any service strategy will have a difficult time supporting it in the marketplace. *Second*, never begin the multisite rationalization and growth stages of the service firm's life cycle with a nonstandard (and high fixed cost) service facility design and layout. Nonstandard facility designs wreck performance and training systems, hurt operational effectiveness, complicate advertising themes and plans, and confuse customers. *Third*, competitors who truly know their CBPs and service delivery systems can learn all they need to know by visiting competitor's stores and experiencing the service delivery process. Competitors can learn much, quickly and cheaply, about competing CBPs and delivery systems. If the CBP and service delivery system are well designed, then the key to success is in the daily execution!

MULTISITE AND MULTISERVICE GROWTH STRATEGIES

An interesting typology was proposed by Langeard and Eiglier concerning strategic options for growth.[10] The study examined 43 European firms from the following service industries: airlines, lodging, banking, restaurants, institutional food, computer software, maintenance, security, insurance, and retailing. The research method included interviews with managers who played a key role in the service development process, and the assessment by top management of the evolution of that service over time.

One result of their research was a multisite–multiservice grid (not shown). The horizontal axis is the number of services (multiservice) available for sale at each service facility. The vertical axis is the number of service facilities (multisite) offering the company's CBPs. They identify three broad growth strategies for service firms to grow.

Scenario 1

The first growth strategy is called Scenario 1 and it is characterized by a narrow and fixed line of services that are duplicated at many different sites. The CBPs and service delivery system are standardized and specialized and a dominant service facility design is established before growth begins. A vertical vector represents this type of growth in the multisite–multiservice grid.

As Langeard and Eiglier note, "For the last 20 years the fast-food industry has sustained a spectacular growth through the development of restaurant chains delivering a limited menu: hamburgers, chicken, pizza, or croissants. When the market is expanding rapidly, aggressive firms, after having simplified their service offering, duplicate their delivery system as fast as they can. Such a (marketing) strategy favoring multi-units over multi-services brings a high rate of sales growth and of profitability."[11]

Scenario 2

Scenario 2 is characterized by many core services offered through a few sites. Disney World theme parks, gourmet restaurants, certain local or regional retail stores, and some medical practices fit this service-firm growth strategy. Excelling at product/ and service/quality usually becomes a key factor in their success. Langeard and Eiglier comment that "the rate of sales growth is usually limited by the narrow geographic boundaries of the market and depends on the ability of adding new services. The percentage of local market share is high and the profitability is good or very good."[12] A horizontal vector represents this type of growth in the multisite-multiservice grid.

Scenario 3

As service firms mature, some venture into a simultaneous multisite and multiservice growth strategy. There growth is represented by a diagonal vector where sites are added as the CBP and supporting facilities are defined and modified. When this strategy, Scenario 3, is adopted, either consciously or unconsciously, there are many dangers awaiting management.

For example, the service facility design may not be standardized because new CBPs are continually being added to the service delivery system. Many heterogeneous facilities may exist, making it more difficult to design training programs, control systems, performance appraisal systems, and the like. Certain retail banks and department store chains exhibited these types of growth patterns in the 43 firms studied. Ultimately, costs may increase while sales growth is slow.

A STORY OF MULTISITE EXPANSION WITH NO STANDARD CBP OR FACILITY DESIGN EARLY-ON

A hotel chain called Best Hotels got its start in the hotel business in the early 1970s by buying an existing apartment building next to a thriving restaurant and bar area in a major US city.[13] The existing building constrained the type of accommodations that hotel management could offer. Instead of a single room, each room offered its guests a living room, dining area, one or two bedrooms, and a kitchen equipped with all major appliances, china, silverware, and cooking utensils.

The appeal of Best Hotel rooms was in its blend of the convenience of a hotel with the freedom and space of an apartment. Management for this first hotel had to fashion a strategy around the physical constraints of the hotel building and rooms. The objective was to offer a true *home away from home* to the business traveler who stayed on the road for long periods of time.

The *all-suite, extended-stay hotel consumer benefit package* was invented by Best Hotels. The all-suite consumer benefit package originated during the entrepreneurial stage of this firm's life cycle. The all-suite service concept represented a *new technology or service innovation* in the lodging industry. By the 1980s, the all-suite hotel service innovation had created a new market niche that was to become one of the lodging industry's hottest segments—extended-stay lodging.

This first Best Hotel was profitable, although initially it lacked food service or a restaurant because hotel guests could walk two blocks to over 100 restaurants, bars, and retail stores. Many hotel customers rented rooms for months at a time. This hotel did lack large public areas such as lobbies, health clubs, conference rooms, and restaurants.

By the early 1980s, Best Hotels had grown to eight hotels. Most of these hotels were in existing buildings very close to high density-traffic with easy access (i.e., walking distance) to restaurants. A couple of the newly constructed hotels had small conference rooms, a single restaurant, and room service. The pure suite-only strategy tailored to the local market had begun to change somewhat at Best Hotels, as reflected in the design of the two new hotels. This was because customers at all the hotels were increasingly requesting food and beverage services at the hotel. In addition, the large hotel chains were entering the suite-hotel market with wider services than just the suites-only concept. And some customers were requesting pools and small conference rooms. Thus, the all-suite hotel CBP was still evolving.

Best Hotels during the early 1980s had left the entrepreneurial stage and was struggling in the multisite rationalization stage of the firm's life cycle. There was no standard hotel facility design among these first eight hotels, and that seemed confusing to the customers. And, the CBP was constantly changing, and it varied by hotel location.

In addition, hotel managers had become more difficult to train and evaluate, due to the nonstandard hotel designs. Advertising on a regional or national level was difficult with no standard building and image to market. The all-suite *rooms* were marketed since they were more standardized than the buildings that housed the rooms. Profits were slim and sometimes hotel debt had to be refinanced. Hotel control systems were not standardized, partly because the hotels were different in physical layout and operating procedures.

One issue facing the management of Best Hotels during the 1970s and early 1980s was "How to grow?" They were entering the growth stage of the service firm life cycle without a clearly defined CBP or standardized hotel facility. Based on Langeard and Eiglier's[24] multisite and multiservice paradigm, Best Hotels is following the diagonal with simultaneous changes in the number of hotel sites and CBP definition.[14] Each hotel's CBP contained many variants as defined in Chapter 4. Both service management paradigms predicted problems with this growth strategy. And Best Hotel management was experiencing many of these very same problems.

Although Best Hotel's first eight hotels did not have a standard facility design, their management did agree on a standard CBP and several optional standard facility designs after the first eight were in operation. But accommodating for standard and nonstandard facilities also caused Best Hotel management some problems. For example, customer surveys and focus groups did show that some business customers felt confused by the different hotel facility designs.

By the late 1980s, the all-suite consumer benefit package had become standardized. Competitors such as Residence Inn by Marriott, Guest Quarters by Beacon Companies, Woodfin Suites, Inc., Homewood Suites, Embassy Suites, and Neighborhood Hotel Corporation had learned from Best Hotels. These competitors had refined the all-suite CBP, each adding peripheral services to fit its market niche and service strategy. As noted in Chapter 2, there are no patents on services. Thus, the all-suite hotel research and development effort was quickly copied. Today, Best Hotels is fighting for market share in an industry it created. Best Hotels is not Number 1 in the all-suite, extended stay hotel market.

CONCLUSION

Today, competitive priorities, positioning themes, CBP designs, and service strategies are global. Designing a global service strategy is even more challenging. There, the whirlpool of service strategy variables and decisions gets bigger and more complex, and increases in velocity. It requires managers in the organization to understand the culture of target markets; the local politics and legal environments; company and country systems, procedures, and global networks; strategic alliances and supplier relationships, and of course, the attributes of CBPs each tailored to local customers.

In Chapter 1 we highlighted the importance of adjusting the CBP and its process and service encounters to group culture, behaviors, and service styles. The sheer magnitude and complexity of defining a global service strategy requires many talented people that exhibit both breadth and depth in understanding these factors. The decision maker who shapes a global service strategy should have an international and service management perspective. This type of global strategic decision maker must be developed if an organization is to be a contributor to The Service/Quality Solution.

Chapter Six

Recent Service Strategy Ideas

H ow can managers conceptualize their business as it grows? How can they examine parts of the organization yet see the big picture? How can they develop a strategy for their organization that is broad and farsighted enough to cover all aspects of producing the good plus providing the service? Four fresh ways to view service strategy are briefly examined in this chapter:

1. The seven P's of service strategy or service management.
2. Service process positioning strategies.
3. Time-based service strategies.
4. The service management and consumer benefit package approach.

These four paradigms help managers configure and synthesize many elements of a competitive service strategy.

THE SEVEN P's OF SERVICE STRATEGY

The original model of the four P's of the traditional marketing mix (product, price, place, and promotion) was founded in the Industrial Revolution. Today, three additional P's (physical evidence, participants, and process) founded in the service sector revolution, have been added.[1] These seven P's of service strategy and management are described in Table 6–1. Two example companies illustrate how one international company used the seven P's to build quality and competitive advantage, and how one regional US company ignored the seven P's and lost its competitive advantage.

WINNING WITH THE SEVEN P's

One international company, Benetton, focuses on producing a universal product—sweaters—in a variety of colors and designs in a niche market. The Benetton consumer benefit package is a powerful mix of the seven P's. It is a focused strategy capable of great cost efficiencies, flexible production capacity, and very quick delivery that produces and delivers a variety of sweaters that best fit the target markets of each store.

TABLE 6–1
Management Decisions Concerning the Seven P's

The Seven Ps of Service Strategy	Example Management Issues
Product (consumer benefit package)	Product ideas and development
	Variety/assortment of products
	Quality of product specifications
	Packaging
	Product logos, trademarks, and public perception
	Supporting/complementary services
	Degree of full- and/or self-service
Price	Competitive analysis
	Strategy—target market, market-will-bear, level, changes, etc.
	Discount, coupon, sales policy
	Methods of payment
Place	Distribution channel strategy and plans
	Shelf space allocation and management
	Inventory and warehouse management
	Degree of vertical and horizontal integration
	Service level policy and standards
	Facility location and convenience
Promotion	Advertising strategy—target market, best media to use, schedules and timing, etc.
	Direct and personal selling
	Market positioning themes
	Brand management and positioning

The first P—*product*—is based on almost a timeless and global set of customer values (i.e., everyone likes basic colorful sweaters). A certain level of product quality is expected. Similarly, a certain *service experience* is expected. The Benetton product logo is a worldwide logo symbolizing certain characteristics of the other six P's.

The second P, the *price* of Benetton sweaters in the United States, is moderate to high, with some sweaters costing up to $150. Discounting is becoming more prevalent in Benetton's 4,500 stores in 60 countries. Prices are always stated in the currency of each country.

The third P—*place*—is where Benetton locates its stores, warehouses (and inventory), and factories. Stores as small as 400 square feet are located in target market areas. Usually a *lead store* is followed by more stores. Recently, Benetton admits it may have made a strategic mistake by locating too many stores too close together. For example, at one time there were 28 Benetton stores in New York City, some on the same city block.

TABLE 6–1 *(concluded)*

The Seven Ps of Service Strategy	Example Management Issues
Physical Evidence	Interior/exterior facility layout, theme, decor, lights, signage, service counters, cleanliness, etc. Employees' appearance and hygiene Equipment/automation convenience, reliability, ease of use, attractiveness Exterior capacity adequate, such as parking lots, loading ramps, etc. Professional credibility, such as licenses for a full-service in-store pharmacy
Facility, Process, and Job Design	Detailed operating procedures, manuals, and job descriptions Procedures for customer problem resolution Training on the technical/procedural part of the job Establish standards of performance for facility, process, equipment, and jobs that create and deliver the CBP Facility design and layout to enhance customer/item movement through process
Participants	Training on human interaction skills and customer problem resolution Employee reward systems and procedures Personal selling Self-service/group participation procedures and norms of behavior Simultaneous execution of technical and human interaction skills at points of customer contact Supported by the other six P's

Factories used to be located only in Italy, but in 1987 Benetton built a US factory in Rocky Mount, North Carolina. Certain sweaters are dyed at the last minute so factories can immediately respond to fashion trends for each store. Factories produce only to order. Warehouses tend to carry sweaters in stable colors and designs, while more fashionable sweaters are shipped directly from the factory to the stores. A flexible and efficient manufacturing and distribution system enables Benetton to minimize fashion risk and inventory investment, and to meet customers' changing fashion needs with a variety of sweaters.

Fifteen years ago, Benetton's name was not known worldwide. Today, *promotion*—the fourth P—has established the *Benetton consumer benefit package* and brand name in the minds of tens of millions of customers all around the world. Advertising at sporting events and in certain youth-oriented magazines is part of managing the fourth P.

These four P's, which define the traditional marketing mix, offer a narrow view and incomplete analysis of Benetton's consumer benefit package(s). It ignores three of the most powerful ways to gain competitive advantage. The three additional P's (physical evidence, process, and participants) complete the management paradigm for competing in the global marketplace in the 1990s and beyond. The three additional P's expand management's solution space to include services, service processes, and service encounters.

The fifth P—*physical evidence*—is vital to Benetton's CBP strategy. Benetton stores are a showplace of color. Store fronts are made of glass, and colorful sweaters are neatly displayed in the front and perimeter of the store. Once in the store, the customer can feel the garment without being waited on or asking a store employee to help. The familiar Benetton signage and store front direct the way to the store with a *splash of color* that stands out compared to other retailers, especially in countries other than the United States.

Benetton franchisees must select one of five types of store interiors. For example, an upscale store might have prepackaged wood-paneling interior and more upscale merchandise, while a trendier store might go for a high-tech interior with more of this season's items. Music that fits the target customer is played in the background. And, store employees (or service providers) when hired are asked to dress to fit the target market and store image.

Process design—the sixth P—includes Benetton's fashion design and store order cycle, the factory and distributor supply cycle, franchising policies and procedures, merchandise payment procedures, and salesperson training procedures. In the early days, these paper procedures were very well planned and executed. Today, many of these processes have been computerized and the stores and factories electronically linked. Other enhancements of their processes include: computer-aided design, a just-in-time production and inventory planning system, and a McDonald's-style franchising system.

The seventh P—*the participant*—whether it is the service provider or other customers in the store, is the final link in this value-added chain of retailing. Customers *do* have an impact on one another! Each P of service management adds value to the final Benetton CBP. Benetton salespersons are trained on the job, usually in established stores. They are trained to mix and match colors and outfits. They must fit the market niche personality for that store, be friendly and polite, and know the procedures of the store.

Benetton is also training the customer, much like McDonald's did in the 1960s. For example, the display and presentation of merchandise is standardized in all stores with the largest sizes on the bottom shelf and the smallest sizes on the top shelf. As customers become familiar with the *Benetton* way, there is less need to rely on the store salesperson. In effect, the place, physical evidence, and process P's all help support this subliminal form of self-service.

Each P can be viewed as an opportunity to build quality, gain competitive advantage, and define business strategy. Competitors will look for any weakness in the seven-P paradigm to exploit. The seven P's also can be used to benchmark one's CBPs and delivery systems with those of competitors.

LOSING WITH THE TRADITIONAL FOUR P's

A regional US fertilizer and grass seed manufacturer (company A) sold most of its products to parks and golf courses. Customers could only slightly evaluate among competitors the technical differences between the primary goods, that is, the fertilizer and grass seed.

Customer service was defined as providing the right product to the right customer at the right time. The focus of company A was on following the physical production and distribution of these goods through distribution channels to the customer's job site. Once these goods were delivered to the customer's premises, Company A thought their job was done. Based on their product-mentality approach, the business transaction between company A and the customer was delivering the physical product to the job site.

The traditional four P's of product, price, place, and promotion were roughly equivalent among industry competitors. Yet, one innovative competitor (company B) began an application service that routinely applied the fertilizer and grass seed for its primary customers. Company B bundled the application service to the primary good and charged a higher price for this bundled CBP.

Meanwhile, Company A did not consider the application service part of what they sold the customer. For their customers, a local subcontractor or the customers themselves applied the fertilizer and seed. These application personnel often did the job incorrectly. The question then became one of which was at fault—the quality of the physical product or the way it was applied. Either way, the customer's lawns were in poor shape.

The CBP strategy of company B required the company to make major changes in how it ran the business. For example, physical evidence—the fifth P—now required that all machinery used to apply the fertilizer and grass seeds be clean, modern, look professional, and not break down. These machines now helped form the customer's perception of company B and its CBP.

Process design—the sixth P—for this job required standardized procedures for applying the products, resolving customer problems and complaints, and billing the customer. Each application crew was evaluated by the customer on how well the application service was executed. Consideration was given to incorporating these customer evaluations into an employee's job performance evaluations. Training programs for these frontroom company employees now had been standardized.

The service provider—the seventh P—that applied the product to the parks and golf courses now wore company uniforms. They had to be well-groomed, polite, knowledgeable, and create a professional lawn-service image. They had to have backroom and frontroom skills, which changed company B's hiring practices, pay scale, and training programs.

Meanwhile, company A, with its product, or four-P, mentality, did not recognize or care about the appearance of the machinery or of the employees who applied their products. The only time the customer saw company A's name or logo was on the physical product—the first P. There was also no standard operating procedure for subcontractors. Most complaints were generated with this triad (customers, subcontractors, Company A) relationship. In addition, there was no formal process to resolve customer problems and complaints.

Although company A stated in its annual report and company literature that customer service was a top priority, the definition focused on the four Ps of the traditional marketing mix. Company A relied on a product perspective that traced the movement of the physical product. It relied on the traditional marketing mix paradigm, which is incomplete when it comes to services.

In its company literature Company B also stated that it valued customer service, but it used the seven P's of service strategy to formulate, differentiate, and sell its CBP in the marketplace. Its bundled CBP guaranteed a no-hassle experience when customers bought it. To the management of Company B, the CBP they sold the customer was a beautiful, green lawn with a promise of no hassles. As might be expected, Company B is taking business away from Company A.

THE SEVEN-P PARADIGM WORKS

Managers everywhere are asking "How can we differentiate our consumer benefit packages from those of competitors to gain competitive advantage?" The seven P's of service strategy are a way to think about this question, rank competitive priorities, define business strategy, format competitive analyses and benchmarking, and answer key strategic questions. Of the seven, the three added P's broaden management's perspective toward what they are (and should be) selling and how they want to deliver the goods and services. The seven P's force management to think service management—Service/Quality Challenge 3 in Chapter 1. What is obvious when using the seven P's paradigm (Benetton and Company B) is not obvious when using the traditional four-P paradigm (Company A).

Finally, the three added P's of physical evidence, process, and participant are situational variables. They are often under the simultaneous control of the marketing, operations, and human resource management functions. They are best described as part of the service management function. The work of top management *is* service management. The analysis and decisions of the seven P's are too important and integrated to be left to any single functional area.

PROCESS MOMENTS OF TRUST: ANALYSIS AND STRATEGY

In Chapter 2, we defined moments of truth or trust, service encounters, frontroom process moments of trust (FPMT), backroom process moments of trust (BPMT), and instantaneous process moments of trust (IPMT). The process-positioning paradigms explained here make use of these ideas and are based on

---

Process-Positioning Strategy #1

FPMT versus BPMT Recovery Capability Strategy

FPMT are more critical than BPMT to the delivery of outstanding customer service because of the customer's immediate consumption and evaluation (perception) of the delivered service and due to the limited time available for recovery from a poorly executed FPMT. Recovery time is the enemy of FPMT and the friend of BPMT, which has implications for designing the service delivery process and the training of employees.

---

past work.[2] Here we shall briefly introduce two of the six example process-positioning strategies described in the original article. Please reference the complete article for a more complete discussion of process-positioning strategies.

When a mistake is made by the service delivery process, the manner and speed in which it is corrected, as described above for process-positioning strategy #1, is very important. The service provider must have the skills, process resources, commitment, and power to resolve the errors quickly and politely. Recovery strategies to cope with FPMT errors include intensive training programs, good employee selection procedures, and separating the front- and backroom work activities. Walt Disney went as far as not allowing the Disney characters who walked around the park to talk with customers. Why do you think he established this no-talking policy for his Disney characters?

Often a skilled frontroom employee can compensate somewhat for a BPMT error. For example, an airline lost my baggage due to a BPMT error. The frontroom airline personnel were well trained in handling my vocal complaint. In time, they found and returned my luggage. Here, the recovery time for a BPMT error was three days while the FPMT attempted to overcompensate immediately and buy time until the backroom error was resolved.

Process-positioning strategy #2 concentrates on when to establish an independent and dedicated service process. Here economic benefits and costs of sharing resources usually can be quantified. Interlinking can help define these key relationships. The cost of poor service also can be estimated from many internal and external sources. These costs include the loss of customer goodwill, lower rates of customer retention, rework costs to correct errors, higher costs to gain new customers, and negative word-of-mouth advertising.

In one major telephone company, for example, the top 10 customers accounted for 70 percent of the revenue. A telephone work-order for a premium business customer should not sit in the same pile as for a private home's telephone work-order. Here, the cost of poor service greatly exceeded the economic benefit of sharing resources. Therefore, a single, dedicated-service delivery process was established for these 10 premium customers.

Process-Positioning Strategy #2

A Single, Dedicated-Process Strategy

When the cost of poor customer service exceeds the economic benefits of sharing resources, an independent and dedicated service delivery process should be designed and used to provide premium service to premium customers.

In one major bank, 20 percent of the business customers accounted for 86 percent of the money on deposit, yet at one time these premium customers shared processes with all other account customers, many with less than $100 average dollar balances. Again benefits and costs were estimated and a premium service process was set up for premium customers. Other examples of needing to adopt a single, dedicated-process positioning strategy include international letters of credit and luxury home sales.

CompuServe, on the other hand, shares its databases and backroom capabilities with over one million subscribers worldwide. Here, the economic benefits of sharing process resources outweigh the cost of service.

Process-positioning strategy is constantly changing industry structure. The US automobile repair and maintenance industry is a good example. Historically, the full-service gas stations did most of these functions, but the industry became fragmented into many *process-driven specialists,* such as Jiffy Lube, Midas Muffler, Grease Monkey, Super America, and NTW Tire Center. Here service process-positioning changed industry structure!

TIME-BASED SERVICE STRATEGIES

Time is an equal-opportunity employer. We all have it. We all can use it to build quality and competitive advantage. Japanese manufacturing companies used time-based strategies and capabilities as ways to gain competitive advantage. Today, American service firms, such as American Express, Cable News Network, Charles Schwab & Co., Citicorp, CompuServe, Deluxe Check, Domino's Pizza, Federal Express, Jiffy Lube, LensCrafters, The Limited, McDonald's, Wal-Mart, and Xerox, have the advantage. They know how to use time as a competitive weapon to create and deliver services. In a service business, a time-based competitive strategy is not complete until it reaches the service encounter level.

In Chapter 5, time was listed separately as a competitive priority. There is no need here to make the case for adopting a time-based competitive strategy because it has been made very well by authors such as Stalk and Hout.[3] Here we shall investigate the impact of a time-based competitive strategy on (1) the traditional product (firm) life cycle, (2) organizational design, and (3) growing profits.

If a firm introduces new consumer benefit packages or major modifications to existing CBPs 2 to 10 times faster than the competitors, the traditional product (firm) *life cycle* never reaches the maturity stage. Or the maturity stage becomes so short relative to the total life cycle time that it is insignificant. The result of a short or nonexistent maturity stage is a set of inverted U-shaped CBP life cycles as depicted in Figure 6–1. Short CBP life cycles inherently mean a differentiation strategy.

Time-compression strategies also attack certain weaknesses in traditional *organizational design.* Chapter 8 will explore a service management approach to organizational design, but for now let's make one point. American companies invented the functional, vertical promotion and information flow, and boundary-laden organizational structure. It worked well for years but not in the environment of today's time-based competition. Such an organizational structure with all its practices is a great impediment to establishing a time-based competitive strategy. Many American firms cling to the outdated functional way to organize work even in the face of extinction. Only management can change the organizational structure.

The third time-based competitive strategy issue we shall address here is its implications for *generating profits* and market dominance. If you examine Figure 6–1, a time-based competitive strategy tries to get profits early in the CBP life cycle before competitors can respond. When competitors do respond, the time-based competitor introduces the newest (second) CBP and tries to repeat this process often. If the customers buy each successive CBP, the time-based competitor builds customer loyalty and grows its cash flow and profits. If the customers balk at the latest CBP creation, in a very short time the time-based competitor introduces a third CBP, and hopes to redeem the company in the customer's eyes.

Traditionally, the maturity stage of the CBP life cycle is where a firm generates strong positive cash flow and profits. With short CBP life cycles traditional ways of generating profits are gone! The cash cow of a mature CBP life cycle is replaced with a relentless succession of new CBP introductions. If you repeat the CBP development to market process described previously in many global markets simultaneously, the multiplicative effect is overwhelming. You build volume and lower costs and introduce new CBPs at a blinding pace. You define global industry structure and performance standards.

In April of 1991, Western Union asked its stockholders to change the parent company's name to New Valley Corporation.[4] It will still use the Western Union name for what's left of its services of money transfers and bill-paying services. The company is *hollowed out* now. In 1861, Western Union built the first transcontinental telegraph and ended the need for the Pony Express. They tried the satellite business and the long-distance telephone business but nothing seemed to work. In 1990 they sold their electronic-mail business to AT&T. Western Union

FIGURE 6–1
Consumer Benefit Package Life Cycles Using a Time-Based Competitive Strategy

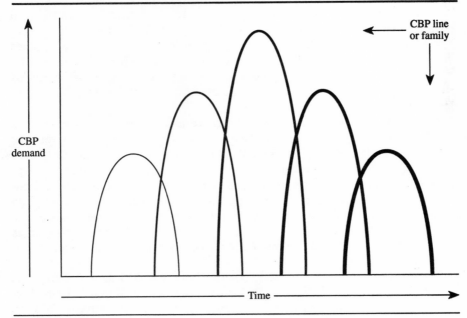

should have understood time better than anyone. American service companies currently understand time and service/quality performance better than anyone. How many of today's American-owned companies will end up like Western Union because they didn't make use of the competitive weapon called time?

Today, the world-class time-based competitor is riding the lighting bolt. To them everything seems normal, the pace acceptable, and the strategic direction clearly defined. Meanwhile, industry competitors are in a daze. They have trouble even seeing the lighting bolt much less catch it or understand it. Some competitors study it and privately just give up.

A SERVICE-MANAGEMENT AND CONSUMER-BENEFIT-PACKAGE APPROACH

An organization's strategic planning process using a service-management and consumer-benefit-package approach includes the following four major steps:

1. Corporate and organizational strategic management.
2. Consumer benefit package management.

3. Service-delivery system management.
4. Service-encounter management.

Step 1 includes all corporate level decisions for each strategic business unit (SBU) under the corporate umbrella. For a single SBU, corporate strategy and goals are identical to Consumer Benefit Package Management strategy and goals. For multiple CBP families and associated SBUs, corporate strategy and goals are a synthesis of each CBP family and SBU's strategy and goals. Example responsibilities and decisions at the corporate level include:

- Defining organizational goals, values, and missions.
- Defining the overall organizational structure, performance systems, and culture.
- Administer SBU capital resource allocations, and overall budgets.
- Align corporate and SBU goals and performance systems.
- Monitor government, regulatory, legal, and environmental developments.
- Delegate all other decisions to the SBU level.
- Evaluate each SBU's performance.

The corporate and organizational strategic-management level exists to support and inspire SBUs to grow profits.

Steps 2 to 4 are diagrammed from different perspectives in Figures 2–3, 2–4, 8–2 and 16–1, and are discussed throughout this book. Decisions in Step 2 include defining target markets, distinctive competence and capabilities, competitive priorities, critical skills needed for success, positioning theme, budgets, and the like. Chapters 1 to 6 describe CBP management.

Service-delivery system design is **Step 3** and includes performance, innovation, and organizational design, and also job, process, and facility design as shown in Figures 2–3 and 2–4. Chapters 7 to 9 discuss the nature of the decisions at this third level of planning. Other chapters (for example, Chapter 12) discuss standards of performance, and Chapters 14 and 15 describe interlinking.

Service-encounter management **(Step 4)** is the execution of all previous strategies, plans, and capabilities. All of the issues discussed in Chapters 10 to 16 are important in creating world-class service encounters. Figure 16–1 also shows how CBP management, service delivery (process) system management, and service encounter management are related. This four-step framework using service-management thinking defines this approach.

CONCLUSION

Chapters 5 and 6, on service strategy, have discussed seven ways to view the business and formulate business strategy with services in mind. Our discussion has been limited, but you are encouraged to examine the references cited here for a more complete discussion of service strategy. The seven approaches to service strategy described here are:

1. Strategic Service Vision Approach.[5]
2. Service Firm's Life Cycle Model.[6]
3. Multisite and Multiservice Growth Strategy Typology.[7]
4. Seven P's of Service Strategy.[8]
5. Process-Positioning Strategies.[9]
6. Time-Based Service Strategies.[10]
7. Service-Management and Consumer-Benefit-Package Approach.

Each service-strategy paradigm offers a different perspective. Some of these strategy paradigms are more useful for the entrepreneurial firm. Other strategy paradigms examined here apply to firms and consumer benefit packages at any stage of development. And all seven approaches add value and fresh perspectives to developing world-class service strategies.

Also, be aware of the great risks of making mistakes by using outdated paradigms in new business environments. For example, the four P's of product marketing may result in very different definitions of the problem and possible solutions than if you used the seven P's of service management paradigm. Or, if you develop your business strategy based on the traditional product life cycle paradigm but discover that the paradigm in Figure 6–1 really applies, you can be in serious trouble. And remember, as discussed in Chapter 5, if service strategy and CBP management are done poorly, all the advice in any of these books and articles won't save the company. Failures at the CBP management level are probably the cause of most quality improvement failures.

Let's now move on to Chapter 7 for the next major step in developing a service/quality solution. That is, designing the structure—facilities, processes, equipment, networks, jobs, service encounters, and organizational design—to execute the strategies and plans of CBP management. Here service/quality performance is *designed into* all aspects of the service encounter.

III

SERVICE DELIVERY SYSTEM DESIGN

If it is not designed in don't expect it to happen.

The Author

Chapter Seven

Facility, Process, and Job Design

G iven a well-defined CBP design and strategy, the next step to achieving world-class service-encounter execution is to design the service delivery system. A service delivery system is a set of outcome capabilities provided through resources such as facilities, processes, equipment, networks, information, and people. Facility design and layout must support process efficiency and effectiveness. Process, equipment, and job design are key ingredients to executing world-class service encounters. How well these resources are configured and managed day to day can elevate service encounters to the world-class level or bury them in structural defeat.

The need for good service process design with supporting facility, equipment, networks, and job design is great. Consider Blackburn's description of service processes in a large insurance company. He notes that "When the layout was superimposed on the (process) flowchart, the team observed that the paper flow crisscrossed two floors of a large office building. The surge of activity moved back and forth between departments in a random pattern rather than in a straight line flow. . . . The firm was surprised to learn it could achieve a 20 percent increase in productivity in the application process simply by getting the forms filled out carefully at the point of sale. . . . As a last symbolic step, walls are being knocked out so that the layout will fit the process, rather than vice versa."[1]

Let's examine a few of the issues surrounding facility, process, and job design from a service management perspective. We begin by gaining some perspective as to where service process design fits with past initiatives on process design.

SERVICE PROCESS MANAGEMENT— TOO LITTLE AND LATE

Operations management has always emphasized facility, process, and job design. One milestone in manufacturing operations occurred in the 1930s when management began to heed Adam Smith (1723–1790), who defined the idea of specialization of labor in his book *The Wealth of Nations*.[2] Today, the body of knowledge on operations management for goods-producing organizations is extensive. Ideas and techniques such as just-in-time, material requirements planning, process and multiple activity charts, design for manufacturability, learning curves, assembly line balancing, ergonomics, and work measurement techniques help managers design and manage the goods-producing processes of today.

The stature of service operations management historically is another story. In 1955, about one-half of the US workforce worked in the service sector. Yet, it wasn't until 1978 when Sasser, Olsen, and Wyckoff wrote a text and case book titled *Management of Service Operations* that service operations management was officially born.[3] Real emphasis on service processes began in the late 1980s. By then, the US service sector accounted for between 70 to 80 percent of civilian jobs in the US economy, depending on what was counted. The Malcolm Baldrige National Quality Award application guidelines also contributed to the national awareness of process management, especially for support, supplier, and business services.

For at least 45 years the service sector and its facility, process, and job design was viewed as a low priority in much of America. The product-perspective is difficult to shed. Services were simply not important enough to spend much time on, so their design and management was delegated to whoever was convenient. Hence, many service processes today are ill-defined, inefficient, fragmented by functional bickering, ineffective, and casually managed. As CBPs continue to proliferate and more information- and service-content is added to CBPs, service process design and management have changed little. Ignoring service processes for 45 years has cost America hundreds-of-thousands of jobs and reduced US productivity, growth and competitiveness.

The good news on process management is threefold. First, management, even Chief Executive Officers, is finally paying attention to service processes. John Akers, the CEO of IBM, for example, is one of many advocates of better process design and management. For most organizations, 50 to 100 percent of their final CBP cost is due to service process costs. Management is discovering the true costs of service processes, and beginning to make them targets for improvement.

Second, the potential benefits of efficient and effective service processes are tremendous. These benefits far outweigh the benefits of improving primary goods-producing processes of the past. Leveraging service process improvement in your organization is a key to increased customer satisfaction, lower costs, increased value-added, and higher profits. Third, service process improvement is one way to get more for less out of the United States's health care and government services. But as you read this book, you can see that service processes are also the most complex processes to design and improve. To really improve service process performance, you must "think and practice service management."

PROCESS TERMINOLOGY

The following process ideas and definitions are from an article I wrote in 1989, "Process Moments of Trust: Analysis and Strategy."[4]

A *process* is the organization and management of resources (i.e., people, facilities, materials, information, equipment, technology) and knowledge (i.e, procedures, know-how) into activities to create the tangible and intangible parts of the consumer benefit package (CBP). An *activity* is a set of work tasks needed to create and deliver the CBP and associated service encounters. *Tasks* are a subset of *activities*, and *activities* are subsets of *processes*. Processes, activities, and tasks consume resources and time.

A process flowchart describes the sequence and logic of all process activities, including feedback mechanisms. A process flowchart is analogous to the script of a movie. All the company's resources must work in unison to provide a top-rated movie (consumer benefit package).

In fact, the process is the service! Examples of service processes include: preparing a bill, renting a car, check and credit card processing, ordering fast food, providing engineering consulting services, checking into a hotel, preparing and delivering meals to hospital patients, shopping for and buying a house, income tax processing, boarding an airplane, writing a will, and insurance underwriting. Management's job in service process design is to provide everyone with a concise picture of what is expected, eliminate confusion for the service provider and [the] customer, and provide the necessary resources to do the job well. The process flowchart is the first step to accomplish this goal.

Process flowcharting has always been the mainstay of operations management. Only in the last 10 years has it been rediscovered, and especially for service processes. Process charts, multiple activity charts, flow diagrams, process yield or bottleneck analysis, work measurement techniques, cause-and-effect analysis, maintenance and repair planning, input–output process analysis, project management and networks, and product- versus process-layout analysis are just a few of the techniques and ideas of operations management.[5] When applied to service processes, process flowcharting has been called service blueprinting or service mapping. These terms and associated methods recognize the points of contact with the customer and sometimes separate the backroom from the frontroom.

THE PROCESS IS THE SERVICE

Service-providing processes are different from goods-producing processes. As noted in previous chapters, service processes may include the customer as part of the process. Human behavior and interaction between the service provider and the customer are critical in service processes. Equipment or labor capacity becomes the way management must inventory their service process capabilities. Customers evaluate quality differently when experiencing a service versus buying a product. Customers can frequently evaluate service/quality more easily than product or technical quality. A service process is often a social process. The performance of the service process concerning information, time, and entertainment takes on increased importance. CBPs with a high degree of information-, entertainment-, and service-content are often indistinguishable from the service process itself.

Service processes must be rigid yet flexible, efficient yet effective, serious business yet fun, controlled yet free, stable yet changeable, objective yet sensitive, and standardized yet customized. Finding the right balance between these service process design characteristics is a service/quality management challenge. These are a few example reasons why designing and managing a service process is more of a management challenge than is designing a goods-producing process.

The basic management issues concerning process design are outlined in Table 7–1. Good process design is a means of execution. Each question posed in Table 7–1 must be answered for any process—goods-producing or service-providing.

Ms. G. Lynn Shostack, CEO, Joyce International, Inc., was one of the first to understand service management and its approach to service process design. Shostack is a former senior manager at Citibank and Bankers Trust Company, and a former managing director of The Coveport Group, Inc. Four of her articles set the stage for a service management approach to process design.[6]

The following comments of Shostack are evidence that, in the early 1980s, she understood the implications of the statement "The process is the service". A service-management thinking person like Shostack sees things the product- or functional-perspective person doesn't see. These quotes come from her later paper, "The Sins of Alfred Sloan."[7]

> A service is not something that is built in a factory, shipped to a store, put on a shelf, and then taken home by a consumer. A service is a dynamic, living process. A service is performed. A service is rendered. The raw materials of a service are time and motion, not plastic or steel. A service cannot be stored or shipped; only the means for creating it can. A service cannot be held in one's hand or physically possessed. In short, a service is not a thing.
>
> Unfortunately, the harder service firms try to make the manufacturing model work, the more cracks appear in it. The real problem is that the functional structure itself is wrong. It reinforces piecemeal management, piecemeal knowledge, and piecemeal experience, because it assumes a divisibility in services that simply does not exist.
>
> All market leaders in service businesses share a common characteristic—they have specified and perfected every detail of the process, the means and the evidence.
>
> To help service firms do formally what great service founders have done intuitively, service firms need a true service design function—one that is a permanent, ongoing part of the business.

TABLE 7–1
Basic Process Design Questions

Basic Process Design Issue	Key Management Questions and Decisions
What?	What are the customer requirements?
	What are the desired process outcomes?
	What are the world-class process performance goals and benchmarks?
	What are the process activities and steps?
	What are the barriers to successful implementation?
Where?	Where are the process boundaries and key interfaces with customers and other processes?
	Where are the resource and knowledge bottlenecks?
	Where are processes shared or dedicated to particular consumer and employee benefit packages (CBP/EBPs)?
When?	When does the process start and end?
	When is each process activity performed?
	When is process recovery action taken?
Who?	Who are the customers?
	Who is assigned process ownership?
	Who is assigned service encounter ownership?
	Who owns that customer?
Why?	Why should this process exist?
	Why design it this way?
	Why automate it this way?
	Why organize around the process this way?
How?	How is the CBP/EBP created and delivered?
	How is process performance measured and rewarded?
	How are service upsets corrected?
	How is feedback used as a basis for continuous improvement?
	How is world-class service/quality performance created and delivered at each customer contact point?
	How to institutionalize process management into the organization?

Within the company, (process) blueprints will serve as an anchor for communication across organizational lines as well as a mechanism for participative management. And blueprints will function as a teaching and training foundation for both workers and managers to increase their understanding of the entire system within which they function.

SERVICE PROCESS PERFORMANCE

Service process performance is normally evaluated at the following two levels: (1) at the CBP/process level, or (2) at the service encounter level. The first level of process performance concentrates on the CBP and its process. Here the CBP/ Process Manager has control and accountability for process performance.

Process performance at the service encounter level must focus on individual customer and service-provider performance. A Comprehensive Customer Contact Plan (3C Plan), as discussed in Chapters 13 and 16, is one way to identify what to measure at the service-encounter level.

For example, the process of a customer inquiring about the design, development, delivery, and price of custom software for scientific information retrieval might include 20 key steps. A key step and point of customer contact is informing the customer that shipment of the finished software and accompanying documentation to the user's site is commencing. At Customer Contact Point #14 the following must happen, as shown in Table 7–2.

A 3C Plan scripts out service provider performance at the service encounter level. It identifies exactly how many points of contact there are in the service delivery process. It plans the ideal "whats" and "hows" of the CBP or EBP delivery process. It makes sure appropriate resources have been committed so frontstage and backstage service providers can do an extraordinary job. It ensures the service process and its people are capable of meeting or exceeding customer expectations. It can be defined as having tight or loose specifications of performance. The previous custom software shipment requirements is an example of a tight customer contact plan. Solution Approach #13 in Chapter 16 describes a loose customer contact plan. At times, service upsets or unusual customer requests will require the empowered service-providers to deviate from the ideal script. But the 3C Plan provides the baseline of performance expectations— what should happen, when, and how.

Service process performance can be evaluated by the following eight measures:

1. Process *outcome* is what the customer receives, experiences, uses, and/ or pays for during a single- or related-set of service encounter(s).

2. Process *inputs* are the resources (i.e., people, facilities, materials, information, equipment, technology) and knowledge (i.e, procedures, know-how) used to create and deliver consumer and employee benefit packages (CBPs/EBPs), and their associated service encounters.

3. Process *quality* is how the process delivers the consumer benefit package(s), and its associated service encounters.

4. Process *capability* is the ability of the process to accomplish its stated design goals concerning the competitive priorities of flexibility, time, price (cost), innovation, product/quality, and service/quality.

5. Process *reliability* is the consistency of outcome and process quality as measured against standards of performance.

6. Process *velocity* is the speed of delivering the completed CBP or EBP and/or one or more service encounter(s) to the customer.

TABLE 7–2
A 3C Plan for Shipping Announcement Requirements
(Customer Contact Point #14)

14.1 The Software Solutions Representative assigned to this job is responsible for all normal and follow-up activities at this customer contact point until the customer is satisfied. Every effort should be made to ensure a close and friendly customer relationship.

14.2 Telephone the customer and inform him or her of the expected date and time (if possible) of shipment arrival, the carrier, and a traceable shipment number.

14.3 Verify with the customer that the shipping information and expected shipment contents are correct and what is expected.

14.3 Follow up the telephone conversation with a faxed copy detailing the contents of the shipment and information previously given over the telephone.

14.4 Contact the customer within 12 hours after the expected shipment arrival time and confirm that the complete shipment has been received.

14.4 Ask the customer what else is required concerning this shipment, if there is any new business, or if there are any other concerns, and document the results of this customer contact in the automated customer profile system.

14.5 Inform the customer as to when and who will arrive on site to help in the installation of this software and in training the customer how to use it. Send follow-up letter, if time, with personnel biographies of the installation team.

14.6 Sign off on the successful completion of this customer contact step in the automated customer profile entry. (Only one service provider can be assigned ownership of Steps 14.1 to 14.6.)

7. Process *agility* is how quickly the process can change, recover, redesign itself, and incorporate feedback for continuous improvement.

8. Process *productivity* is a measure of input-output relationship(s), normally stated in terms of output per unit of input.

It is not unusual for process improvements to accomplish any or all the following example performance goals:

- Decrease rework costs by O%.
- Increase value added per employee by P%.
- Decrease employee turnover by Q%.
- Increase capacity utilization by R%.
- Decrease service upsets or errors by S%.
- Reduce labor hours by T%.
- Decrease total process cycle time by U%.

- Reduce costs per process cycle by V%.
- Decrease average inventory levels by W%.
- Reduce the number of non-value-added process steps by X%.
- Reduce facility space and costs by Y%.
- Increase repeat business or customer satisfaction by Z%.

The surprising fact is these percentages are higher than you think—often above 50 percent! Improving process performance can reduce costs and increase revenue, productivity, and customer satisfaction. Quality improvement is the driver of these improvements. Chapters 9 and 12 also discuss how these performance categories are related.

Much of this reduction in processing time is due to eliminating process idle time. Just like with pre-just-in-time manufacturing systems with lots of idle inventory; the customers, paper, and information sit idle waiting to be worked on in many service processes. In fact, they wait as much as 95 to 99 percent of the total processing time. So it's no wonder that "time" has become a key competitive priority and its reduction the basis for so much process reengineering.

Many other design issues must be addressed when undertaking a process improvement effort. Example service process design and improvement decisions can focus on any of the following issues: make or buy, flexibility, capacity and bottlenecks, training, simplification, self-service, employee empowerment, interfaces and boundaries, duplication, recovery strategies, consolidation, performance feedback mechanisms, horizontal and vertical integration, job specialization or enlargement, process and service encounter ownership, reproducibility, customer entrance and exit scenarios, automation, and reward and compensation for performance. If all this makes service process design and management seem challenging, it is!

The automation of a service process creates special challenges. For example, some process activities are eliminated while others now occur at the speed of light. It is important that we automate only the essential and value added process activities. The objective here is to eliminate non-value added activities in the process. This suggests that a comprehensive process analysis be performed before automating the process. Automating an inefficient or ineffective process is like putting your best foot forward, and then dragging the other.

PROCESS FLOWCHARTING

Process diagrams come in many forms.[8] Armed with these process diagrams, and a service management viewpoint, the task of designing a service process begins. Process flowcharting is one of 16 service/quality tools defined in Chapter 11. It is a tool that visually displays how things get done and a good basis for continuous quality improvement discussions. It is one of the most powerful tools of service/quality management. It can also consume significant amounts of time and money, and must be carefully managed. Clear process analysis objectives, well defined CBPs and EBPs, accurate process boundaries, and careful definition and sequencing of process activities and tasks are prerequisites to a successful process flowcharting and analysis initiative.

A process flowchart is shown for automobile repair service in Figure 7–1. Here a macro view is taken of this service process with more detailed steps and subsystems not presented. The line of customer visibility roughly separates activities and tasks the customer sees versus those basically invisible or not readily available to the customer. One could characterize this separation as frontroom versus backroom or frontstage versus backstage. But as discussed later in this chapter, the backroom in this example is really a service factory the customer visits. Therefore, the automobile repair service backroom directly affects the customer's perceptions of service. The backroom must be clean, colorful, and neat because the customer is in your factory. Likewise, the role of the mechanics must change to include both technical and customer interaction skills. As noted in Chapter 2, the backroom has been hurled into the frontroom in many cases by technology or aggressive service strategies. There are no backrooms anymore in many service businesses—everything is frontroom. The automobile repair service depicted in Figure 7–1 is a good example of a ''there are no backrooms anymore'' philosophy.

Other basic ideas of process management are illustrated by Figure 7–1. For example, process performance is measured in seven places in the service process, as denoted by the circles with numbers 1 to 7. This automobile repair service performance measurement system provides both customer satisfaction data (external) and process performance data (internal operational data). This provides opportunities for interlinking external and internal performance, and identifying areas for improvement.

Also, note that two service providers, the customer service representative and the mechanic, are assigned ownership of specific customers. They are responsible for everything that happens to that customer and his or her car in this service process. Other service-providers such as the automobile parts personnel and the cashier have important but peripheral roles.

Finally, there are many other ways to display and enhance process flowcharts. Some process flowcharts place value-added or processing-time numbers on the flowchart. Facilitating and primary goods and services can be separately identified on the flowchart. Steps in the process where service upsets and failures (fail points) are most likely to occur can be identified on the flowchart. And specific activities and steps in the process can be defined in detail by ''zooming out'' from a macro flowchart to a smaller level of detail.

FIGURE 7-1
Automobile Repair Service Process Flowchart Example

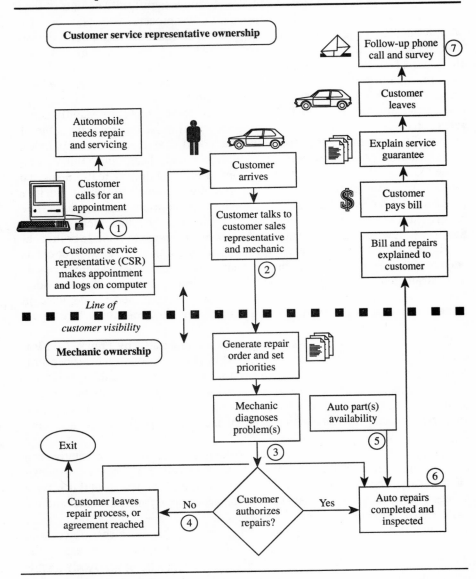

FACILITY LAYOUT AND PROCESS INTEGRATION

Especially in service process design, facility layout is so integrated with job and process design they must be done simultaneously. They must be integrated and support each other. As described at the start of this chapter, a large insurance company had to knock down walls to get the facility and process designs congruent.

Broadway Pizza (discussed in Chapter 5) tried to combine robotic entertainment with a pizza food service. In effect, Broadway Pizza had two different consumer benefit packages under the same roof. We reported that Broadway Pizza went bankrupt in 1984. Incompatible store layout and service process design contributed to the failure of Broadway Pizza. A service management perspective is needed to "see" these incompatibilities. The more you study the Broadway Pizza case, the more you learn about service management and its approach to facility, process, and service encounter design.[9] Management designed this failure!

Let's briefly preview a successful integration of service facility layout and process design before we examine other issues. (But first, some background on the US optical eyeglass industry.)

The US optical eyeglass and contact lens market could be divided into three retail markets and optical providers. They are: (1) small, independent optometric physician offices; or (2) large-volume specialty shops that send customer orders to an outside lab for optical production; and (3) special-service shops that do almost all production on-site. The first two types of optical providers use a store (frontroom only) layout, displaying a variety of eyeglass frames and customer fitting stations. The third type of optical provider links the frontroom and backroom together in a single site with greater emphasis on fast, convenient service.

Using the ideas of Chapter 4, all three optical providers sell a core good with various combinations of peripheral services. Detailed diagrams for each optical provider, such as shown in Figures 4–1 to 4–7, can be developed for each CBP design and configuration, but will not be shown here.

The competitive priorities discussed in Chapter 5 are all important in this industry, but the general order of priority is approximately as follows: price (top priority), time, product and service/quality, flexibility, and innovation (lowest priority). The small independent optometric physician office is typically high on price. The large-volume specialty shops that send customer orders to an off-site lab for optical production are usually volume discounters. The special-service shops that do almost all production on-site also charged high prices—but they justify their high prices based on extra value-added services, such as one-hour delivery time.

Given this industry background, let's examine how LensCrafters integrates facility and process design to enhance service encounter effectiveness. Lens-Crafters is a US national optical chain of almost 600 special-service shops with on-site production capabilities. Over 90 percent of their customer orders are on time. The other two types of optical providers quote 4 to 14 days to send an eyewear order to the off-site optical lab and get it back to the store.

LensCrafters' service guarantee states that, "If for any reason you are not completely satisfied with eyewear or service you receive from LensCrafters, we will make any adjustments you consider necessary, including replacing your lenses or frames at no additional charge."[10]

Figure 7–2 is a schematic of a typical LensCrafters' layout. Let's take a brief tour of their facility layout and process design. Inspection of the layout reveals it strongly supports the CBP delivery process. The greeter directs customers as they enter the store each to the appropriate service area. The optical lab area (backroom) is separated from the retail area (frontroom) by large glass panels. The backroom becomes a showroom to enhance the customer's perception of the total delivery process. Many customers stay and witness their individual pair of glasses being made. The store is spacious, open, clean, carpeted, with very professional merchandise display areas, modern furniture in the frontroom, and modern equipment in the show- or backroom.

Two clocks on the wall allow customers to evaluate the total processing time of their service encounter. And customers *do* watch those clocks! LensCrafters built their entire business around the value of time to its customers. First, Lens-Crafters decided that the competitive priority of time was their way to differentiate themselves from competitors. Then the facility layout and service processes had to be designed to support this time-based competitive strategy.

All customer-contact personnel are well trained, friendly, and knowledgeable about their consumer benefit packages. The lab production specialists are professional and well-dressed. Employees are called associates and efforts made to cross-train associates.

The store's information system tracks customer history and eyewear preferences. The information system sends customers reminders to get a checkup at certain intervals to encourage repeat business. It also routinely sends a feedback questionnaire to a sample of customers.

One objective of LensCrafters' service delivery process is to enhance the purchase of goods by outstanding service/quality and time performance. Prices are high but customers are willing to pay a high price for extra service- and time-related performance. Their time-based service encounters are very much dependent on good facility and process design. As noted in previous chapters, it is almost a given in the customer's mind that goods or technical CBP content is competitive.

LensCrafters' facility, process and job design demonstrate all of the key service management ideas of this chapter. Ideas of "the process is the service," facility layout and process integration, self-service, waiting for service, perception management, the showroom factory, and a service strategy positioned around time and service/quality performance as key differentiators are all inherent in Lenscrafters' designs.

FIGURE 7–2
A Schematic of a Typical LensCrafters Layout

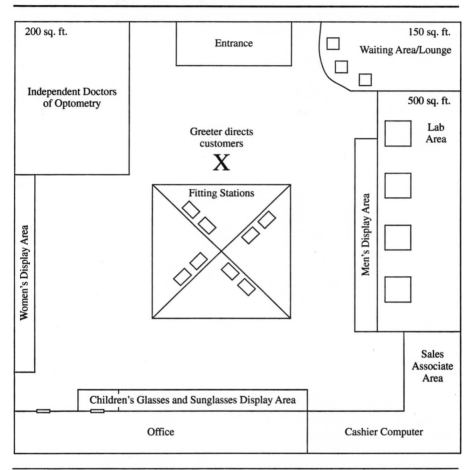

SELF-SERVICE

The use of customer labor—self-service—in service process design is an American service innovation. Customers share in the responsibility to create and deliver their CBPs and related service encounters. When a customer produces and consumes a service they are called *prosumers*. Depositing a check, selecting food in a supermarket, cleaning up after eating in a fast-food restaurant, and completion of medical forms before medical service, are some of the thousands of service processes that have self-service requirements.

"Service managers must decide exactly what the customer should experience and how the customer will or will not participate in the creation of the service. The degree of self-service desired in a service process affects capacity requirements, service levels, training requirements for employees, and cost control. Customer labor is a decision variable for organizations that provide services."[11]

Experiments with self-service are an example of research and development efforts in service industries. Many service industry R&D efforts are out in the field, not in the lab. Innovative service process designs are constantly field-tested.

For example, Amoco Corporation and Burger King Corporation announced they were testing out a combination gas station and fast-food restaurant in a suburb of Chicago. You can pump your gas while ordering food. The customer orders from a menu posted above the pumps and places his or her order through an intercom. Once inside, customers can pay their fast-food and gas bill together. Burger King built and runs the restaurant and Amoco paid for installation of the gas pumps. As one restaurant consultant said, "Now the problem is, are you going to wash your hands after pumping gas or are you going to eat your burger with high-test?"[12]

Is this bundled CBP configuration another Broadway Pizza-type failure or a Super America-type success? Where are the CBP and service process conflicts? What facility and service process design are appropriate?

The organization benefits from self-service by capturing the customer once they have committed themselves to self-service tasks. The organization expects to reduce costs with self-service. Also, self-service is a time-based strategy to speed delivery and enhance customer convenience at the service encounter level.

The risks to the organization of incorporating self-service into their CBPs and processes are difficult to measure. For example, customers might switch to other providers who offer full service for comparable prices. Customer resentment, customer mistakes, liability claims, and loss of organizational control are other dangers of using self-service.

How the customer views self-service is also difficult to evaluate. One empirical study investigated six self-service scenarios that were defined as follows:[13]

1. At a service station—pumping your gas versus having an attendant do it for you.

2. At a bank—using an automatic teller machine versus using the services of a human teller.

3. At a quick service restaurant—getting your own food at the counter versus receiving table service from a waiter or waitress.

4. At an airport—carrying your bags onto an aircraft with special storage facilities versus checking your bags.

5. At a hotel—using a self-service food and drink dispenser versus obtaining the same food and drink from room service.

6. At a travel agent—purchasing traveler's checks from an automatic teller machine versus buying them from a clerk.

Two different questionnaires were mailed to 2,500 customers. A total of 1,349 questionnaires were used in the statistical analysis.

The results of this self-service study suggest that, for some customers, participating in providing one's own service is very attractive. These customers were prepared to work in the service process without reward of any kind. For this group, no added inducement is necessary, such as a lower price. Thus, some customers are inherently participative in the service process.

Other customers needed a slight inducement to use self-service such as faster processing time or a lower price. Still others did not use or intend to use the self-service options in some of the scenarios listed. For certain services, these customers were low- or non-participators and viewed self-service as unattractive.

The data analysis also showed that customers may develop a propensity to participate. That is, customers may carry over self-service from one service to another, say, from pumping gas, to film developing, to do-it-yourself legal services.

The challenge for service process managers is to know their customers well enough to design the appropriate degree of self-service into the CBPs and associated processes. As this study suggests, there are at least three groups of behaviors and feelings toward self-service. These three groups are: (1) participative, (2) need a slight inducement, and (3) low- or non-participators. The absence or inclusion of self-service in your service process design can differentiate your CBPs from competitors. The degree of self-service to use is a key CBP, process design, and service encounter decision.

WAITING FOR SERVICE

We rush to wait! We leave the house in an attempt to catch our airplane flight, only to wait at countless traffic intersections. Then we wait for an airport parking lot ticket so we can park our car. We wait for someone to carry and check in our luggage. We wait at the airline ticket counter to get our boarding pass. We wait to use the airport restrooms and automatic teller machines. If time permits, we wait to be seated and served in the airport restaurant or cafe. We wait at the airport security checkpoints. We wait to use the telephone. We wait to board the plane. We wait for airport control tower clearance to depart the gate and, again, to use the runway. We wait for cabin food service to begin. And we reverse this entire process as the plane begins to reach its destination and you try to reach your final destination.

And the truth is, the waiting game is worse at many other service-providing organizations, such as hospitals. The minute the waiting starts, the customer may perceive his or her worth to diminish. The customer asks, "Am I so unimportant, that I have to wait? Don't they value my time?" If the wait is long, the customer begins to feel a social injustice has been committed by the service delivery process. Some customers have even sued a company because of too long a wait.

Of course, life begins and ends with a series of queues. If you have to wait too long in one queue, it may hurt your waiting time performance in all subsequent queues. Waiting for service can wreck anyone's day!

In the average US manufacturing firm, less than 5 percent of the total time required to manufacture and deliver a product to a customer is spent on actual work. For service processes, the actual time working compared to the total time required to complete the process is also very small. Data, people, and paper all sit in the service process waiting on someone to act and process it.

What can a service management's approach to service process design do about waiting? Can the process be designed to minimize waiting time? How?

First, management must excel at CBP design and integrating this with excellent process design. We have already examined CBP design and strategy in Chapters 4 to 6, and cited ideas of service process management in this chapter.

One technique that we have not mentioned is queueing or waiting-line models and analysis. Recognizing that manufacturing or service processes are a series of queues, queueing analysis can provide useful insights into how alternative service process designs behave. Like any technique, queueing techniques must be carefully applied. Many books on queueing methods are available.[14]

When queueing models are inappropriate, simulation methods can be used. Burger King, for example, is well known for using simulation models to examine alternative store layout and process designs. Many other industries use queueing and simulation models to help them better understand their facility and layout designs (e.g., the banking and telecommunications industries).

Management must also excel at perception management to minimize waiting time and customer dissatisfaction. Let's investigate what the master of perception management does—who else—but Walt Disney!

Walt Disney designs a CBP with associated facilities and processes configured to support the goals of the CBP. The Disney orientation handbook notes, "You already know you've been Cast for a Role, not hired for a job, and you'll work either On Stage presenting the Show or Backstage preparing and supporting the Show. As Cast Members, we're Hosts and Hostesses to our Guests—not customers—and they're an Audience, not a crowd. We don't have rides, we have Adventures and Attractions, each carefully "Imagineered" to provide family entertainment unparalleled anywhere in the world."[15]

Dan Kent, manager of show quality standards for Walt Disney Imagineering, illustrates that facility design is process design in a service business. He states that the "park's design makes the most of guests' ability to appreciate subtleties.

Take, for example, the way Main Street is designed. The distance between the Central Plaza (the hub of the park) and the Town Square (just inside the park) appears shorter from the Central Plaza end than it does from the Town Square end. That's because the buildings along Main Street on the Central Plaza end are a little farther apart than the buildings along Main Street on the Town Square end. It gives the impression that the park is opening up to guests as they enter and that the exit is a little closer when they're leaving."[16]

One airline at the Houston, Texas airport provides a good example of perception management. Customers were complaining about waiting to pick up their luggage at the baggage carousel. Actual waiting times averaged six minutes at the baggage carousel until the baggage began to arrive. It took passengers one minute to walk to the carousel from the airport gate. The airline moved the baggage carousel area to the farthest corner of the building. Now it took the passengers six minutes to walk from the airport gate to the carousel. Now the passengers had to wait an average of two minutes for their baggage to start arriving. Customer complaints decreased though total process time increased from 7 minutes to 8 minutes.[17]

Mechanisms to reduce or improve the customer's perception of waiting are varied. The dominant mechanism, of course, is a well-designed and managed service process and facility layout. Other examples of ways to design waiting into the service process or manage its occurrence are as follows:

1. Design a series of queues, each hidden from the other.
2. Place TVs or reading material in customer waiting areas.
3. Fill out forms before patron's arrival.
4. Express lanes in banks and supermarkets.
5. Provide airline frequent-flyer VIP lounges.
6. Provide express reservation and hot-line telephone numbers and processes.
7. Design salad bars that rely on self-service.
8. Use mirrors in elevators.
9. Use an appointment system.
10. Process customers in batches.
11. Sell tickets before the event.
12. Triage medical patients.

World-class service process managers think like the customer and know every detail of when, where, and why a customer may have to wait. They anticipate human behavior and the customer's situation through every stage of the service process. When the widget being processed is a human being, perception management is a critical part of service process management.

SERVICE PROCESS TOURS

There are many ways to differentiate one consumer benefit package from another. One way is to use the goods-producing or service-providing facility to help show off and sell your consumer benefit package to the customer. A tour helps build customer loyalty and encourages word-of-mouth advertising. One visit to a modern, clean, well-managed facility with professional, friendly people is worth many dollars in advertisements and salesperson calls. Many companies have done this for years.

In manufacturing, Honda of America considers its plant tours one of its best advertisements. In health care, one major hospital encourages new arrivals to the city and potential patients to visit the hospital for personal tours. In retailing, The Limited takes suppliers and customers through their centralized backroom distribution and order processing center. In financial services, a major bank pays for its larger corporate credit card customers to visit the processing center.

Chase and Garvin identify four ways to use what they call the service factory to enhance customers' perceptions of the company and its products.[18] Although their discussion focuses on companies that offer for sale a primary good with supporting services, service-providing companies also can use tours as a competitive weapon. This is especially true when the backroom of a service process is isolated from its customers—as in credit card and bank check processing, reservations systems, information and distribution services, and maintenance and repair services.

Chase and Garvin note that "the showroom factory can serve as a working demonstration of the systems, processes, and products it manufactures. It can also dramatize the company's manufacturing superiority and, by implication, its superior quality or reliability."[19]

The tour itself is a service process with its own unique CBP design, process steps, service encounters, and employee training implications. The questions in Table 7–1 should be answered for this service process. The tour process should be flowcharted, objectives set, service recovery strategies and customer-employee script dialogues defined, and employees trained to handle customer questions.

Using the factory or service facility as a way to impress the customer has its challenges and risks. First, the facility must be modern, clean, and well-maintained. It must clearly proclaim to the visitor that there is great attention to detail. LensCrafters' for example, lets customers tour the factory simply by looking at their eyewear being made in the backroom.

Second, employees who conduct the tours and employees who interact with visitors, must be knowledgeable, friendly, confident, and communicate well. They must get the customers excited about what they are seeing. The employees are the ultimate guarantee that visitors like what they see on the service facility tour. A third, more sublimable message must be communicated to the customer, and that is, trust us and our CBPs and processes. The visitor must walk away with a positive, exciting, and trusting perception of the organization.

The challenge for management is to arrive at the point where their facilities, processes, and people are ready to meet the demanding showroom requirements. These traditionally backroom managers and service providers have now been propelled to the frontroom. On frontstage, they must begin to execute a service management philosophy that also requires them to be good at human interaction and marketing skills.

PROCESS DESIGN IMPLEMENTATION

Chapter 13 outlines a service management approach to implementing a world-class service/quality management system. The seventh step (Action Step #7) in the 16-step implementation plan is to design a service process and its performance system simultaneously. Each of the 16 action steps has certain sub-steps. For an example, Table 7–3 here defines the sub-steps for Action Step #7. These sub-steps must be tailored to the unique characteristics of the organization and provide a greater level of detail.

For multisite service firms with hundreds or thousands of service facility sites, process design and procedures must be reproducible at all sites. For centralized service processes such as credit card or reservation processing, the service process reproducibility criterion is not as important.

Finally, the Malcolm Baldrige National Quality Award criteria define important guidelines for process design and improvement. To be world-class in process management, the approach must include a sound, systematic prevention-based system refined through evaluation/improvement cycles and must exhibit excellent integration. Deployment must be in all major areas and support areas and for all operations. Results must be excellent in all major areas and good to excellent in support areas, and results must be clearly caused by approach.

CONCLUSION

Service/quality performance depends on facility, process and job design. Execution is inherent in the design. If the design is lacking, management is asking its employees to execute with one hand tied behind their backs. World-class process design is the responsibility of management. Examples abound of the right and wrong way to integrate facility layout with job and process design, assuming you view it from a service management perspective.

For example, LensCrafters' facility and process design is a way to market their CBP to customers and differentiate their CBP from that of competitors. Their integrative facility and process design are the means for achieving their time-based competitive strategy. This backroom and frontroom configuration

TABLE 7–3
Action Step #7 Sub-Steps on Service Process and Performance Design

Sub-Step 7.1:	Define all process work tasks and activities and flowchart the service delivery process in detail, ignoring organizational boundaries and taking the customer(s) viewpoint. Inherent in this sub-step is defining who are the internal and external customers and suppliers.
Sub-Step 7.2	Identify all customer contact (service encounter) points per process, define performance measures, and the degree of organizational control for each service encounter.
Sub-Step 7.3	Simplify, automate, or eliminate all work tasks, activities and customer contact points that do not add value to the CBP/EBP or are a major source of service upsets.
Sub-Step 7.4	Redefine and flowchart the improved process with continuous improvement loops and document each work task, precedent relationship, training and resource requirements, and how performance will be measured and rewarded.
Sub-Step 7.5	Assign service-providers and manager's ownership of all process work tasks and the overall process itself. Communicate who is responsible to all people, suppliers, customers, and organizational entities. Make it easy to contact (access) all process and service encounter owners. (This is part of developing a Comprehensive Customer Contact Plan (3C Plan) for critical service encounters—Action Step #10 in Table 13–1).
Sub-Step 7.6	Collect data that allow you to compute the value of a loyal customer, the cost of poor quality, and the type and number of service upsets. Incorporate this information into sub-step 7.7.
Sub-Step 7.7	Evaluate performance frequently, based on objective and pre-agreed-upon standards of performance at the CBP, process, and service-encounter levels.
Sub-Step 7.8	Check to see if process performance and improvements are aligned with planned CBP performance attributes, and other work unit and organizational objectives. Frequently benchmark your process against world-class process performance.
Sub-Step 7.9	Build continuous improvement and nurturing cycles into all aspects of improving the process. (Action Step #14 in Table 13–1).

also enhances the service encounters by allowing the customer to see their eyewear being made.

If facility, process, and job design are integrated and well-managed, value added per employee can be increased. For example, world-class performers report $74,000 value added per employee while organizations just getting started on total quality and process management efforts report less than $47,000 value added per employee.[20] Good design and management of all of your primary, business, supplier, and support processes is a competitive advantage that works on both sides of the profit equation!

Service process design also requires the disciplines of marketing, operations, and human resource management to coalesce into a concoction called service management. When the widget processed is a human being, perception management becomes an important part of service process management and an integrator of functional areas.

Process design and management must be integrated with the organizational structure. The problem is that processes have more of a horizontal, across-functional-boundary, and throughput orientation that does not fit with traditional vertical and functional hierarchies. Something has to change here; processes and functions cannot both dominate the organization's design and decision making. A service management approach to organizational design, the subject of the Chapter 8, has help for correcting this structural problem.

Chapter Eight

Organization and Performance Design

T he most difficult challenge for management is to change an organization's structure, culture, and associated performance systems. It tears up the very fiber of the old organization and upsets traditional behaviors and management styles. But no one else has the power to do it except top management.

A service management approach to organizational design requires such a change. It is absolutely critical that top management understand the philosophy of service management, its ramifications, and use it as a rationale and guide for change. Everything else can be perfect but if the organization's structure and performance system are at odds with service management principles—service/quality and service encounter excellence are difficult to achieve.

Here we will examine representative issues surrounding organization and performance design, especially as it applies to service/quality. Given the limits of a single chapter, many important issues are not addressed. Example topics not fully addressed here include service-provider selection and empowerment, leasing service providers, multisite management, service-based performance and compensation systems, self-directed quality teams, training of high- versus low-contact service providers, and evaluating the performance of franchise units.[1]

WHY MUST THE ORGANIZATIONAL DESIGN CHANGE?

The major reasons organization designs must change to a service management approach are explained in this section. The reasons are based on service management ideas and principles. For example, service is now a much larger portion of what the customer buys and values than when functional organizational designs were founded in the early 1900s. More information-, service-, and entertainment-content in the CBP requires new approaches to organizational design and its performance systems. Many implications of this change in CBP content were discussed in previous chapters. For example, Chapter 1 defined these three service/quality premises:

Premise # 1   Service/quality performance is the best competitive
                  weapon.

Premise # 2   Service/quality performance is more difficult to manage
                  than product/quality performance.

Premise # 3   To truly understand service/quality, one must truly
                  understand service management.

Chapter 2 defined service management as follows. ''Service management is the study of how marketing and operations come together through technology and people to plan, create, and deliver consumer benefit packages and their associated service encounters. It is the fusion of many disciplines, and therefore, service management is extremely interdisciplinary. Service management tries to match the art it intends to serve. That is, the realities of managing a service at points of contact with customers.'' This definition itself is enough to justify a service management approach to organizational design.

Functional areas view functional goals and performance as top priority, while service management views organizational goals and performance as top priority. Optimization of functional goals may get functional managers promoted but it often leads to suboptimization of the total organization goals. Functional areas view integration as a second priority, while service management sees it as top priority. A service management designed organization doesn't make a big deal out of integration because it is inherently in the design and always there. Functional approaches often lose sight of who is the customer. A service-management-designed organization absolutely assures that the organization knows their true customers.

Chapter 2 also discussed the differences between goods and services. For example, services require quick response to fixing problems immediately in the presence of the customer, that is, prompt service recovery skills. In a service-management-designed organization, service recovery skills and policies are part of a time-based service strategy at the service encounter level.

Chapter 4 showed how to think about bundling goods and services together. It provided a framework to design CBPs and EBPs. Chapters 5 and 6 showed how service is a major part of almost any competitive strategy. Chapter 7, for example, discussed the notion and implications that ''the process is the service.'' The information and capability to compete reside in the process, not a functional department. Much of the energy of a functional organization is spent resolving problems at the interfaces among functional areas.

Functionalism has served us well in past operating environments. Now it is frequently a barrier to service encounter and service process success. The curse of functionalism is destroying world-class service strategies and service-encounter execution. Today's organizations must organize by process and by using a service management approach as defined in this book.

Another reason organizational designs must change is that after World Wars I and II, the world competitive environment more readily accepted inefficiencies and ineffectiveness. Most consumers were happy just to have the goods. Service was not a major competitive weapon until the mid-1960s. Functionalism formalized certain inefficiencies into Western-based management systems. With limited foreign competition and little regard for the role of service/quality, functionally designed organizations produced billions of products that a material-deprived world needed.

Until the 1970s it was a seller's market, which competed mainly on product quality and price. Japan began to give the United States and other Western industrial powers their wake-up-call during the 1970s. It is a buyer's market today for developed nations. Now the non-goods part of the CBP plays an important strategic role in an increasingly competitive world economy. The organizational structure must change to meet these new realities.

THE SERVICE MANAGEMENT WAY TO ORGANIZE WORK

Figure 8–1 depicts the traditional functional approach to organizational design. The functional approach in Figure 8–1 depicts some traditional departments such as marketing, production, and human resource management. For this functional organization to deliver a consumer benefit package (CBP), and its associated service encounters to the customer, many work activities must be done as shown by the A's, B's, and C's in Figure 8–1. For example, each functional department must complete its respective A1, A2, A3 activity and pass it on (like passing the baton in a relay race) to other departments, according to some management-specified sequence of activities. The output is a bundle of value-adding A activities that comprise CBP and Process A. And work activities for CBP/Process B and CBP/Process C are going on simultaneously in each functional area.

What CBP to work on first, second, etc., starts out as a functional (departmental) manager's decision. As consumer demand varies and many other things disrupt the way things get done, higher levels of management must intervene and resolve functional (departmental) conflicts and make decisions. Information and decisions begin to flow up and down the management hierarchy, not because it is more efficient but because it is designed that way. Little real value is added to the CBPs by the vertical hierarchy and resolution of interface issues. The functional organizational design ensures that management isn't left out by requiring that key decisions and information flows are vertical in nature. From the service providers' viewpoint, one customer is management.

Work intended for customer use tries to flow across the organization in almost a horizontal or lateral manner. If we reference any basic operations management textbook, we will find that "operations management refers to the systematic direction and control of the processes that transform inputs into outputs (finished goods and services)."[2] There are many types of transformation processes such as continuous flowshops, assembly lines, batch processing, projects, and routine

FIGURE 8–1

A Functional Approach to Organizational Design

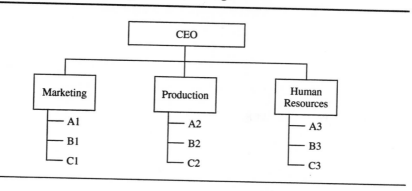

and professional job shops. The point is that operations management always has focused on processes, and their inputs and outputs.

Somehow we forgot or ignored the basic definition of operations management and its focus on process design and management. We flowcharted goods-producing processes for decades but not service-providing processes. The service operations managers and workers were never asked or allowed to design the organizational structure or performance system. If they had been allowed to, we might have had a process-dominated organizational structure and performance system 50 years ago. Functional areas would have never become so dominant.

Functional organizational designs do have advantages in some operating environments. Example advantages are:

1. Works best with only a few products.
2. Clearly defined functional career paths with in-depth skill development.
3. A concentration of functional expertise often centrally located.
4. Economies of scale within functional departments.
5. Employees in each department adopt similar values, goals, and orientations.
6. Best in small to medium-size firms.
7. Highlights the accomplishment of functional goals.[3]

Figure 8–2 depicts a service management approach to organizational design.[4] There are several ways to depict this idea but this is the simplest graphically. The organization in Figure 8–2 is now organized by process. Each process typically creates and delivers to its customers a single CBP/EBP or family of CBPs/EBPs. Process managers have complete responsibility and control over all inputs, transformation processes, and outputs of their process.

FIGURE 8–2
A Service Management Approach to Organizational Design

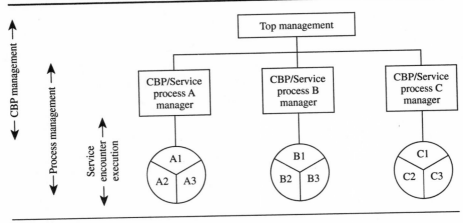

Service management makes no attempt to separate functional activities, especially as we get closer to the customer. Thus, the functional dimension exists only at the corporate levels for speciality services such as legal, tax, finance, and information systems. The customers of these corporate services are the CBP/process line managers.

Most functional types now reside in the process facilities and report to the appropriate process line manager. This positions managers and service providers closer to their customers and execution of the process. All employees are recognized and rewarded based on how well the process meets efficiency and effectiveness goals.

The circles below each process manager in Figure 8–2 represent service management process activities (e.g., A1, A2, A3). That is, marketing, operations, and human resource management skills and work activities are so intermingled that no attempt is made to separate them. Here the primary boss is a true customer, not a functional manager.

Processes sometimes share common resources as discussed in Chapter 6. At other times, each process is a single, dedicated process tied to certain CBPs or target customer groups. Only one (not many) higher level of management is needed to oversee CBP family groups, allocate resources to competing processes, and resolve process conflicts. Normally, this is senior management's responsibility.

Another result of adopting a service management approach to organizational design is to flatten the organizational structure. Information, decisions, and power reside at the CBP/process level. Several levels of management are cut out of the traditional functionally based organizational design. The organizational design is much less hierarchical and may consist of three to five levels.

A service management approach to organizational design has no more than the following five levels: (1) top management, (2) CBP family/line managers, (3) process line managers, (4) process supervisors, and (5) service providers. Often the second and third levels are combined into one level titled CBP/process manager. The leanest type of service management organizational structure has the following three levels: (1) top management, (2) CBP/process managers, and (3) empowered service providers. This structure has the capability to be the fastest and least costly design. It also requires world-class application of service management principles.

Top management and CBP family managers make key CBP management decisions and allocate scarce resources among competing CBPs and processes. The process line managers are fully responsible for everything (from A to Z) that relates to their process and the CBP(s) it delivers. Process line managers are clearly in a powerful position in the organizational design. Finally, supervisors and service providers are given much more responsibility and authority to create and deliver excellent CBPs and service encounters. They are highly skilled and empowered employees who work at the service-encounter level.

The service management approach places decision-making capability much closer to the customer. There are fewer levels in the organizational hierarchy but much more responsibility and power per level. This structure requires multiple communication channels to disseminate quality values, missions, performance standards, and continuous improvement initiatives.

The old span-of-control rules of 5 to 10 subordinates per supervisor or manager are not appropriate in a service management organizational design. Why? First, empowering the employees relieves managers and supervisors of many past responsibilities. Second, an electronic information and communication system is overlaid on this flat service management organizational structure. This capability allows a larger span of control and reduces the need for layers of management. As Chapter 9 points out, a service management approach to organizing work fits well with the capabilities of today's information systems and technology.

WHERE ARE THE QUALITY CONTROL POINTS IN A SERVICE PROCESS?

Finding the quality control decision points in goods-producing organizations was easy in the 1950s to 1970s. Somewhere on the factory floor was a sign identifying a room where the quality control function was performed. The quality journey followed the physical product much like the example given in Chapter 6 about the regional grass seed and fertilizer company. This company defined their job as done, once the physical product was unloaded at the customer's site. The journey of the physical product was traceable, measurable, consistent, and well-defined.

Service-providing process definition is more difficult than goods-producing process definition for reasons noted in earlier chapters. The following example illustrates the consequences of not using a service management approach to process and organizational design. A regional US hospital found that salary expense for their dietary food service department was more than double that of other comparable hospitals. In addition, one hospital patient almost died because a dietary tray delivery aide gave the wrong tray to a patient. Poor cost and service/quality performance triggered a quality audit of the dietary department. The objective of this hospital's dietary department was to *provide timely, neat meals with no errors, at competitive hospital costs per meal.*

A national consulting firm was hired to evaluate the dietary department's situation and make recommendations to improve cost and service/quality performance. The consulting firm sent in a team that did work measurement studies, flowcharted the tray production, assembly, and delivery processes, and so on. They found the dietary department to be overstaffed and in need of a training program for dietary production, assembly, and tray delivery personnel; and more quality checks were needed in the kitchen, the tray assembly area, and by each tray delivery team. Most of these recommendations were implemented, the consulting firm got paid, and the costs per meal decreased 1 percent whereas 8 percent was promised.

One year after this consulting firm's audit, costs were slightly lower but service/quality performance had greatly deteriorated. There were many more complaints by patients and family members—such as patients' meals being late or not picked up promptly, or by rushed and impolite tray delivery aides. It was privately known that there had been more tray mix-ups and a couple of close calls where patients were in danger because they had eaten the meal delivered to their rooms.

What was the problem? Why had patient's complaints increased? Where were the quality control points in this hospital's tray production, assembly, and delivery processes?

The consulting firm had missed one key area—Patient Services. They had followed the *food* through the hospital's processes. They had partially ignored the information flow and service-side of the dietary food service process.

For example, eight full-time employees in the Patient Services area took the diet cards filled out by each patient or doctor and processed them each day. These clerks assemble the diet cards by room and floor and checked to see that all menus were properly filled out. They also handle the myriad of changes that take place each day due to surgery, discharges, new admittances, or doctor-prescribed diet changes.

The clerk's office did this manually for three meals each day for all hospital patients. Clerks give this information to the kitchen, tray assembly, and tray delivery areas. Due to the short time between meals (i.e., a service window), some clerks are working on the breakfast diet cards while others are working on the lunch cards. The average age of the eight Patient Services clerks was 58 years old at the time of this incident. They received no training, and their salary was about equal to that of a tray delivery aide.

What is the significance of Patient Services in this hospital? What is the CBP for this hospital's dietary department? How important is their performance to labor utilization, cost containment, and service/quality performance? How important is their job to process performance? How many processes were there? How was each process defined? Was each process defined correctly? How were these processes coupled (linked) together?

A second study done from a service management perspective arrived at the following example conclusion. The eight clerks in this hospital's Patient Services area are (1) the service/quality control managers, (2) the master scheduler's for shop orders (dietetic patient menu orders), (3) the engineering change control managers, and (4) the best source of patient demand and admissions information in the hospital. They were the service management nerve center and information processor for the hospital's dietary department.

The implications of this discovery were immense. For example, these eight clerks working in Patient Services couldn't always finish their work between meals (i.e., overlapping and conflicting service windows). The volume, timing, and complexity of this information flow would surprise you. Thus, Patient Services needed an information system to handle the huge volume of data that passed through the area daily.

Patient Services job descriptions, titles, and salaries were upgraded. Training programs were designed. The entire Patient Services area was elevated in the hospital's organization chart. Patient Services began to be viewed as a top priority activity, not as a backroom, low-grade, paper-pushing activity done by eight elderly clerks. Many process improvements were implemented between Patient Services, the hospital kitchen, the tray assembly area, and the tray delivery teams. Only management with a service management perspective could make the changes necessary to improve the performance of Patient Services and the hospital's dietary department. The truth was that these eight clerks were doing an outstanding job in spite of being almost totally ignored by hospital management and doctors for 30 years.

Once service management thinking was applied to this situation, the roles of Patient Services personnel, dietary tray delivery aides, patients' family members, hospital nurses, dietitians, tray assembly personnel, and doctors were also redefined. The hospital's patients' food service became a competitive weapon that differentiated the hospital from its competitors. Of course, patients could readily evaluate the dietary department's performance and complaints went down dramatically. Overall, the patients' perception of the hospital improved due to improvements in this peripheral service. If you cannot see it, you cannot fix it!

THE POWER OF SKILLFUL SERVICE PROVIDERS

The Cooker Restaurant Corporation has the following guarantee on every menu in their successful chain of restaurants.

---

100 % Satisfaction Guaranteed

Yes—that is exactly what we mean. Your satisfaction is guaranteed by all of us here at The Cooker. Our goal is high-quality food, friendly and efficient service, and comfortable and clean surroundings. If you find we haven't reached that goal, please let us know. If we fail to make you happy, then we don't expect you to pay. It's that simple. We value you as a guest and a friend, and your happiness is our primary goal. Thank you.

Source: Cooker Restaurant Corporation, Columbus, Ohio, 1991. Used with permission.

To execute this policy of immediate reconciliation of customer complaints, Cooker management hires employees with a commitment to high standards of customer service. Employee personalities must be compatible with the company's philosophy, and able to handle much responsibility and autonomy. Therefore, Cooker's employee interview process is very extensive.

For example, company policy is to give the customer(s) free menu items, and sometimes, free meals for service failures. For example, if from the time the customer order is placed on the cook's order board until it is delivered is more than 15 minutes, Cooker employees can give the customer free desserts, drinks, and so on. They may ask store management what to do but they don't have to. They have been empowered to do, on the spot, whatever in their judgment will make the customer happy. At times, good routine service providers must be selectively disobedient.

The all-important capability to execute a *service recovery strategy* rests most often with the front-line service providers—here, the table server. Give the store manager a skillful workforce that is properly trained, and excellent customer service is (almost) assured. As one senior-level manager explained, "the availability of top-quality people to hire and execute our policy is our biggest constraint to growth."

HUMAN PERFORMANCE SYSTEMS

CBP management, service delivery system design, and service encounter execution all depend on human performance. CBP management and service delivery system design have set the stage—now it is time to perform. Figures 2–3 and 2–4 show how it fits together. Many books are available on designing and managing high-performance people systems.[5] Here our purpose is narrow compared to complete books on this subject. We shall briefly address the following example issues:

1. Empowering service providers is a necessity.
2. The need for service management career paths.
3. Service providers as key sources of service innovations.

Empowering Service Providers Is a Necessity

As we discussed in Chapter 2, a service is a performance. Managing a performance, like the director of a play, is very different from managing a factory. As you get closer to service encounter execution, the ability of management to influence service encounter performance decreases rapidly. When managers adopt a service management approach to organizational design and human performance management they need to empower their employees. At first, empowerment seems like a polite gesture but it is not. Empowering service providers is a necessity if you organize the service management way.

For example, Beth Israel Hospital in Boston, Massachusetts, is a world-class hospital renowned for its medical research and its patient care and service performance. Nurses are the dominant service providers in this hospital's service delivery system. "Each patient is assigned a registered nurse as his or her primary nurse within 24 hours of admission. That nurse is made responsible for and empowered to manage the patient's hospital experience from admission through discharge or transfer to another unit of the hospital. So much care-planning and decision-making has been moved to the frontline that Beth Israel has eliminated two tiers of management in its nursing staff. The nurse is now both care-giver and care-manager."[6] Here the nurse is assigned process and service encounter ownership.

Federal Express, a 1991 Malcolm Baldrige National Quality Award Winner, provides another good example of how management style, organizational design, empowered employees, and technology are integrated to provide world-class service encounters. How do they do it? First, they define the core of their business and their consumer benefit package as "the anxiety relief business." This is a human need. The movement of the physical letter or package is the means of eliminating customer anxiety (i.e., customer wants and needs). This is how they define their business, and accordingly, their service encounter capabilities. Their CBP definitions are well-defined—a first step to a service management approach.

Then this process-dominated and flat organizationally designed company goes to work. They measure performance on a real-time basis at all levels of the company—the CBP, process- and service-encounter levels. Federal Express's world-class technology also facilitates information flows and human communication requirements.

Technical capability and organizational design create the opportunity for human performance perfection. Here is where Federal Express goes from being an industry leader to truly world-class. Competitors may duplicate technical capability and organizational design but, ultimately, well-trained and empowered employees create and deliver world-class service encounters. A friendly smile or a concerned and knowledgeable voice over the telephone or an immediate solution to the customer's problem are the cornerstones of Federal Express's "anxiety relief business." When it all fits together right, it is easy to gain competitive advantage.

As Fred Smith, the CEO and Founder of Federal Express, noted, *"Probably the most important thing that we have to add to the body of knowledge is what we've learned about the involvement of our employees at the customer-contact level of the quality process.* There are probably many companies that know as much or more than we do about automation and statistical process control systems and things of that nature, but I think we know a lot about how to get a large service organization committed to first-rate service. That will be our primary focus."[7]

Empowering employees is more than a cheerleading conference, customer service buttons, token focus group and marketing plans, publicity stunts, and making performance promises to customers. Employee empowerment requires the following eight commitments.

1. Growth and service strategies must not outpace empowerment and execution capabilities, and availability of qualified people.

2. Management defines the organizational structure and it must be organized the service management way.

3. Information system and technical capability must be provided to support empowered employees at the process- and service-encounter level(s).

4. Management must authorize and assign process, service encounter, and customer ownership to specific employees and managers.

5. The committment of resources for outstanding training for each empowered job in the organization is an essential requirement.

6. Management must make sure each employee understands his or her role and contribution in the overall process, the organization, and national competitiveness.

7. Empowered employees must know their customer's wants and needs, and be a source for innovation and change. Then management must listen to their employees and seriously evaluate employee ideas.

8. Management must build an employee selection and performance system that hires the right people, rewards correct employee behavior, decisions, and actions; and provides feedback for continuous improvement.

Many of these empowerment characteristics and requirements have been illustrated here by examples from Cooker Restaurants, Beth Israel Hospital, and

Federal Express. These eight minimal requirements of empowerment give you some idea of what true employee empowerment means. It is not an easy service strategy to successfully implement.

The Need for Service Management Career Paths

A service management career path demands more flexibility from the organization and the employee. Table 8–1 presents potential changes in management orientation and philosophy by comparing a service management career path with a traditional career path. A traditional career path in Table 8–1 is typical of a functional or matrix-organized company. Federal Express uses a combination of growth, compensation, promotion, recognition, and grievance systems to accommodate the need for career management. Delta Airlines and Marriott Corporation also use many service management career path ideas noted in Table 8–1.

Most of the comparisons in Table 8–1 are self-explanatory but a few general comments help explain these ideas. The service-management-organized firm has few organizational levels, and it values interdisciplinary expertise as a prerequisite to promotion. Managers and service providers will rotate among different jobs. The idea is that once they see the cause-and-effect relationships among successive stages of the process, they will be better able to raise the performance levels of their stage in the process or overall process performance. Worldwide economic competition can no longer tolerate the inefficiencies and practices of the past. These highly qualified people with broad interdisciplinary experience are now ready to be CBP/process line managers. Finally, several of the comparisons in Table 8–1 refer to the style of management. Those managers and service providers not capable of making this transition in management style will be cast aside by the service requirements, structural changes, and technological capabilities of the Servomation Age.

Service Providers as Key Sources of Service Innovations

Several things change when the organization uses the service provider as a source for CBP, process- and service-encounter innovations. First, CBP designers and managers begin to listen to service providers and value their insights. Service providers are normally the first to recognize major or subtle changes in customer preferences. Historically, this source of information was undervalued and seldom used.

Second, the role and reporting relationships of the marketing, and research and development functions must accommodate service providers as a key source of CBP, process- and service-encounter information. Traditional roles require the marketing area to design customer surveys and focus group sessions to evaluate changes in customer preferences. Traditional methods of marketplace intelligence are frequently characterized as slow, discrete, costly, and independent

TABLE 8–1
*Comparing Traditional versus Service Management Career Path Issues
and Styles*

Traditional Career Paths	*Service Management Career Paths*
Vertical advancement	Circular advancement
Functional expertise and education	Interdisciplinary expertise and education
Short cycles between job changes	Longer cycles between job changes
Promote up and out and never return	Rotate among different jobs and return
Specialists' job titles	Generalists' job titles
Know part of the CBP	Know all of the CBP
Focus on the customer and the boss	Focus on the customer, then the boss
Faith in structure and bureaucracy	Faith in continuous change and adaptability
Work for one or two organizations	Work for many organizations
Match career goals with narrow functional and organizational goals	Match career goals with broad personal goals
Supervise and control	Coach and inspire
Few communication channels	Multiple communication channels
Functional management	Process management
Emphasize individual management	Emphasize collective/team management

events. Service-provider information and ideas are fast, continuous, cheaper, and interconnected events. The basis for competitive advantage may be found in one idea from a service provider. For example, over 50 percent of new-product ideas originate from the employees at 3M. Milliken & Company relies on customers for over 50 percent of their new-product ideas.

A third issue that changes when service providers are involved in CBP design is the chance of implementation success. Schneider and Bowen studied the role of service employees in new service design, development, and implementation. They offered six propositions based on previous research and ideas.[8]

One proposition they offer is: "The more employees are involved in service (as defined by their service cube) the more important it is to involve them in the design, development, and implementation of new services."[9] They cite examples where management was out of sync with customer needs while service employees knew what needed to be improved. Evidence is presented that implementation is more successful if service providers are a part of the design process.

TABLE 8–2
Service Management Action Starter Questions

1. What does a service management approach to organizational design look like in your organization? What is your implementation plan and timetable to restructure your organization the "service management way"?

2. How is human performance tied to CBP, process, service encounter, and service/quality performance? What employee hiring and training programs are in place to ensure service management skill capability? How will your organization achieve the eight minimal requirements of employee empowerment?

3. Define ideal service management career paths in your organization. How does the performance system reward successful completion of each of these career paths, or does it?

4. How can a service management approach to organizational design drive a time-based competitive strategy? Develop an agenda for action at the CBP, process, and service encounter level for this time-based competitive strategy.

5. What organizational mechanisms, communication channels, and systems are in place to use service providers as a key source of service innovation ideas and service/quality improvement?

CONCLUSION

The key ingredients to establishing a service management approach to organizational design include: (1) creating a world-class service management culture, (2) empowering people to deliver world class service encounters, (3) adopting process management and organizing as in Figure 8–2, and (4) harnessing the power of information technology and service innovations. Table 8–2 identifies five example Action Starter Questions concerning organization and performance design from a service management perspective.

A service management culture is a business strategy and objective in itself. Competitors see or experience it but have trouble copying it. It puzzles competitors. It excites customers. It reenergizes employees. You know it when you see or experience it but cannot totally explain why it was so superb. Companies such as Federal Express and Walt Disney use their service management culture and well-trained and empowered employees as sources of competitive advantage.

A service management approach to organization design, as shown in Figure 8–2, can help guide companies in their restructuring efforts. It can provide direction and a broad goal as to what the organization should look like in X years. CBP, process, and service-encounter management dominates the service management designed organization. Also, it is inherently the basis for a time-based competitive strategy.

The organization defined in Figure 8–2 is a time machine. It moves fast both vertically and horizontally. It is lean, fast, and adaptable. The organization's playing field has only three general levels—CBP Management, CBP/Process Line Management, and Service Encounter Execution. Functional areas of expertise reside at the corporate level only for very specific purposes such as tax or legal advice. The last ingredient of a service management approach to organizational design is how service innovations and information technology are integrated into the organizational design to help support service-encounter execution. This is the subject of Chapter 9.

Chapter Nine

Service Innovations

T echnology drives the future. It creates new consumer benefit packages, service encounter capabilities, markets, and industries. But technology is only as good as the management team that discovers, directs, and uses it. And technology in a service business can take forms very different from industrial-based definitions.

In Peters and Austin's book, *A Passion for Excellence*, they identify two edges of excellence. The first is to take exceptional care of your customers via superior service and superior quality. The second is to constantly innovate.[1]

In a service business, service innovation and service/quality performance are inseparable. A service innovation can inherently result in better service/quality performance. For example, the test kitchens of luxury hotels prepare prototype dishes and meals. Taste-testing experts and selected customers evaluate these new dishes. Once the new dishes are approved, waiters and waitresses are taught what is in the new dish and about how it is prepared. They are also trained in how to serve customers the new dish, and what might be typical questions the luxury hotel guest will ask. Here the service innovation (the new CBP), how to serve it (process quality), and the final result in the customer's mind (outcome quality) are inseparable. Also note that this service innovation requires backroom and frontroom coordination.

An excellent collection of essays on service technology is a book edited by Bruce R. Guile and James Brian Quinn, *Technology in Services*.[2] These essays address the issues of service productivity, employment, international trade, policy, industry comparisons, and past myths and future challenges. The book is rich in facts to support specific premises about the status and role of service technology in the world economy.

Our purpose here is much narrower. This chapter surveys management issues surrounding service innovation. Service innovations take many forms and are not fully recognized in most research and development performance statistics. So, documenting and reporting service innovation activity is difficult. Besides nonexistent or insufficient service innovation measurement systems at the company, association, and government levels, the process of creating service innovations has not been well defined and described.

WHAT IS A SERVICE INNOVATION?

A new idea is exciting to some people in an organization but disheartening to others. If the idea is developed, tested, and implemented, it may improve productivity and change the nature of the service encounter and work itself. The wheel, automobile, refrigeration, airplane, telephone, satellite, automatic teller machine, space shuttle, personal computer, digital tele(vision)computer, micromachine, plastic automobile bodies, and rapid manufacturing prototyping represent advances in hard technology. These hard technology examples are physical apparatus that help create and deliver CBPs. They are easy to recognize. People can see and touch these physical items. They usually represent our physical world and material well-being.

At the other end of the technology spectrum, soft technologies also increase productivity and improve our standard of living. Soft technologies here are more than computer software. Soft technologies include human intellect and ways of thinking and acting. The written word, self-service, customer service script dialogues, the Bill of Rights, insurance, service guarantees, corporations, service-provider empowerment training, object-oriented software, and health maintenance organizations are examples of soft technologies. They are not so easy to recognize. They are usually associated with a novel procedure such as self-service or an intangible characteristic such as a person's psychological well-being.

Marketplace technologies are normally an artful combination of hard and soft technologies. The art is human ingenuity and intellect. A good example is Vision System. It is an interactive tele(vision) computer that offers customers instant refunds, coupons, and recipes at supermarket checkouts.

An electronic network is a combination of hard and soft technology. Many information-based primary and supporting services are created and delivered through electronic networks. Here electronic networks, information technology, and information systems are approximately the same thing. The hard technology consists of optical fiber wires, electronic switches, computers, satellites, and so on. Soft technology includes the configuration of the network and its design, network software—some approaching artificial intelligence, user-friendly process design, computer terminal training and skill development, and the like.

Network architecture has to do with how the network is designed. Again there are two major components of a network. They are hardware architecture, and human communication and interaction relationships. Hardware architecture can be configured in simple chain, wheel, circle, and all channel arrangements. The human side of network relationships is even more complicated. Human communication, for example, can be to accomplish work or for social interaction objectives.

The social, electronic, and organizational networks form a conglomerate that influences innovation and service/quality performance. Federal Express is a good example of a conglomerate network that is itself a service innovation.

Other conglomerate networks that represent service innovations include buyer and computer clubs, health maintenance organizations, and newspaper wire-service associations.

Table 9–1 is a reprint from a 1983 article on the issue of recognizing service automation and its implications. The title of the article was "The Service Sector Revolution: The Automation of Services."[3] A subsequent book was titled *Service Management: The Automation of Services.*[4] The examples of service automation shown in Table 9–1 have purposely not been updated since 1983. They *understate* a service management view of service innovation.

Webster's Dictionary defines *automation* as "the technique of making an apparatus, a process, or a system operate automatically."[5] The ability to do physical and intellectual tasks often unassisted by human beings is automation. *Technology* is defined "as a technical method of achieving practical purposes."[6] *Innovation* is "something that deviates from established doctrine or practice; something that differs from existing forms."[7] Quinn defines innovation as "creating and introducing original solutions for new or already-identified needs."[8]

Service innovations, in this book, are any means by which the seven P's of service management establish a new or modified doctrine, practice, or form of creating and delivering service encounters. Here innovation includes discovery and the practical application or commercialization of a device, method, or idea. The seven P's of service management, as defined in Chapter 6, are product (consumer benefit package) price, place, promotion, physical evidence, process, and participants.

Service innovation reflects the broadest view of technology. It is most appropriate for services. Service technology or automation is a subset of service innovations. The examples in Table 9–1 are only part of the total picture of service innovation.

For example, Wendy's salad bar in the US fast-food industry is a service innovation. The salad bar service innovation is not automated (at least not yet). But it did combine at its time of introduction many new ideas of process design and self-service.

Another example of a service innovation (described in Chapter 5) is the Best Hotels invention of the all-suite hotel room idea. Within the seven P's of service management framework, it changed the role of the participants—the hotel employees and the hotel guests. It also reengineered and reconfigured the consumer benefit package (product, if you must) and price, place, promotion, physical evidence, and process. This facility design-based innovation created a new CBP, type of service encounter, and market segment in the lodging industry.

Service innovations don't have to include new physical layouts or the use of new technology. A process-based service innovation coupled with existing technology can sometimes differentiate one's CBPs and service encounters from that of competitors. For example, shop-at-home-by-phone capabilities have been in existence for a long time. Kroger's offers The-Shoppers-Express where a customer places an order verbally over the telephone or by fax machine. The cus-

TABLE 9–1
Examples of Automation in Service Industries

Service Industry	Example
Financial services	Electronic funds transfer systems
	Automatic teller machines
	MasterCard II—the electronic checkbook
	Encoded check processor machine
	Pneumatic delivery systems
	Automated trust portfolio analysis
Utility/government services	Automated one-man garbage trucks
	Optical mail scanners
	Electronic computer-originated mail
	Mail sorting machines
	Electric power generating plants
	Airborne warning and control systems
Communication/electronic services	Information systems
	Two-way cable television
	Teleconferencing/picturephone
	Telephone switching systems
	Phone answering machines
	Word processing
	Paper copying machines
	Voice-actuated devices
Transportation services	Air traffic control systems
	Auto-pilot
	Boeing 747
	Automatic toll booths
	Space shuttle
	Containerization
	France's RTV trains
	Ship navigation systems
	Rapid transit system
Health care services	CAT scanners
	Pacemakers
	Fetal monitors
	Ambulance electronic dispatching systems
	Electronic beepers
	Dentists' chair system
	Medical information systems
Education services	Personal/home computers
	Audio-visual machines
	Speak and spell/speak and read
	Electronic calculators
	Language translation computers
	Library cataloging systems

continued

TABLE 9–1 *(concluded)*

Service Industry	Example
Restaurant/food services	Optical supermarket checkout scanners Assembly line/rotating service cafeterias Automatic french fryer Vending machines
Wholesale/retail trade	Telemarketing Point-of-sale electronic terminals Dry cleaner's conveyors Automatic window washers Newspaper dispenser Automatic car wash Automated distribution warehouse Automated security systems
Hotel/motel services	Electronic reservation systems Elevators/escalators/conveyors Automatic sprinkler systems Electronic key/lock system
Leisure services	Television games Video-disc machines Movie projectors Disney World (Hall of Presidents, Country Bear Jamboree, Circle-Vision 360) Beach surf rake

Source: D A Collier, "The Service Sector Revolution: The Automation of Services," *Long Range Planning* 16, no. 6, 1983, pp. 12–13. Reproduced with permission.

tomer can call 24 hours a day, 7 days a week. Temperature-controlled vehicles deliver the groceries right to the customer's door with same-day or next-day service. Prices vary according to delivery requirements, faxed orders get a discount, and so do senior citizens. Senior citizens and time-starved yuppies are two target markets for this time- and convenience-based CBP. This service innovation is *process-based*, using existing telephone technology.

Service innovations are also not fully recognized in US accounting, productivity, and budgeting methods, and US research and development statistics. For example, *Business Week* magazine includes an R&D Scoreboard every summer.[9] Products dominate these R&D statistics. Products are easy to see and count. Accounting and financial systems are set up to recognize and count product-based R&D activities. Service innovations in *Business Week's* R&D Scoreboard are undercounted and underrepresented because they are not as easily recognized and it is more difficult to define service innovation boundaries.

Example service organizations not included in the *Business Week's* R&D Scoreboard, but using one or more service innovations include American Airlines, American Express, American Red Cross, Citicorp, Domino's Pizza, Federal Express, Girl Scouts of America, Harvard University, Hyatt Legal Services, L. L. Bean, The Limited, Marriott, McDonald's, US Internal Revenue Service, Wal-Mart, Walt Disney, and Wendy's. The problem is not *Business Week's* R&D collection procedures. They, and others, are doing the best they can, given the current sources of accounting and R&D data, and the dominance of a product-perspective.

One final point about service innovations before we move on to other management issues. Picking the right time to introduce a service innovation is critical to marketplace success. The market must be ready. The customer must be willing to pay for and use the new CBP. Because service innovations can be so personal, they can outpace customer needs. For example, bank-at-home services have had trouble in the marketplace due to nonreceptive customers. Huntington Bancshares Inc. and American Telephone & Telegraph have announced a new effort at making at-home banking work. (Huntington was one of the first banks to offer and to pull out of home banking in the early 1980s.)

The new home banking service uses a newly developed and interactive Smart Phone. It has all the characteristics of a telephone plus a touch-sensitive television-like screen. The screen is reprogrammable so the placement and format of each icon can be easily changed. As William M. Randle, senior vice president of corporate marketing at Huntington said, "The Smart Phone appeals to people who are time poor. We think it's a delivery system whose time has come."[10]

PROTECTING SERVICE INNOVATIONS

Goods-producing firms use patents and licensing agreements to protect their products. The chemical formula for fluoride in toothpaste is precise and is defendable in the courts. As the world economy develops, American firms are finding it much harder to protect those ideas. For example, Carla Hills, the top US trade representative, notes that "foreign piracy of US trademarks, copyrights, and patents steals $40 billion a year from American sales. She wants the General Agreement on Tariffs & Trade (GATT) expanded to ensure that all nations honor intellectual property rights."[11]

The intangible portion of a service makes it more difficult to protect service innovations. Services are legally less defensible than goods. Copyrights, trademarks, and the establishment of a standard facility design or standard CBP provides some protection in US courts. More practical ways to protect service innovations include buying prime sites for hotels or the rights to satellite communication channels or security systems for computer software.

Another way to protect rights of service or service innovations is to use the court and legislative systems. The US cable industry is currently using the US courts and Congress to protect its access to American homes. The local and regional telephone companies are also lobbying the US Congress for greater access to these homes. Both the cable and telephone industries want to provide a wide array of CBPs, using voice, video, and information services through fiber optic cables.

Exporting services also improves the US balance-of-payments problems. However, many nations object to free service trade or to honoring US intellectual and service rights. Sometimes a nation's entire service industry might be eliminated in the face of global service competitors. A legalistic approach to protecting service trade is one of many avenues the United States is pursuing. For example, the Bush Administration's Structural Impediments Initiative (SII) tried to reduce the barriers to exporting CBPs to Japan. Where the Clinton administration will lead on this issue will soon be known.

MOBILE AND GLOBAL SERVICE PROVIDERS

Where work takes place is becoming irrelevant in today's electronic global village. Service firm managers and service providers don't need a permanent workplace. For information-intensive jobs, electronic networks allow this work to be done anywhere in the world. The time and place of service-encounter execution becomes portable. The portable CBP or service encounter is a reality today.

Technologies such as a portable personal computer, a fax machine, and a car telephone define a mobile office for many professional and routine service providers. Consultants, engineers, lawyers, and so on are mobile and now have the capability to leverage every minute of their time. Routine service providers such as a Federal Express courier are in constant communication with central offices, managers, and one another. Their electronic communication and information systems make them an intelligent, real time, and moving mail service.

As discussed in Chapter 5, the management issues of multisite management are dramatically changed due to electronic network and information system capabilities. This geographical dispersion and high mobility of managers and service providers presents several challenges to managers. For example, how do you control service/quality performance at hundreds or thousands of temporary sites scattered around the world? How much of one's business can or should be done via teleworking? Should the service provider be part-time or full-time, salaried or paid by project? Should electronic monitoring of managers and service providers be the major way to evaluate job performance? What type of training programs are best? How does the service encounter change? Do we need fewer levels of management for global operations?

A service/quality challenge is how to manage those other managers and service providers effectively who seldom come into a traditional and permanent workplace. The distinction between work and nonwork is becoming blurred. Technology allows service providers to vary their place and time utility daily. It allows service providers to spend more time with their customers. It also allows teleworkers to avoid traffic jams and accidents, and the costs of child care and fuel for transportation.

One good model of the future of electronic multisite management is F International of the United Kingdom. This software systems company founded by Stephanie "Steve" Shirley in 1962 employs over 1,100 workers in 800 different sites and serves approximately 400 clients at any one time. Almost all professional service providers are part-time but control does not seem a problem. As Shirley says, "Through the machine, through the kind of product, through the documentation, through the client's payment. That is the final quality control— the amount of repeat business."[12]

For routine service providers, there are also many examples of mobile or at-home electronic offices.[13] Examples are: mobile health care vans, some of which contain a CAT (computized axial tomography) scanner; service providers with an electronic office at home; Federal Express trucks with CRT screens and computers; mobile and electronic insurance disaster response vehicles; ambulance and emergency vehicles; and mobile libraries.

Where work is performed—the site—is becoming more irrelevant each day. Each day's workplace now can be a time line of work activities moving through many sites and never to be repeated. The capability to create and execute service encounters can now follow the customer. The term *convenience* (time- and place-utility) takes on a new meaning when you are hooked up to the global electronic network or take your service encounter resources with you.

SIMULTANEOUS SCALE, SCOPE AND TIME ECONOMIES

Information technology and systems have allowed some companies to change the service/quality performance plateau in two ways. These companies now offer (1) better levels of service at lower cost and (2) broader CBP lines and options. Information is easy to move, divisible, easily shared, expandable, fast, and a corporate asset that is not readily identified on the firm's financial statements. The truth is we are still learning how to manage, record, and use information to gain competitive advantage.

The following example companies have gained economies of scale, scope, and time from their information system(s):

- American Airlines's SABRE and CRS information, reservation, and yield management systems.
- Caterpillar's total maintenance and repair service systems.
- Federal Express's COSMOS system.
- The Limited's merchandise scanning, ordering, production, and distribution management systems.

- Marriott's CONFIRM hotel reservation system and guest service index system.
- MBNA America's affinity credit card information system.

These service innovations may offer totally new CBPs or shift the service/quality performance plateau upon which competition takes place.

Information technology helps shape organizational structure and complements organizational designs as were shown in Figure 8–2. Technology helps set the boundaries on the degree of centralization and decentralization, and the degree to which employees and customers can be empowered with information. Typically, the decentralized frontroom has smaller and smaller facilities and point-of-sale devices that are convenient and close to the customer. Ultimately, frontroom decentralization will continue marching all the way to the customer's home and even to the individual's person. Meanwhile, the backroom is centralized, far removed from the customer, and becoming superefficient and powerful.

The Limited, for example, was quick to gain a competitive advantage by developing an information system for store sales tracking, order processing, inventory management, and fast factory-to-store shipment. This electronic capability is essential when customizing merchandise and orders by store; and for stores-within-stores as quickly as possible. MAST Industries Inc., for example, is a subsidiary of The Limited. MAST operates a dozen factories, subcontracts to 300 other factories, and distributes apparel items to The Limited's only distribution center in Columbus, Ohio. This center services about 4,200 Limited stores.[14]

MAST industries excels at speed-sourcing apparel items from the time a fashion item or trend is identified until the item gets into the customer's distribution channels in significant numbers to meet demand. Today, MAST delivers most orders within 800 hours or 33 days. This time includes design and production time. The goal is to average 500 hours. MAST also bids for all of The Limited's business, and no Limited division is required to purchase products from MAST.

At MAST, a centralized information system is available to employees and customers 24 hours worldwide. Everyone communicates through this system. Electronic invoices, order receipts, factory orders, order quotations, messages, and so on, are done through this global information and communication system. The Limited and MAST Industries' information systems allow them to achieve backroom economies of scale, frontroom economies of scope, and economies of time compression. Flexibility, speed and service are top competitive priorities at The Limited.

IS TECHNOLOGY DELIVERING
SERVICE PRODUCTIVITY?

The service sector of the US economy owned 84 percent of the US economy's total stock of information technology capital in 1985. About 38 percent of this capital is found in the communication industry, 11 percent in the financial and insurance sectors, 10 percent in the real estate sector, 10 percent in the wholesale and retail trade sectors, 3 percent in public utilities, 1 percent in the transportation sector, and the remaining 11 percent in a host of other service industries.[15]

Yet, depending on what sources you use, US service sector productivity has lagged goods-producing productivity even though a huge infusion of technology has entered service industries. Table 9–2 summarizes one set of performance data.

As Stephen Roach notes concerning the data of Table 9–2, "Service providers as a whole, with an information technology endowment that is at present two and one-half times the size of the endowment in the goods sector (as shown by TIM2 in Table 9–2), have experienced a clear slowdown in productivity growth so far this decade. Moreover, that deterioration follows a period of relatively meager productivity increases over most of the 1970s."[16] Roach concludes by saying, "So far, the service sector has little to show for its spending binge on technology. Quite simply, massive investments in information technology have failed to boost national productivity growth in the 1980s."[17]

Why hasn't US service sector productivity improved like manufacturing productivity? There are many explanations for this service sector productivity problem, four of which are given here.

The *most popular reason* for this disparity in US national productivity performance is that it's a problem of measurement. That is, the US government and industry association measurement systems don't do a very good job of measuring and valuing service output. Are the numbers contained in Table 9–2, for example, valid? Can white-collar productivity be measured the same way as factory-worker productivity? Can we count pages of creative output like we do refrigerators? How do you measure the productivity of a security guard or a lawyer?

Even simple service innovations improve service productivity, but it is not clear whether government, corporate and association reporting systems pick this up. At Sleep Inns, for example, the nightstands are bolted to the wall so cleaners don't have to vacuum around the legs. The closet lacks a door to open and shut. The shower stall has rounded corners to eliminate corners that collect dirt. The result is that it takes only 20 minutes to clean a room versus the industry average of 30 minutes.[18] The ample use of shrubbery and asphalt paving reduces the amount of grass to mow. The hotel night watchperson also does some hotel laundry.

The US Bureau of Labor Statistics has been trying for years to improve government productivity measures. Standard Industrial Classification (SIC) codes are outdated and need a major overhaul. Still, the US Congress keeps cutting funding for these improvement efforts. Meanwhile, a patchwork of special government and independent association surveys are the key sources of performance information for the US service economy.

You cannot have a world-class US government policy by using inferior information. Information-driven government is as important as information driven

TABLE 9–2
Technology and Productivity Disappointments in the Services

Business Sector	Technology Intensity Measures		Average Productivity Growth (%)		Change* (percentage points)
	TIM1	*TIM2*	*1973–1979*	*1979–1985*	
All industries	1.0	1.0	0.6	1.1	0.5
Goods-producing	1.4	0.5	0.5	2.2	1.7
Services-providing	0.9	1.2	0.7	0.4	−0.3
Transportation	0.9	0.1	1.5	−1.2	−2.7
Rail	0.4	0.0	1.1	3.5	2.4
Nonrail	1.3	0.1	1.7	−1.8	−3.5
Communications	0.6	4.3	4.3	3.9	−0.4
Public utilities	1.3	0.3	0.3	1.8	1.5
Trade	2.1	0.9	0.8	1.3	0.5
Finance and insurance	2.7	2.2	−0.1	−1.3	−1.2
Real estate	0.7	0.8	−0.2	−1.4	−1.2
Miscellaneous services	0.9	1.3	0.2	0.7	0.5

*Difference in percentage points between 1973–1979 period and 1979–1985 period.

NOTE: TIM1 is each industry's change in technology endowment form the 1970s to 1985, relative to the average change for all industries. TIM2 is each industry's 1985 technology endowment relative to the all-industries average. Technology intensity measures are Morgan Stanley estimates derived from the Industry-Commodity Capital Stock Matrix of the US Department of Commerce; productivity detail is taken from Multiple Productivity Indexes, published by the American Productivity Center based on US government statistics.

Source: S S Roach, "Technology and the Services Sector: America's Hidden Competitive Challenge," in *Technology in Services: Policies for Growth, Trade, and Employment*, ed. B R Guile, and J B Quinn. Copyright © 1988 by the National Academy of Sciences. Published by the National Academy Press, Washington, DC, p. 133. Reprinted with permission.

corporations. Information-intelligence is the foundation for any world class strategy and plan of action.

Second, traditional productivity measures seldom consider the quality of service outputs, nor do they incorporate the complexity of the service encounter. Consider an orchestra that always takes three hours to play its music. It can play Mozart poorly or well and neither outcome will affect service productivity as we currently define it. We may pay for the orchestra performance, an automobile repair, a sporting event, a home mortgage loan service, a movie, a kidney operation, or writing our last will and testament, but the price of these services may or may not reflect true long-term customer satisfaction and value.

A *third* reason why US service-sector productivity is so difficult to measure is that these service industries are currently going through a restructuring period much like the US goods-producing industries did in the 1980s. The service management organization of Figure 8–2 overlaid with information technology capabilities will be far more productive than previous structures. Information technology changes the structure of how things get done.

Also, information networks, once they reach a critical mass, should begin to show productivity gains. We hope it is simply a matter of time before we see productivity improvements in the information-intensive service industries. In fact, there are signs that information technology is finally improving productivity in US service industries. Service industries during the 1980s spent more than $800 billion on information technology. But, since the bottom of the 1991 recession, service-sector productivity gains are outpacing national economic growth. For example, "in the eight quarters since the (1991) trough, output per hour has increased at an average annual rate of 2.3 percent, its best showing in 20 years. Most encouraging: Service-sector productivity finally sprang to life, matching the gains that began in manufacturing in the 1980s."[19] According to one study by MIT's Sloan School of Management, "the return on investment in information systems averaged a stunning 54 percent for manufacturing and 68 percent for all businesses surveyed."[20] So the elusive issue of US service sector productivity may be showing the early signs of a service sector explosion in productivity.

Fourth, CBP proliferation, as discussed in Chapter 4, is a major contributor to poor service sector productivity. Service firms such as banks are notorious for not eliminating noncompetitive CBPs from their CBP line. Service firms need to do a better job at CBP management. They can learn much on this issue from their goods-producing counterparts.

The fact is that quality, productivity, customer satisfaction, revenue, value, and costs are all related in complex ways. For example, a process improvement can increase (improve) quality, productivity, customer satisfaction, revenue, and value while decreasing costs. If our process performance and measurement systems were perfectly accurate, we might find that Federal Express's Supertracker, for example, improved all performance criteria simultaneously. Or that new procedures for reducing infections after surgery improved all performance criteria simultaneously. Complex interlinking methods are the only way to develop the quantitative relationships between these performance categories.

STRATEGIC AND STRUCTURAL ISSUES

Strategy and structure decisions go hand-in-hand, and therefore, are examined here together. When Federal Express decided to establish COSMOS (Customers, Operations, and Services Master On-Line System) and related technology such as the Supertracker hand-held wand, it made both strategic and structural decisions. Federal Express's information technology and strategic plans developed together. Management's challenge is to develop them at the same pace and resolve any temporary mismatches.

Strategic and structural decisions reside at the base of the Service Encounter Cone shown in Figure 2–3. Mistakes of strategy or structure can doom a business quicker than mistakes in designing and implementing a quality management system.

Consider the ongoing example of Eastman Kodak Company whose core business has been film production and developing. In 1981, Eastman Kodak Company received a technology shock. Sony introduced the Mavica camera that stores pictures on a floppy disk. Sony had seen the future and they thought it was theirs. Customers could take their pictures and instantly play them on a computer or television. Reporters, desktop publishers, and others took notice of this filmless technology but they ultimately found the pictures to be fuzzy.

Electronic pictures challenge the core technology and organizational structure of Eastman Kodak. All CBP designs, configurations, strategies, processes, and so on, have to be rethought. The picture of future competition only slightly resembles that of the past. In this situation, service/quality and service process performance is elevated in stature. Picture processing responsibility shifts more to Eastman Kodak than, say, to an intermediate film processor such as K mart. Service encounter criteria such as convenience, process reliability, processing time, and customer contact relationships all take on new meanings.

Thousands of Eastman Kodak employees must shift to a service management way of thinking. Will the shift be quick enough or will the advancement of technology outpace the company? How would service encounters change? Can processors electronically deliver the pictures to the customer's home and vice versa? What are the implications for training, retraining, job shift, and job displacement? Would the old research and development methods still work? Do we have the electronic expertise? How should service processes be redesigned? Could a film-knowledgeable sales force sell electronic-expertise CBPs?

By 1988, Eastman Kodak had decided on the Photo CD. With Photo CD, pictures are taken with film, but the customer can choose normal film developing or having the pictures electronically stored on compact disks. The Photo CD picture can be displayed on the television by using a special Photo CD player. Here a dual technology, film and electronic storage, is the basis for a dual strategy, film or electronic processing. Clearly, the Photo CD is a transition strategy. The risk is that Sony and Canon may leapfrog Kodak's methodical strategy.

The technological change in the photography industry illustrates several lessons of strategy, structure, and technology.

1. All competitors will eventually reach parity concerning product quality (outcome quality). The key to competitive advantage will then be service/quality (process quality) performance. The customer also may be more capable of evaluating service/quality than product/quality performance.

2. Service process capability exists to process and distribute family pictures to and from the home. The home telecomputer will be capable of manipulating electronic images in a wide variety of ways. The first to correctly configure product and service/quality performance into a new CBP will have the competitive advan-

tage. Photographic film could be in the museum right beside the drafting board and paper check. And where will Canon, Eastman Kodak, and Sony be?

3. Information and telecommunications services go from a support role to a strategic service management role in Eastman Kodak. Process management through electronic (not paper) mediums becomes the key to marketplace success.

4. Eastman Kodak's management must also redesign the organizational structure to accommodate the new and evolving capabilities of information technology and systems. Planning and synchronizing these changes in organizational structure and technological capabilities is crucial to outstanding service/quality performance. Ultimately, Eastman Kodak's organization may look much like the organizational design that was shown in Figure 8–2.

SERVICES ARE FAST FOLLOWERS

Once product technology can create and deliver a new CBP, many pure services quickly hop a ride. The piggybacking of a service onto a new technology-based CBP is illustrated by the current battle for the digital tele(vision)computer, or smart TV, market. Although the digital telecomputer will create the technical and physical capabilities, most of the profits from this technology development will reside in the value-added services bundled with the technology. Even though product technology creates the business, the final CBP sold to the customer requires service management expertise to build market share. This is an important lesson frequently overlooked.

Consider the forces that are helping to shape the US telecomputer marketplace:

1. Personal computers are becoming more powerful and visual.

2. Televisions are beginning to look more like computers.

3. Optical fiber technology allows massive amounts of data to be moved quickly within a fiber optic network.

4. Digital information replaces analog signals.

5. Technology breakthroughs for compressing data and for computer chip miniaturization add the needed technical capabilities.

6. Telephone and cable TV companies are merging and forming strategic alliances.

When these capabilities converge, the telecomputer is born.

The telecomputer would allow customers to purchase, for example, any entertainment or educational broadcast. Smart TV inquiries initiated by the customer might search for all library books on genetic engineering published within the last year, for a roofing contractor to redo a roof, or for the closest US stamp

TABLE 9–3
Service Management Action Starter Questions

---

1. Identify key service innovations in your organization and compute their dollar benefit and development costs. Compare the return on investment for service versus product innovations. What did you learn? What are the strategic and tactical implications of this analysis?

2. How can the organization's accounting and financial systems do a better job of recognizing, measuring, and reporting service innovation related benefits, costs, and productivity levels? Define an agenda for action.

3. How can your organization protect its service innovations? If it cannot, then what should you do?

4. Are your research, development, and commercialization processes for service innovations well defined, documented, and managed? If not, develop an agenda for action. If they are, how can they be improved?

5. What opportunities exist for piggybacking a service onto a new technical capability or product in your industry? How will you price the piggybacked service?

---

collectors' monthly workshop. The customer can then store, edit, and transmit information. Two-way or multiple-way service encounters would transform the traditional television from a passive to an active learning, entertainment, and communication device. Picturephones coupled with interactive technology could substitute for face-to-face meetings.

What are the implications of the telecomputer on the printed word, libraries, banking, the telephone yellow pages, and the lodging and transportation industries, just to name a few? You can be sure that services and service/quality performance will quickly follow these expected technical innovations. And services are what will grow market share and profits over the long-term.

CONCLUSION

Service innovations help define the capabilities of the consumer benefit package (CBP), and its service process and service encounters. Because service innovations have less copyright and patent protection than product innovations, service firm managers must be very alert to new ideas. Innovations in all forms encapsule human knowledge. Constant innovation, as Peters and Austin found, is a predictor of marketplace success. There must be a constant stream of service innovations to keep a service organization alive and well. Table 9–3 identifies a few example service management action starter questions concerning service innovations.

American service firms are world leaders in service innovation expertise. It's time to recognize it, document world-class service innovation research and development approaches, collect comprehensive performance statistics about it, and try to leverage it to build quality and competitive advantage in world markets.

For example, the Industrial Design Excellence Awards (IDEA) sponsored by *Business Week* and the Industrial Designers Society of America honor outstanding product designs, such as Goodyear's Aquatread tire and Apple Computer's Powerbook computers. Each year American products are scrutinized for user-friendly and innovative designs. In 1992, 111 IDEA medalists were recognized for their product design expertise.[21]

Service innovations seldom are recognized in any award program except periodically at the firm and industry levels. One reason for ignoring the vast US service economy is that CBPs high in service content, and their associated service processes and service encounters, are difficult to evaluate. You can kick, measure, and hold a product. You can even revisit the same product. But service innovation design is more elusive. And sometimes service innovations are so beautiful in their simplicity that they are not recognized. But surely, some of the great American service organizations are candidates for "The Service Innovation/Encounter Design Excellence Award."

P A R T

IV

SERVICE/QUALITY MANAGEMENT

"Service/quality management must be proactive, predictive, and anticipate customer wants and needs in everything from service strategy to service encounter execution."

The Author

Chapter Ten

Service/Quality Definition, Design, and Approach

S ervice/quality performance is a function of good consumer benefit package management and service delivery system design. Service encounter execution, normally through people, is the third stage. The fourth and final stage is continuous service encounter follow-up and recovery activities. The first nine chapters highlighted the importance of strategy, definition, and design, using service management thinking. Now we can focus on service/quality performance and execution as shown in Figure 2–3 (page 48).

Design and execution must grow and develop together. They must be harmonious. When design elements outpace or underpace execution capability, the organization's economic and service encounter performance suffer. World-class organizations do both design and execution better than do competitors.

In this chapter, we first define service/quality in three ways. Service/quality is too interdisciplinary and complex to depend on a single definition. The more ways we view service/quality the better we will understand it. Then we examine the following issues: (1) internal and external service/quality criteria; (2) service encounters by design, (3) a service management approach to the House of Quality, and (4) four approaches to service/quality improvement. These topics set the conceptual framework for examining service/quality management in later chapters.

DEFINING SERVICE/QUALITY

The underlying question of service/quality definition and measurement is "what constitutes value in the Servomation Age?" The answer is increasingly becoming the information-, entertainment-, and service-content of the CBP, and its associated process and service encounters. Goods and services are slowly switching places as to the focal point (center) of the CBP.

Popular definitions of quality are:

1. Quality is conformance to specifications.
2. Quality is the degree to which customer specifications are satisfied.

3. Quality is a fair exchange of price and value.

4. Quality is fitness for use.

D A Garvin also describes five approaches to defining product quality and eight dimensions for measuring quality performance.[1]

Basic ideas and premises about product quality are not always directly transferrable to service/quality.[2] For example, Parasuraman, Zeithaml, and Berry point out that (a) service/quality is more difficult for the consumer to evaluate than goods quality, and (b) service/quality perceptions result from a comparison of consumer expectations with actual service performance.[3] They also note that (c) quality evaluations are not made solely on the outcome of a service; they also involve evaluations of the process of service delivery, and (d) the customer has fewer tangible cues when purchasing a service than when purchasing a good.

Requisite variety is a term that also helps us understand service/quality. Requisite variety suggests that the sources and variety of your information must match the complexity and multiple criteria nature of the outcome. Requisite variety demands that service/quality definition and measurement match the complexity of the service process and service encounter outcomes. Within this multiple criteria framework, let's examine three generic views of service/quality.

Lewis and Booms in 1983 *defined service/quality* this way: "Service quality is a measure of how well the service level delivered matches customer expectations. Delivering quality service means conforming to customer expectations on a consistent basis."[4] Here service/quality is a comparison by the customer between his or her expectations before experiencing the service with actual service delivery system performance. The objective of each service encounter is to meet or exceed customer expectations by actual performance.

Customer expectations can be established by advertising, previous personal experience, conversations with other users of the service, by the local culture, and the like. The actual performance level of the service delivery system depends on many controllable factors, such as process design, employee reward and compensation programs, training programs, and employee scheduling. In addition, uncontrollable factors—such as the behavior of other customers in the service delivery system, weather, competitors' performance and influence, traffic congestion, and labor shortages—can affect the performance level of the service delivery system.

Table 10–1 defines a *second view of service/quality*. Here service management thinking is incorporated into the definition.

A *third view of service/quality*, and possibly the most sophisticated, recognizes that there are several ways to misspecify and mismanage the definition and delivery of excellent service/quality. Parasuraman, Zeithaml, and Berry call these *gaps* and identify five of them in their service/quality model, shown in Figure 10–1.

TABLE 10–1
Defining Service/Quality

Excellent service/quality is consistently meeting or exceeding customer expectations (external focus) and service delivery system performance criteria (internal focus) during all service encounters.

Excellent service/quality is achieved by the consistent delivery to the customer of a clearly defined consumer or employee benefit package, and associated process and service encounters, defined by many internal and external standards of performance.

Service/quality is where:

- *Excellent* means achieving all performance standards 100 percent of the time.

- *Customer* is the next entity (person/department/firm) that receives, pays for, uses or experiences the output of the service (or manufacturing) delivery system. The customer includes entities within as well as outside your primary organizational identity.

- *Service* is any primary or peripheral activity that does not directly produce a physical product, that is, the nongoods part of the transaction between buyer (customer) and seller (provider).

- *A consumer or employee benefit package* (CBP/EBP) is a clearly defined set of tangible (goods-content) and intangible (service-content) attributes (features) the customer (or employee) recognizes, pays for, uses, or experiences. A CBP/EBP includes the purchase or receipt of a primary good with peripheral goods and/or services or of a primary service with peripheral goods and/or services.

- *Quality* is the distinctive tangible and intangible properties of a CBP that is perceived by the customer as better than a competitor's CBPs.

- *Consistent* means continuous conformance (low, or no variability) to all standards of performance.

- *Delivery* means getting the right CBP in the right way (process quality) to the right customer at the right time.

- *Internal* standards of performance focus on in-house or backroom operating and marketing criteria that are hidden or decoupled from the customer. Measurement can be more objective against numerical specifications.

- *External* standards of performance focus on out-in-the-field or frontroom operating and marketing criteria that the customer expects/perceives while using or experiencing the CBP. Measurement is usually more dependent on human perception and judgment.

- *Service encounter* is one or more moments of truth. A moment of truth is an episode in which a customer comes into contact with any aspect of the organization, however remote, and thereby has an opportunity to form an impression.

- *Defined* means by management and employees.

Source: This table is a modified version of Figure 1 in David A Collier, "The Customer Service and Quality Challenge," *The Service Industries Journal* 7, no. 1 (January 1987), p. 79. Reproduced with permission of Frank Cass & Co. Ltd., London, England.

FIGURE 10–1
A Gap Model of Service/Quality

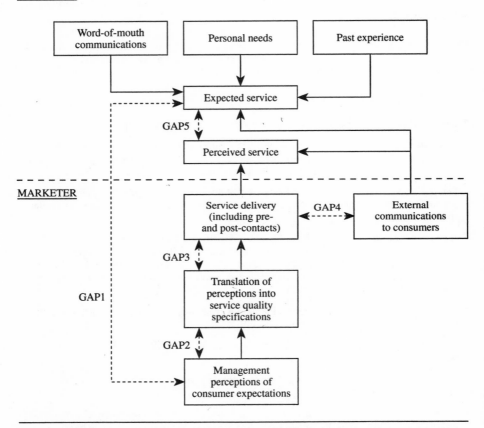

Source: A Parasuraman, V A Zeithaml, and L L Berry. Reprinted from *Journal of Marketing* 49, (Fall 1985), p. 44, published by the American Marketing Association. Reproduced with permission.

A Gap Model of Service/Quality

1. The first gap is the discrepancy between consumer expectations and management perceptions of those expectations. Managers may think they understand why the customer buys their service, and based on this perception, try to define the service/quality specifications. But what if management's perception is wrong?

2. The second gap is the discrepancy between management perceptions of what features constitute a target level of service/quality and the task of translating these perceptions into executable specifications. Even if Gaps 1 and 2 are

congruent and well managed, Gap 3 recognizes that the service delivery system must deliver these service/quality specifications.

3. Gap 3 then, is the discrepancy between service/quality specifications documented in operating and training manuals and their implementation.

4. The fourth gap is the discrepancy between actual service delivery system performance and external communications to the customers. The customer should not be promised a certain type and level of service/quality unless the service delivery system can achieve or exceed that level. Here is where a service management approach is superior to independent efforts by marketing and operations.

5. Finally, the service/quality perceived by the customer depends on the magnitude and direction of the fifth gap, that between expected service and perceived service. The fifth gap depends on the other four.

Parasuraman, Zeithaml, and Berry make an important contribution to the service/quality literature by proposing this gap model of service/quality. The model clearly shows the complexity and interdisciplinary nature of service/quality management. It also shows that there are many opportunities to make mistakes. The gap model of service/quality demands an interlinking approach to data analysis.

RECOGNIZING INTERNAL AND EXTERNAL SERVICE/QUALITY CRITERIA

Measuring service/quality performance can be within (internal) or outside (external) the organizational entity that provides the CBP and associated service encounters. Whoever receives the output (outcome) of the process is the customer. The customer is an *internal customer* if the process is within the parent (umbrella) organization and serves another person, process or department within this parent organization. If the customer is outside the parent organization we call this an *external or ultimate customer*. Computer and information processes, for example, normally serve many internal customers and sometimes, for a price, several external customers. Both internal and external customers should be treated equally and subject to similar performance reviews, customer satisfaction surveys, and the like.

In Chapter 3, we briefly presented the seven performance categories for the 1993 Malcolm Baldrige National Quality Award (MBNQA). Although not a perfect match, internal performance is evaluated mainly by MBNQA Category 4 on human resource development, Category 5 on management of process quality, and Category 6 on quality and operational results. MBNQA Category 7 on customer focus and satisfaction evaluates external performance. Of course, the customer can be an internal or external customer. Many MBNQA criteria items and notes also ask how internal (process) performance is related to external performance measures.

MBNQA Category 2 on information and analysis clearly recognizes the differences between internal and external performance measures. It also asks how internal and external data are linked for improved decision making. (See 1993 MBNQA Item 2.3 criteria Notes 1 to 5.) The crucial interplay and relationships among criteria are vitally important for the MBNQA; this is the subject of Chapters 14 and 15.

Our discussion of internal and external measures of performance is a predecessor to service/quality measurement and interlinking. For every external, marketing- and perception-based performance measure, there are one or more internal, operational- and transaction-based performance measures. These internal and external metrics of performance must be quantitatively linked together to identify critical success factors, align organizational performance goals, and drive continuous improvement initiatives.

Internal performance measures typically relate to any of the following criteria: cost per unit of output, output per unit of input(s), on-time delivery, output as a function of total capacity, errors per unit of output, employee turnover rates, budget versus planned cost variances, the degree of cross-selling activity, internal failure costs, and statistics on development, waiting, setup, and processing time. Internal measures of performance are most closely related to accuracy, efficiency, and productivity.

The most well-established instrument for measuring the external customer perceptions of service/quality is SERVQUAL, developed by Berry, Parasuraman, and Zeithaml.[5] Their initial reasearch identified 10 dimensions of service/quality performance. These 10 dimensions of service/quality were: (1) reliability, (2) responsiveness, (3) competence, (4) access, (5) courtesy, (6) communication, (7) credibility, (8) security, (9) understanding/knowing the customer, and (10) tangibles.

The original 10 service/quality criteria were reduced to 5 criteria based on further research. Of the five revised criteria, *tangibles, reliability and responsiveness* remained intact. A single performance variable called assurance consolidated the competence, courtesy, credibility, and security attributes. A new variable called *empathy* consolidated the access, communication, and understanding the customer attributes. Assurance was defined as the ''knowledge and courtesy of employees and their ability to convey trust and confidence.'' Empathy was defined as ''caring, individual attention the firm provides its customers.''[6]

The danger of a smaller set of service/quality performance measures is that you may miss or hide a critical performance attribute. For example, these five performance measures could be consolidated into two tangibles—reliability and flexibility. Here, flexibility supposedly captures the dimensions of responsiveness, assurance, and empathy. Of course, this consolidation should be based on sound research and not what looks conceptually attractive. Hedvall and Paltschik, for example, took the original 10 determinants of service/quality and collapsed them into 2 aggregate measures.[7] Their two-concept service/quality performance model included (1) the willingness and ability to serve and (2) physical and psychological access. Other reseachers also find that the definition of service/quality performance depends on the type of service(s) studied.[8]

Berry, Parasuraman, and Zeithaml are also refining the definition and use of the SERVQUAL instrument.[9] The lesson here is that defining abstract dimensions of service/quality performance must be based on sound research at the industry and process level; otherwise, the results can be misleading.

A list of possible service/quality performance measures creates a large multiple criteria solution space. Examples of performance attributes include accuracy, advocacy, appearance, attitude, articulate, clear audit trail, commitment, completeness, convenience, control, courtesy, documented, durability, entertaining, fairness, fast, flexible, friendly, fun, honesty, immediate, innovative, listening, privacy, repairability, satisfaction, safety and security, status, timeliness, value, and workmanship. Many of these service encounter performance attributes are present in even simple service processes.

Add these service/quality performance measures into a solution space with performance criteria such as price (cost), product quality, market share, customer retention, and profits; and only multiple criteria interlinking techniques can model this degree of complexity. Yet, most organizations tend to rely on one- and two-way performance criteria linkages such as X versus Y scatter plots, trend analyses, and statistical process control. These one- and two-criteria comparison methods are incapable of modeling the complexity of real service processes.

For example, why have so many measurement systems lost their relevance to strategic and tactical decision making? One reason is that they rely solely on one- and two-criteria data analysis methods when only multiple criteria methods can capture the complexity and performance of a real process. Chapters 11, 14, and 15 will briefly describe these simple and complex data analysis methods.

The data analysis challenge in the Servomation Age is to interlink internal and external performance criteria and to model these complex relationships with the objective of improving organizational learning and decision making, so the organization will make a profit and survive. Interlinking is a powerful competitive weapon that uses data as its fuel and smart multiple criteria modelling techniques as its engine.

SERVICE ENCOUNTERS BY DESIGN— COURTYARD BY MARRIOTT

A well documented and publicly available study of designing a consumer benefit package, associated service encounters, and physical facilities based on the customer's wants and needs is Courtyard by Marriott. It is a glimpse into the future of how CBPs and services can be designed and configured. The source for this discussion is an enlightening article by Wind, Green, Shifflet, and Scarbrough, "Courtyard by Marriott: Designing a Hotel Facility with Consumer-Based Marketing Models."[10]

Marriott Corporation in the early 1980s identified two segments of travelers who might need a new type of hotel chain. These two segments were (1) business travelers who travel at least six times a year and stay in mid-level hotels or motels, and (2) pleasure travelers who travel at least twice a year and stay in hotels or motels. The challenge was to design a new hotel chain for these target markets, using the customer's perceptions for a hotel that wasn't built.

Table 10–2 defines the possible physical features of the hotel and services to be offered. The seven major facets of CBP attributes were (1) external factors, (2) rooms, (3) food-related services, (4) lounge facilities, (5) services, (6) facilities for leisure-time services, and (7) security factors. A total of 167 optional CBP attributes are shown in Table 10–2.

A sample of potential target-market customers was surveyed and various statistical techniques used to match (a) the customer's perceptions of what an ideal hotel might look like to (b) the 167 CBP attributes in Table 10–2. The result was a final set of CBP attributes that are underlined in Table 10–2.

If you look closely at Table 10–2, you will see much detail in design options. For example, under rooms' amenities (in the second column) there were four design options:

1. Small bar of soap only.
2. Large bar of soap, shampoo packet, and shoe shine mitt.
3. Large bar of soap, bath gel, shower cap, sewing kit.
4. Large bar of soap, bath gel, shower cap, sewing kit, shoe shine mit, shampoo packet, toothpaste, deodorant, and mouthwash.

Ultimately, option #2 was chosen. Think of the hotel job, process, and service/quality design implications for each of these room amenity options. How much room cleaning capacity is needed for each option? What happens to the chance of making errors for each option? What is the cost per room-night for each option? What are the service/quality standards for each option? How much importance do customers place on each room amenity option? What does the customer not want to pay for? How do these options affect service encounter and CBP efficiency and effectiveness?

The postscript on this story of quality by design is a very successful one. By 1991, Marriott Corporation had built over 200 *Courtyard by Marriotts*. This chain contributed to Marriott's continued growth, financial health, and increasing stock values. It also created many thousands of new jobs, provided cross-advertising benefits and economies of scale, and enhanced the Marriott image both with investors and Marriott employees.

Courtyard by Marriott employees also knew that their hotel chain was designed based on customer perceptions of what the customer wanted in a travel-

TABLE 10–2

Designing a Consumer Benefit Package and Associated Service Encounters Called "Courtyard by Marriott"

EXTERNAL FACTORS
Building Shape
  L-shaped w/landscape
  Outdoor courtyard
Landscaping
  Minimal
  Moderate
  Elaborate
Pool type
  No pool
  Rectangular shape
  Free form shape
  Indoor/outdoor
Pool location
  In courtyard
  Not in courtyard
Corridor/View
  Outside access/restricted view
  Enclosed access/ unrestricted view/ balcony or window
Hotel size
  Small (125 rooms, 2 stories)
  Large (600 rooms, 12 stories)

ROOMS
Entertainment
  Color TV
  Color TV w/movies at $5
  Color TV w/30 channel cable
  Color TV w/HBO, movies, etc.
  Color TV w/free movies
Entertainment/Rental
  None
  Rental Cassettes/in-room Atari
  Rental Cassettes/stereo cassette playing in room
  Rental Movies/in-room BetaMax
Size
  Small (standard)
  Slightly larger (1 foot)
  Much larger (2½ feet)
  Small suite (2 rooms)
  Large suite (2 rooms)
Quality of Decor (in standard room)
  Budget motel decor
  Old Holiday Inn decor
  New Holiday Inn decor
  New Hilton decor
  New Hyatt decor
Heating and Cooling
  Wall unit/full control
  Wall unit/soundproof/full control
  Central H or C (seasonal)
  Central H or C/full control
Size of Bath
  Standard bath
  Slightly larger/sink separate
  Much larger bath w/ larger tub
  Very large/tub for 2

Sink location
  In bath only
  In separate area
  In bath and separate
Bathroom Features
  None
  Shower Massage
  Whirlpool (Jacuzzi)
  Steam bath
Amenities
  Small bar soap
  Large soap/shampoo/ shoeshine
  Large soap/bath gel/ shower cap/sewing kit
  Above items + toothpaste, deodorant, mouthwash

FOOD
Restaurant in hotel
  None (coffee shop next door)
  Restaurant/lounge combo, limited menu
  Coffee shop, full menu
  Full-service restaurant, full menu
  Coffee shop/full menu and good restaurant
Restaurant nearby
  None
  Coffee shop
  Fast food
  Fast food or coffee shop and moderate restaurant
  Fast food or coffee shop and good restaurant
Free continental
  None
  Continental included in room rate
Room service
  None
  Phone-in order/guest to pick up
  Room service, limited menu
  Room service, full menu
Store
  No food in store
  Snack items
  Snacks, refrigerated items, wine, beer, liquor
  Above items and gourmet food items
Vending service
  None
  Soft drink machine only
  Soft drink and snack machines
  Soft drink, snack, and sandwich machines
  Above and microwave available
In-room kitchen facilities
  None
  Coffee maker only
  Coffee maker and refrigerator
  Cooking facilities in room

LOUNGE
Atmosphere
  Quiet bar/lounge
  Lively, popular bar/lounge

Type of people
  Hotel guests and friends only
  Open to public — general appeal
  Open to public — many singles
Lounge nearby
  None
  Lounge/bar nearby
  Lounge/bar w/ entertainment nearby

SERVICES
Reservations
  Call hotel directly
  800 reservation number
Check-in
  Standard
  Pre-credit clearance
  Machine in lobby
Check-out
  At front desk
  Bill under door/leave key
  Key to front desk/bill by mail
  Machine in lobby
Limo to airport
  None
  Yes
Bellman
  None
  Yes
Message service
  Note at front desk
  Light on phone
  Light on phone and message under door
  Recorded message
Cleanliness/upkeep/ management skill
  Budget motor level
  Holiday Inn level
  Nonconvention Hyatt level
  Convention Hyatt level
  Fine hotel level
Laundry/Valet
  None
  Client drop off and pick up
  Self-service
  Valet pick up and drop off
Special Services (concierge)
  None
  Information on restaurants, theaters, etc.
  Arrangements and reservations
  Travel problem resolution
Secretarial services
  None
  Xerox machine
  Xerox machine and typist
Car maintenance
  None
  Take car to service
  Gas on premises/bill to room

Car rental/Airline reservations
  None
  Car rental facility
  Airline reservations
  Car rental and airline reservations

LEISURE
Sauna
  None
  Yes
Whirlpool/jacuzzi
  None
  Outdoor
  Indoor
Exercise room
  None
  Basic facility w/weights
  Facility w/Nautilus equipment
Racquet ball courts
  None
  Yes
Tennis courts
  None
  Yes
Game room/Entertainment
  None
  Electric games/pinball
  Electric games/pinball/ ping pong
  Above + movie theater, bowling
Children's playroom/ playground
  None
  Playground only
  Playroom only
  Playground and playroom
Pool extras
  None
  Pool w/slides
  Pool w/slides and equipment
  Pool w/slides, waterfall, equipment

SECURITY
Security guard
  None
  11 a.m. to 7 p.m.
  7 p.m. to 7 a.m.
  24 hours
Smoke detector
  None
  In rooms and throughout hotel
Sprinkler system
  None
  Lobby and hallways only
  Lobby/hallways/rooms
24-hour video camera
  None
  Parking/hallway/public areas
Alarm button
  None
  Button in room, rings desk

Note: The 50 factors that describe hotel features and services and the associated (167) levels are categorized under seven facets. The underscored items were included in the final design of the hotel.

Source: J Wind, PE Green, D Shifflet, and M Scarbrough, "Courtyard by Marriott: Designing a Hotel Facility with Consumer-Based Marketing Models," *Interfaces* 19, no. 1 (January–February 1989), p. 26. Reprinted with permission.

related hotel. Thus, the hotel's physical facilities and CBP amenities support the employees in doing their job right. What a splendid example of service definition, design, and strategy being in harmony with day-to-day execution. America's service expertise at work!

A SERVICE MANAGEMENT HOUSE-OF-QUALITY EXAMPLE

In Chapter 2 we defined outcome, or technical, quality and also process, or functional, quality. In Chapter 4 we defined consumer benefit packages (CBPs) and configurations, and the traditional House of Quality. We used an example company called Slide-Master to demonstrate CBP definition and configurations. In Chapter 6 we introduced the seven P's of service management and frontroom and backroom positioning strategies. In Chapter 7 we focused on process management. In Chapters 8 and 9 we presented a service management view of organizational design and service innovations, respectively. These chapters and the ideas in them focused directly or indirectly on design.

There are many ways to manage the design process. The traditional House of Quality is one of them. Service management ideas can be incorporated into the House of Quality format.

In Chapter 4, we defined the basics of the House of Quality (pages 75–77) and a broader idea called quality functional deployment. In the House of Quality matrix (Figure 4–5), each row represents a customer requirement or want and need. Each column represents a technical requirement of the CBP from the company's viewpoint. Customer requirements can be thought of as *what* the customer requires (i.e., customer wants and needs). Technical requirements are *how* the company will meet these wants and needs. The strength of these relationships are shown by various symbols and relative weights. Many other columns, rows, computations, and matrix areas can be added to the basic house of quality format. Any set of *whats* and *hows* can be disaggregated into greater detail by taking the *hows* from House of Quality A and making them the *whats* for House of Quality B.

Figure 10–2 is an example Service Management House of Quality format (called format B). Service Management House of Quality Format A, which is not shown here, uses the dimensions of customers' wants and needs (whats) versus final CBP attributes (hows). Final CBP attributes fulfill customer wants and needs. Format A matches up well with traditional notions of the House of Quality. Format B (shown in Figure 10–2) goes to a second level of detail beyond Format A. The *hows* of format A become the *whats* of format B.

The dimensions of format B in Figure 10–2 are final CBP attributes (whats) versus design, outcome, and process quality (hows). In format B, the major vertical and horizontal dimensions of the House of Quality have also been reversed so the sources of quality performance (hows) can be easily listed. Here the whats

FIGURE 10–2
The Service Management House-of-Quality Format B

Source of Quality Performance	CBP Family A		CBP Family B	
	CBP #1 Attributes	CBP #2 Attributes	CBP #3 Attributes	CBP #4 Attributes
Design quality: Facility layout Signage Uniforms Decor Service counters Parking lots Lighting Storefront Other CBP design attributes				
Outcome quality: Doing things right Meet/exceed expectations Value (customer satisfaction/price) Other attributes				
Process quality: Meet/exceed expectations Procedure correct Service style Service recovery Other attributes				

Note: Scoring and symbol methods are similar to traditional house-of-quality methods.

are at the top of the figure and represent the final CBP attributes. Design, outcome, and process quality represent how to satisfy the final CBP attributes.

Design quality is how the infrastructure is set up to accommodate service encounters. The infrastructure includes tangible attributes such as the facility, equipment, uniforms, and system design. Outcome and process quality are focused on the execution of the service encounter. Here the human and intangible side of creating and delivering CBPs and associated service encounters are emphasized. As with the traditional House of Quality, competitive benchmarking and analysis also can be done using Figure 10–2.

Typical objectives of the Service Management House of Quality are:

1. Match customer wants and needs to final CBP attributes.

2. Ensure that final CBP attributes are carefully matched up with design, outcome, and process capabilities.

3. Provide a format for benchmarking and competitive comparisons.

4. Identify and rectify inconsistencies between organizational capabilities and CBP definition.

5. Provide a checklist to ensure completeness of service encounter and CBP design.

The most important aspect of the Service Management House of Quality is to use service management thinking. Service management thinking leads to different problem definitions and, therefore, solutions.

SERVICE/QUALITY IMPROVEMENT APPROACHES

Service/quality improvement approaches are centered on certain ideals, values, resources, and themes. Usually a dominant theme evolves as the organization strives to be world-class at results, approach, and deployment. Here we look at service/quality improvement approaches, using two perspectives (dimensions). The first perspective identifies the dominant means of execution. These four approaches are called (1) communication, (2) people, (3) systems and standards, and (4) service management. In practice, a dominant means of execution can be hard to identify, especially as the organization's improvement efforts grow and mature. World-class organizations typically excel at three or four of these means of execution.

A second perspective is the degree of sustained organizational commitment to see that quality goals and agendas get done, executed well, and are fully deployed. Figure 10–3 shows how the approach (means of execution) and organizational commitment dimensions are related.

Actual company performance resides all over the 16-square grid depicted in Figure 10–3. Stage 1 is superficial communication. Stage 2 has four possible states, including superficial communication, cautious communication, superficial people approach, and cautious people approach. To make it beyond Stage 1, the organization only has to "talk and look like a quality program is in place."

Many more organizations reside somewhere in the nine cell solution space of Stage 3. Organizations that are making a serious effort toward all three quality improvement approaches—communication, people, and systems and standards—reside at the Stage 3 performance boundary. Here, improvement issues should be related to integrating these three approaches, growing them at the same pace, and fully deploying them to all areas. Other organizations not at the performance boundary of Stage 3, for example, may be rated serious on communication, and systems and standards, and cautious on their commitment to the people approach. Organizations in Stage 3 might be applying for the Malcolm Baldrige National Quality Award (MBNQA), but none are winning it.

FIGURE 10–3
Service/Quality Improvement—Approach and Commitment

Dominant Improvement Approach (Means of Execution)	Degree of Sustained Organizational Commitment			
	Superficial	*Cautious*	*Serious*	*World-Class*
Communication	Stage One			
People		Stage Two		
Systems and Standards			Stage Three	
Service Management				Stage Four

In Stage 4 the organization has a world-class commitment toward their quality improvement goals and agenda. Communication, people, and systems and standards approaches are all strong and integrated. Results are caused by approach. Deployment is good. All primary processes and most secondary processes are well designed and managed. At the performance (best practice) boundary of Stage 4 reside the MBNQA Winners and industry leaders. Here the Service Management Approach is the framework or glue that integrates these other quality improvement approaches. And a service management improvement approach is a form of glue.

The four distinct types of quality improvement approaches are known as:

1. The Communication Approach.

2. The People Approach.

3. The Systems and Standards Approach.

4. The Service Management Approach.

As Figure 10–3 suggests, an organization's world-class commitment toward its communication processes, people, and systems and standards are tied together with a service management approach. It is within these four broad approaches that the details of service/quality management are executed.

The Communication Approach

The Communication Approach is a communication assault on the organization. It should be initiated and supported by the chief executive officer and top management. Characteristics of this approach include many speeches, meetings, company newsletters, television videos, bulletin boards, teams, mission statements, and advertising announcements concerning the quality initiatives within the organization. The communication approach is an essential part of any service/quality improvement approach if properly done and integrated with other approaches. As a stand-alone approach, it is a sure way to create confusion and disappointment within the organization.

The Communication Approach is a core organizational capability for embarking on a continuous improvement initiative. The organization's communication system must be receiver-oriented. The receiver must be educated and trained to understand and use the information to improve organizational performance. Without clear, accurate, and timely communication, quality improvement initiatives often fail. The types and frequency of communications must be well defined. Multiple communication channels must be designed into the organization's structure. The organization's communication approach must promote quality awareness and sharing of ideas and actions, must inform the workforce about competitor performance, and lead to an understanding of quality values, goals, and practices within the organization. The communication approach helps establish the quality culture.

One piece of evidence that a superficial or cautious communication approach is alive and well comes from an American Society of Quality Control and Gallup Survey.[11] They found the gap between talk and action to be large. For example, on the question of making quality everyone's top priority, 53 percent said the company says it is important, whereas only 35 percent thought the company follows through with action—a gap of 18 percent.

The People Approach

The People Approach is the dominant means of achieving service/quality improvement in many organizations. Three subsets of this general approach are the *fun approach*, the *reward and recognition approach*, and the *charisma approach*. We can learn several lessons about the means of execution by briefly examining these approaches.

The fun approach is a way to keep people excited and interested in superior service/quality performance. Domino's Pizza's Olympics is a good example of the fun and reward and recognition approaches.[12] At first it may seem this approach is not a serious quality improvement effort. But at Domino's Pizza it is a way to encourage excellent service encounter performance. Domino's Olympics places team members from across the United States in competition according to 15 jobs common to their pizza stores. The jobs included doughmaking, driving delivery trucks, telephone receptionist, purchasing and inventory control, and team leaders or supervisors. Store, area, and regional competitions take place before the final contestants reach Domino's Olympics.

Domino's Pizza approach to quality improvement incorporates the reward and recognition approach. Besides the medals, ovations, lapel pins, music, winners' jackets and patches, and write-ups in company and home town newspapers, winners of the Olympics receive checks for up to $4,000. Every effort is made to recognize and honor those who are outstanding performers.

The benefits of Domino's fun approach to quality improvement include: (1) employee excitement and interest in their jobs and outstanding performance, (2) building a quality culture within the organization, and (3) enhanced communication among all employees and management. Their approach to quality improvement also resulted in measurable improvements such as a reduction in expenses from 18 to 16.5 percent of sales, or a savings of $9 million.[13]

The charisma approach is also a people approach and depends almost entirely on a charismatic leader who continually inspires people to excel. For small or entrepreneurial firms the approach works well. These highly motivated and empowered employees can then monitor quality performance themselves. As the size and complexity of the organization increases, frequent pep talks or keen interest and action by the CEO, or managing by wandering around, begins to lose its impact. Now there are too many functional areas, processes, levels of management, and sites. Other approaches are needed to complement a charismatic leader and direct the company toward world-class performance.

Roger Milliken, Chairman of the Milliken Company, is credited with this passion for excellence and charismatic leadership style. The late Sam Walton of Wal-Mart, Inc., and Fred Smith of Federal Express are other leaders that fit this category. But, for large organizations, the charismatic approach must be backed up by other approaches, such as systems and standards.

The Systems and Standards Approach

The Systems and Standards Approach is founded in the logic of the scientific method. Specialists are usually advocates of this approach. Here everything can be diagrammed, quantified, measured, and objectively analyzed to arrive at a rational solution. This works well in the backroom of a service process. But in the frontroom the systems and standards approach needs fine tuning.

Over 700 performance measures, for example, are used at First National Bank of Chicago in its Product Quality Measurement Program.[14] Each performance measure has two thresholds—minimum acceptable performance and an outstanding performance goal. Actual performance is charted against these standards, which are based on what the customer says is important and on banking industry standards. Weekly performance review meetings are held throughout the bank to evaluate performance, identify problems and take corrective action. Many other communication and people programs surround their systems and standards approach.

The problem with relying solely on a communication or people or system and standards approach is that the integrative mechanism to tie it together is missing. An integrated design is the key to nature's success. The entity invented by humankind called "the organization" frequently forgets this truism. A service management approach provides the philosophy and glue to coordinate and direct these other three approaches toward common goals and continuous improvement. The synergistic effect of a service management approach is very powerful. It can build service/quality and competitive advantage.

The Service Management Approach

The Service Management Approach to quality improvement can be described in many ways. It can be defined as all the ideas, paradigms, methods, and approaches contained in this book and the references cited. Courtyard by Marriott, LensCrafters, and Walt Disney (described in Chapter 7), Cooker Restaurant Corporation, Federal Express, and Beth Israel Hospital (Chapter 8), and F International and The Limited (Chapter 9), are examples of a service management approach. They all use some combination of the communication, people, and systems and standards approach that best fits their organization. The "glue" of these three approaches is a cultural change that uses service management paradigms and thinking.

Walt Disney is one of the few service-providing organizations that fully demonstrates a service management approach. For example, how do Walt Disney theme parks keep their premises so clean? The answer is based on three major steps, where attention to design and detail are paramount.

First, they do a world-class job of CBP, process, and service encounter definition and design. It's frequently called "imagineering" at Disney. Disney does its imagineering from the customer's perspective. They get into the customer's mind. They ride the customer's thought waves through their theme parks. Service encounters are elevated to their proper status in the organization.

The *second* step focuses on execution in terms of outcome and process quality. Design quality sets the stage on which outcome and process quality is played. For example, every theme park has an intricate system of pneumatic tubes that allow litter-pickers to quickly discard any refuse they pick up. You never see a smiling Disney litter-picker dragging a heavy trash bag around. This high level of service/quality performance is made possible because it is designed into the park's systems and standards of performance.

The *third* step highlights continuous improvement cycles. Disney experts do such a good job in the first two steps that you seldom hear much about Disney's continuous improvement cycles. But employee suggestions and customer complaints are incorporated into their service/quality improvement cycles. Walt Disney uses a service management approach to build quality and competitive advantage.

TABLE 10–3
Service Management Action-Starter Questions

1. What are the best internal and external performance criteria for each consumer/employee benefit package, and the associated process and service encounter(s), in your organization? (Use the final consumer/employee benefit package attributes as the basis for service/quality performance measures.)

2. For each of your organization's consumer/employee benefit packages (CBP/EBPs), can you identify and critique each gap, using the service/quality gap model of Figure 10–1? What gap(s) provide the greatest opportunity for error? How can these interfaces/gaps be improved? How can interlinking methods help drive these improvement efforts?

3. What would the Service Management House of Quality Formats A and B look like for each of your key consumer/employee benefit packages? How well do CBP/EBP attributes match up with process and service encounter capabilities?

4. Can you define your total quality management agenda for action for the Communication, People, and Systems and Standards approaches in your organization? How can you keep these approaches aligned?

5. Where does service/quality design and approach expertise reside in your organization? What level of expertise is found at the consumer/employee benefit package, process, and service encounter levels of the organization? What strategies and actions can you take to protect, grow, and leverage this expertise?

CONCLUSION

The future of service/quality definition and design is exciting. Table 10–3 identifies five example service management action-starter questions concerning service/quality definition, design, and approach. This knowledge base is evolving quickly. Customers, for example, are beginning to design their consumer benefit package(s) with associated process and service encounters based on *future* needs. The risks are becoming too high in today's competitive business environment to do otherwise. You will see how a future (predictive and proactive) orientation fits into a service/quality performance measurement system in Chapter 11.

A service management approach helps justify redefinition, renewal, reorganization, and redirection the "service management way." The communication, people, and systems and standards approaches can now be aligned with the service management blueprint. For example, interlinking can help align process performance measures with recognition and reward systems. Organizational capabilities are now linked and more powerful. What seems impossible becomes possible with a service management approach.

Chapter Eleven

Service/Quality Measurement, Control, and Analysis

A merican Airline's powerful Sabre information system and yield management techniques have helped them develop service innovations, identify and capture target markets, minimize costs, and grow revenues. They also have leveraged their smart data analysis capabilities to market hotel rooms, rental cars, show tickets, and packaged tours.

Otis Elevator has used information analysis to wrap more service- and information-content around its products and their maintenance and repair. Their OTIS-LINE information system has become part of the consumer benefit package. They informate and servomate their CBPs to help them gain competitive advantage. Such information helps Otis dispatch maintenance personnel, expand service times to 24 hours per day, improve response time, reduce the number of callbacks, identify problem elevators and component parts, predict equipment failures, and improve the accuracy of field service data. Better performance evaluation, identifying new market opportunities, and electronic monitoring of elevator breakdowns are just a few of the many spin-off benefits from OTISLINE.

MBNA America's Customer Needs Assessment Network (CNAN) tracks, measures, reports, and helps people evaluate performance and CBP features. MBNA America is one of the fastest growing bank credit card issuers in the United States. Their primary business is issuing and administering credit cards to affinity groups. Extensive data analysis allows MBNA to customize their credit card services to each group. Interlinking lets them link group satisfaction to CBP features and performance. Like American Airlines, they also could market their group customization skills to noncompetitors.

American Airlines, MBNA America, and Otis Elevator use smarter and faster information systems than their competitors to manage and direct service encounters toward world class performance. Good information systems are cornerstones of 1992 Malcolm Baldrige National Quality Award Winners AT&T Universal Card Services and The Ritz-Carlton Hotel Company. AT&T Universal Card Services uses over 100 measures of service/quality performance, and the Ritz-Carlton maintains computerized guest profiles on its premium customers. Without a world-class performance measurement and analysis system, it is impossible for these large organizations to provide superior customer service day in and day out.

All performance in a service business is relative. If every competitor has it, even if it's perfect performance, that CBP feature becomes a market qualifier. This CBP feature or process capability is neutralized. A new CBP feature quickly becomes the performance attribute that differentiates it from competitors and becomes the order winner.

In summary, a world class quality information system must measure the right things, be quick in its analysis, interlink complex performance relationships, and incorporate these insights into decision and improvement cycles for prompt action. It must be continually adaptive and broad in scope. It must reach the strategy development and service encounter levels of the organization. It must link quality-related performance to business results. Everyone must understand these metrics of performance and know how to use them to build quality and competitive advantage. In the Servomation Age, strategic and tactical decisions must be linked to customer requirements. Information-intelligence has become the source of sustained competitive advantage. The topics of Chapters 11 to 15 describe some of these issues and capabilities.

REACTIVE AND PROACTIVE PERFORMANCE EVALUATION APPROACHES

Quality-related performance, and particularly service/quality performance, can be viewed as shown in Table 11–1. The interdisciplinary nature of service encounter and service/quality performance demands the broad scope defined by Table 11–1.

Reactive measurement approaches occur after the execution of the service encounter. They are reaction-based lagging indicators of performance. Here we are evaluating historical results. Proactive and prevention-based approaches occur before the execution of the service encounter. Here we anticipate and predict future customer needs, CBP features and service encounter designs, and process performance.

You can use Table 11–1 to evaluate your organization on each category by awarding from 1 to 10 points per category. The scoring guidelines are as follows:

1. Ten points are world-class performance reflecting a #1 or #2 industry ranking or being in the top 5 percent of competitors in your industry worldwide, whichever is the more demanding criterion.

2. Six, seven, eight, and nine points are progressively awarded when the organization is approximately equal to or within one-half standard deviation positive increments from mean worldwide industry performance. For example, eight points would mean the organization is one to one-and-one-half standard deviations above mean worldwide industry performance on that criterion or set of criteria.

TABLE 11–1
*Service/Qualtity Performance Evaluation Approaches**

		Maximum Score	Your Score
Reaction-Based Approaches			
1.	Internal historical measures	10 points	
2.	External historical measures	10 points	
3.	Statistical process control	10 points	
4.	Predictive interlinking models based on history and past relative performance	10 points	
Proactive and Prevention-Based Approaches			
5.	Quality by design	10 points	
6.	Quality by systems and standards	10 points	
7.	Quality by leadership, rewards, and recognition	10 points	
8.	Quality by education and training	10 points	
9.	Quality by empowerment	10 points	
10.	Predictive interlinking models based on customer's *future* needs and perceptions	10 points	
	Total points	100 points	

*Evaluation can be done at the strategic business unit, department, facility, consumer or employee benefit package, process, and/or service encounter levels.

3. Five points are awarded when the organization is very close to mean worldwide industry performance.

4. Four, three, two, and one point(s) are progressively awarded when the organization is approximately equal to or within one-half standard deviation negative increments from mean worldwide industry performance. For example, two points would mean the organization is one to one-and-one-half standard deviations below mean worldwide industry performance on that criterion or set of criteria.

5. No points are awarded reflecting the bottom of the worldwide industry ranking on that performance category or being in the lower 5 percent of competitors in your industry worldwide.

A perfect score totals to 100 points as shown in Table 11–1.

Most organizations rely heavily on reactive measurement and control mechanisms. Examples of reactive approaches are: (1) an internal historical measure is the number of errors per thousand transactions; (2) an external historical measure is the number of customer complaints per period; (3) statistical process control uses historical data to track and evaluate performance; and (4) a predictive interlinking model based on history is a linear regression model. It could define the relationship between an internal performance measure such as average processing time and an external performance measure such as customer satisfaction.

Proactive approaches such as those noted in Table 11–1 don't wait to see what is going to happen. They are future-looking and preventive-based leading indicators of performance. They are anticipatory and predict customer satisfaction and system performance. Proactive mechanisms 5 to 9 are self-explanatory. They match up well with Malcolm Baldrige National Quality Award criteria. Other chapters in this book describe each of these proactive mechanisms. For example, quality by design is the subject of Chapter 4 on CBP definition and design and Chapter 7 on job, process, and facility design.

Proactive approach #10—predictive interlinking models based on customer's future needs and perceptions—in Table 11–1 tries to predict CBP design and modifications based on customer's future needs and precepts. The key difference between reactive approach 4 and proactive approach 10 in Table 11–1 is the former's use historical data whereas the latter uses the customer's assessment of future wants and needs. The Courtyard by Marriott CBP design example described in Chapter 10 is a good example of a proactive, prevention-based approach using interlinking metric analysis to design the hotel delivery system(s).

Proactive approaches are becoming more important because the cost of a major definition or design error is becoming higher. The tolerance for error within the global marketplace is decreasing. One major mistake and you don't survive, or you seriously hurt your competitive position. Also, under the umbrella of time-based competition or service encounter upsets that require immediate action, reactive approaches simply aren't fast enough.

Proactive approaches require skilled people at all levels of the organization. Here is where the training and educational systems of the company and country become important. Companies and education-providing organizations must communicate closely, not only on what the company thinks they need, but also in terms of what is possible. Adopting a proactive and prevention-based approach places new demands on top management and educators.

WHAT PERFORMANCE ATTRIBUTES DO WE MEASURE?

The final attributes (features) of each consumer benefit package offered for sale by your organization provides the performance criteria to measure. Chapter 4 on CBP definition and a list of CBP attributes such as shown in Figure 4–6 are sources of knowing what to measure. In Chapter 7 we saw that in a service business many performance criteria are process related. In Chapter 10, we listed some of these internal and external performance criteria. We also introduced the Gap Model of Service/Quality and the Service Management House of Quality in that chapter.

CBP definition and design is where service/quality performance measurement begins. It is here during the design of the final CBP, and its associated service encounters and processes, that the performance attributes are finalized. Good CBP definition and design is the key input to a good quality measurement system.

Some organizations define and design their CBPs with inadequate thought and up-front coordination. Once their CBPs are out in the marketplace, they begin to ask (1) What are the CBP performance attributes? and (2) How should we measure CBP, process, and service encounter performance? By then, it is normally too late. CBP redesign and correction costs increase dramatically once the CBP is introduced to the marketplace. Up-front CBP definition and design lay the framework for all subsequent activity.

SIXTEEN TOOLS OF SERVICE/QUALITY MEASUREMENT AND ANALYSIS

Once we measure and collect mountains of data, we must know how to analyze and evaluate these data. Here the methods of service/quality measurement help us assign cause and effect, predict future performance, model process performance, define relationships and priorities, and plan corrective action. Some of these methods are appropriate for front-line employees while others are appropriate for management, corporate staff, or internal consulting units. But each level and area of the organization must have clearly defined methods of data analysis and be trained to use them effectively.

The objectives of service/quality measurement and analysis are to: (1) maximize revenues and customer satisfaction while minimizing costs, (2) integrate the results of these data analyses into the organization's decision and improvement cycles, (3) make wiser and faster decisions than competitors do, and (4) improve service-provider and manager's intuition and decision making. The 16 tools of service/quality measurement and analysis include:

1. Cause and effect diagrams
2. Checklists
3. Histograms
4. Pareto charts
5. Trend charts
6. Scatter diagrams
7. Process flowcharting
8. Statistical process control
9. Statistical sampling and testing
10. Quality improvement teams and empowerment
11. Queuing and perception management
12. Employee feedback
13. Customer feedback
14. Benchmarking
15. Interlinking models—simple
16. Interlinking models—complex

These 16 tools of service/quality measurement and analysis are briefly defined here. References are cited for these tools during our overview discussion. Evans and Lindsay, Juran and Gryna, Rosander and Gitlow et al. are example references on the first nine tools of quality measurement and analysis.[1]

The first seven methods are frequently called "The Seven Tools of Quality Control." These seven basic tools should be used at *all levels of the organization* while the other nine tools have special roles and places in the organization.

Cause-and-Effect Diagrams

A cause-and-effect diagram identifies potential causes of a problem or circumstance that may have caused a certain outcome or result. The diagram looks like a series of successive treelike branches denoting the hierarchy of the analysis. Data analysis results and logic eliminate causes until the most likely sources of the problem emerge. These causes become candidates for corrective action.

Checklists

Checklists simply list things that must be done before, during, and after executing a service encounter. Checklists also can be used to list all possible causes of a certain outcome or result. Checklists and cause-and-effect diagrams help ensure completeness.

Histograms

Histograms show the distribution of performance of measured data. Bar charts are one way to show the shape and dispersion of the data. The mean, median, mode, quartile, variance, skewness, kurtosis, minimum, and maximum of a performance measure are often reported with histograms.

Pareto Charts

Pareto charts show that a small percentage of the causes typically account for a large percentage of the problems. These charts visually depict the relative importance among cause-and-effect measures. Pareto analysis separates the vital few from the many. Concentrating on the vital few or A items should result in the greatest benefit, for a constant amount of improvement effort.

Trend Charts and Scatter Diagrams

Trend charts plot performance data in time-ordered sequence. Scatter diagrams are two-way criteria plots that show graphically the relationships between these data. Scatter diagrams are one of the simplest methods of interlinking. Correlations between two variables can be computed and observed graphically.

Process Flowcharting

Flowcharting service processes defines the sequence and relationships among process activities and steps. As noted in Chapter 7, process flowcharting is an essential method for quality improvement. Figure 7–1 showed a service process flowchart. Process design begins with process flowcharting. Harrington's book on business process improvement,[2] Shostack's, and Shostack and Kingman-Brundage's, work on flowcharting and service blueprinting[3] are example sources of information on this topic.

Statistical Process Control

Statistical process control charts are methods to see if the variation in performance is due to identifiable factors or assignable causes. If the process or performance measure is in "statistical control," it is said to be in control. If actual performance ventures outside prescribed limits, the process is said to be out of control. Control charts come in many forms, such as x- or R-charts for continuous variable data and p-charts for attribute (yes/no) type data. Process capability analysis and ratios also fit in this tool category.

Control charts have been used primarily for monitoring internal measures of performance. But they can also be used to monitor external, perception-based measures of performance. Of course, interpreting the results poses new challenges.

Applying control charts in a service business is not always as straightforward as in a goods-producing business. For example, control-chart measurement requires many observations or much time to observe what is going on. Service encounters need immediate feedback. If you wait for a statistically significant sample size and run length, corrective action can take too long. You can lose many customers who will tell many more about their poor service encounter experience. This favors proactive measurement and control methods such as employee empowerment, especially at the service encounter level. Statistical process control is a reactive method as noted in Table 11–1.

Finally, the results of continuous improvement, new technology, better processes, and so on, can quickly shift or increase service/quality plateaus of performance. As performance tolerances and means shift, statistical quality control finds it difficult to assume a *stable* service process. For example, our journey to zero defects can be viewed as a wavy continuous improvement or step-function curve with many local optima and a global optima equal to zero. The phenomena that one is measuring with statistical quality control methods assume a stable process over the analysis period. If the rate of improvement (learning) is great, then statistical quality control is simply tracking trends and variances. Rapidly increasing, decreasing, or shifting service/quality performance plateaus are a problem for traditional statistical quality control methods.

Process stability, adequate run lengths, changing service providers, and correct sample sizes are more difficult to verify in service processes. Statistical process control is a very valuable tool to evaluate cause and effect. But you must clearly understand its role and limitations in a service-intensive setting, and when and where to use it.

Statistical Sampling and Testing

Statistical sampling and testing determines the appropriate sample size and statistical criterion for acceptance or rejection of lots from which the sample was taken. There are many types of sampling plans but they usually fall into four categories—single, double, multiple, and sequential.

Statistical process control and sampling evaluate one performance variable at a time. Unfortunately, service/quality performance is measured using many different criteria and requires multidimensional analysis tools. That is why Solution Approaches #8 and #9 in Chapter 16 will point out that we must move beyond one- and two-way criteria comparison methods in practice. The 16 tools of service/quality measurement and analysis include higher forms of data analysis. The service and information (Servomation) Age demands that we use data analysis methods capable of modelling complex relationships between multiple performance criteria.

Quality Improvement Teams and Empowerment

A quality improvement team is a method of organizing people to analyze a situation, make recommendations for improvement, and then do it. It is an approach that brings people together to brainstorm, gather data, identify the problem, develop alternative solutions, make a final recommendation, and implement it. Improvement teams are a major contributor to the organization's quality and corporate culture.

The Deming cycle of plan-do-check-act (PDCA) is a framework of analysis frequently adopted by improvement teams. Coupled with the 16 tools of quality measurement and analysis noted here, these teams are an important way to achieve continuous quality improvement. Over the years, quality improvement teams have had many forms and names. Aubrey and Felkins, and Crocker et al. are example references on teamwork and group processes.[4] We examined the topic of empowering employees in Chapter 8.

Queuing and Perception Management

Queuing methods describe the nature and performance characteristics of waiting for service. People, information, paper, and products all have to wait sometime during their life. In Chapter 7 on process management we discussed the design issues of waiting. Manufacturing or service delivery processes can be thought of as a series of queues. Therefore, queuing models and analysis can provide key insights into process performance. Queuing analysis is an internal, transaction-based method of analysis. Hall, for example, presents an overview of queuing methods.[5]

Perception management, as described in Chapter 7, is also an important part of any queuing analysis. For example, the facility layout and process flow must accommodate waiting lines and make the wait seem as short as possible. Airports, automobile repair, banks, factories, government services, hospitals, libraries, professional services, restaurants, retail stores, universities, and telephone service and information centers, for example, must accommodate waiting lines of people, things, and information. How management configures these interrelated queues has a major impact on service/quality efficiency and effectiveness. Perception management and queuing analysis are close companions in any practical situation. They are powerful tools for evaluating service/quality performance.

Employee Feedback

Employees in the United States have only in the last decade been used as a primary source of service encounter design information. The cumulative insights of thousands of employees who interact daily with internal and external customers are a valuable source of information. What your employees tell you affects both the revenue and cost sides of your business. It is management's job to harness this powerful source of service/quality performance information.

Employee feedback mechanisms take many forms, such as employee self-directed teams, suggestion systems, videotaped focus groups, and surveys.[6] These mechanisms can provide the seeds for service innovation by defining new or modified consumer benefit packages. They can identify possible problems with current performance and suggest ways to improve service encounter efficiency and effectiveness. And employee feedback can provide information for supervisor performance evaluation and encourage a quality culture.

In 1979, Federal Express recognized that considerable benefit could be derived from surveying employee satisfaction, complaints, and suggestions for improvement. Federal Express's Barvo Zulu awards, for example, allow managers to award cash or theater and dinner tickets to employees who exhibit world-class performance. Their Guaranteed Fair Treatment Program also provides employees with a process to handle any grievance with the right of appeal. Federal Express's Survey-Feedback-Action (SFA) process evolved into a semi-annual employee survey. Today, a 30-question survey is administered by the personnel department twice a year to all Federal Express employees. Employees discuss issues and problems identified in these surveys at mandatory feedback sessions. Managers and employees work on the SFA process together. Over 99 percent of Federal Express employees participate in the SFA process. An SFA Leader's Guide outlines the SFA process and the responsibilities of everyone involved.

Another Federal Express employee feedback mechanism is their Leadership Index. The first 10 items on the SFA questionnaire make up a Federal Express Leadership Index. The index is used in the performance appraisal of front-line supervisors and middle managers. The Leadership Index is a quantitative method of executing the quality philosophy that "customer satisfaction begins with employee satisfaction."

Customer Feedback

Customer feedback mechanisms include survey questionnaires, customer comment cards, focus groups, mystery shoppers, and complaint-handling processes.[7] Banc One Corporation, for example, uses many of these measurement methods. Federal Express measures customer satisfaction through a series of external, perception-based studies. Telephone surveys, mailed surveys, and customer comment cards are the primary methods used at Federal Express. Federal Express also has an extensive complaint-handling system with a standard response time to the customer within 24 hours.

Besides the SFA, customer complaint-handling, and customer satisfaction survey methods at Federal Express, they developed an internal-based measure of service/quality performance. The Service/Quality Indicator (SQI) is a 12-criteria index. Example indicators are: abandoned calls, complaints reopened, damaged packages, lost packages, missed pick-ups, right-day late deliveries, traces, and wrong-day late deliveries. Each criterion is weighted according to its relative importance. Continuous improvement goals for the SQI are set each year. SQI is really a measure of process effectiveness. Meeting SQI performance goals also can account for as much as 40 percent of a manager's performance evaluation!

Federal Express's service/quality performance measurement and analysis systems are comprehensive, multiple-channeled, interdisciplinary, and fully deployed. They measure performance multiple ways. They build redundancy and speed into their measurement systems. They provide a model of not only how to collect timely data but also how to analyze and use it for continuous improvement. Their measurement systems are highly integrated with their recognition, reward, and grievance systems.

Benchmarking

In 1989, Robert C. Camp defined the topic of benchmarking.[8] Benchmarking has accelerated organizational learning and improved performance worldwide. Camp's definitions of benchmarking are:

1. "Benchmarking is the continuous process of measuring products, services, and practices against the toughest competitors or those companies recognized as industry leaders."[9]
2. "Benchmarking is the search for industry best practices that lead to superior performance. . . . In this regard it pursues *dantotsu,* the best of the best practices, best of class, or best of breed."[10]

Benchmarking is part of a broader approach to continuous improvement initiatives, and is often found under the umbrella of total quality management, performance measurement or continuous improvement management. Benchmarking is viewed, in many cases, to be a "driver" of continuous improvement initiatives.

Four generic questions addressed in benchmarking studies include: (1) Who is best? (2) What constitutes best practice and the best practice frontier? (3) What performance targets should be used for a nonperforming benchmarking partner to help them achieve best practice performance? (4) What are the rates of improvement over time? The generic benchmarking process is divided into (a) benchmarking metric analysis and (b) benchmark best practices.

Three factors made benchmarking a hot topic in the late 1980s. The first factor was intense foreign competition. Second, Robert C. Camp's book on benchmarking highlighted its importance. Third, benchmarking became an important part of the Malcolm Baldrige National Quality Award (MBNQA) criteria. Benchmarking directly influences at least 300 points out of 1,000 points in the 1993 MBNQA scoring scheme, depending on how you count it.

For example, Motorola studied Domino's Pizza and Federal Express to learn how to shorten processing time between order receipt and delivery of its cellular telephones. The United States Internal Revenue Service benchmarked itself against American Express to try to improve its billing processes. General Electric and others visited Merck Sharp & Dohme, the US pharmaceutical marketing area of Merck & Co., to study how Merck trains its sales force. Benchmarking helped reduce these organizations' learning cycles and encouraged improvement initiatives.

Benchmarking requires *relative* measures of performance. One determines "who is best" given a set of observed outputs, which were achieved by using a set of observed inputs (resources) for each organizational entity or decision making unit (DMU) in the comparison.

A decision making unit (DMU) can be any organizational entity, such as a company, a function, a factory or service facility, a department or work unit, a consumer benefit package, a process, a person such as a surgeon, or a critical service encounter. A benchmarking partner can be viewed as a comparative DMU. Benchmarking can be done at the strategic or macro level, such as the company or service facility level, or at micro levels of detail, such as at the work unit, process or service encounter level. Some argue that only micro level benchmarking results in actions that actually improve performance.[11]

Ideally, DMUs internal and external to the organization are compared in benchmarking studies. The difficulty in benchmarking worldwide performance is getting comparable data from all internal and external DMUs. Internal benchmarking typically uses DMUs (branch banks, a health maintenance organization's surgeons, etc.) that are all part of a larger organizational structure. Best in the organization is the focus with internal benchmarking. The advantage with internal benchmarking is quick access to comparable performance data and poor performing DMUs can immediately learn from their best of class DMU counterparts.

The dominant way to measure DMU performance in practice is by ratio analysis, using inputs and outputs. Example ratios used for benchmarking are: cost per unit, service upsets (breakdowns) per customer, processing time per unit, customer retention rates, revenue per unit, return on investment, and customer satisfaction levels. Other ways to benchmark DMUs include using standard cost systems or international standards of excellence and comparing actual DMU performance to these standards. Audits and reviews also are ways to benchmark DMU performance. Using the MBNQA scoring system for self-assessment is an example of the audit and review approach.

Graphs, histograms, ratios, performance gaps, basic statistics, and standardizing and weighting performance criteria are the normal methods of doing benchmarking metric analysis. For two-way (criteria) comparisons, these methods are adequate. Unfortunately, the performance of most CBPs and EBPs, and their associated processes and service encounters, require many input and output performance criteria. Most benchmarking information or performance matrices have multiple rows identifying each partner (DMU) and multiple columns identifying critical performance measures for all DMUs. Two-way criteria (pairwise) comparison methods quickly break down or ignore key interrelationships when confronted with the multiple criteria data analysis problem. Here is where a data envelopment analysis approach to benchmarking can accommodate multiple inputs and outputs in a systematic and objective manner.[12]

Applying data envelopment analysis (DEA) to benchmarking. Research on applying data envelopment analysis (DEA) to benchmarking is ongoing.[13] Although a full discussion of a DEA approach to benchmarking is not possible here, we shall review some of the characteristics of DEA that make it an attractive and objective method for benchmarking metric analysis:

- Applicable to any organizational entity, big or small, that uses inputs to create outputs.

- Identifies the best performing DMU(s) and defines them as 100 percent efficient; and identifies the degree of inefficiency of the other nonperforming (i.e., not on the best practice frontier) DMUs in the data set.

- Defines efficiency or effectiveness in terms of multiple performance measures (i.e., the composite model) as well as two-dimensional input/output performance models. Two dimensional models can be graphed and are easy to explain, and the extension to higher-dimensional models is easily handled.

- Accommodates service-providing processes and organizations that provide a complex mix of goods and services—a consumer benefit package—typically, at many sites, with many noneconomic, qualitative, nominal, and ordinal performance measures.

- Uses actual performance results and does not require relative prices or market values for the inputs and outputs. Many services such as corporate in-house training programs, environmental protection programs, the quality of health care, and government services are difficult to price. DEA can also use perception-based data and rankings.

- Identifies the elements of "best practice" for each DMU, in terms of the mix of resources, and sets targets (standards) of performance for each nonperforming (inefficient) DMU to help them achieve best practice performance levels.

- Determines the extent of inefficiency (performance gap) for a DMU as a measure of its distance from the best practice frontier.

DEA has many unique terms, alternative ways to formulate the model, and ways to present the results. A few of DEA's most basic terms and ideas applied to benchmarking can be observed in Figure 11–1, which depicts two input levels, at a given level of output, for five service processes, A to E. This multiple (two) input model results in a concave frontier where better performance means moving toward the origin and using less of each input (minimizing inputs) for the same output level.

Inefficient service process E's performance is measured along ray OE, to its hypothetical "best practice" point E'. In this case, "efficiency" assessment is based on proportional reductions of both inputs for this single output level. The geometrical measure of E's efficiency, therefore, is given by the simple proportion of OE'/OE.

The *performance gap* for service process E is the difference between its performance (OE) and that of the "best in the industry or world" (OE'). The corresponding DEA concept is that of *relative efficiency*, which is a measure of the distance a DMU's performance is from the "efficient frontier" determined by the "best practice" DMUs. The best practice or efficient frontier in Figure 11–1 is defined by service processes A, B, C, and D. Note that these four DMUs are 100 percent efficient, although each DMU uses a different mix of resource inputs 1 and 2.

DEA results also give the amount and direction of target input resources for each DMU to achieve 100 percent relative efficiency (i.e., best practice performance). Of course, over time the best DMUs and the efficient frontier itself will change. DEA also can be used to help measure and evaluate these changes over time, that is, the dynamic nature of continuous improvement initiatives.[14]

Benchmarking needs better and smarter ways to do metric analysis. DEA is particularly well suited for service processes with a complex mix of inputs and outputs. Simple ratio analysis, weighted average comparisons, and one- and two-criteria comparisons are not powerful enough to handle the multiple criteria

FIGURE 11–1
The Best-Practice Frontier for a One-Output and Two-Input Data Envelopment Analysis Model

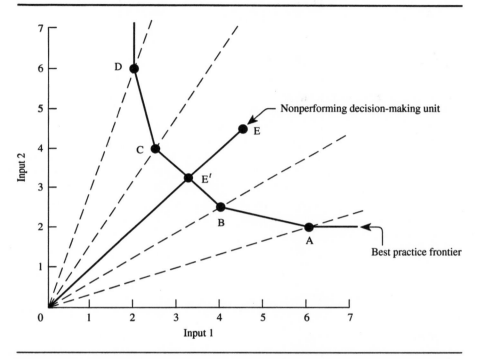

Note: Decision-making units A, B, C, and D are all on the best-practice frontier. Each uses a different combination of inputs to produce the same output performance level.

problem posed in benchmarking studies. A DEA approach to benchmarking metric analysis provides the decision makers with a management-by-fact basis for a well directed and smart improvement strategy. A DEA approach to benchmarking is a complex interlinking approach. DEA is a technique whose time has come. The need is there—it is now simply a matter of education and training.

Interlinking—Simple and Complex

Chapter 1 defined interlinking. Chapters 14 and 15 will describe both simple and complex interlinking models in more detail. For the purposes of this overview of measurement methods, a few basic points about interlinking are in order.

Interlinking tries to define a quantitative relationship between at least one internal performance measure and at least one external performance measure. It emphasizes managerial insights gained from the modeling approach over the technical details of the models themselves. Example methods most appropriate for *simple interlinking models* include scatter plots, histograms, gap analysis, correlations, parametric or nonparametric statistical tests such as the *t*-test or Wilcoxon Signed Rank test, learning curves, and linear and nonlinear regression models. Some of the elements of quality functional deployment and the House of Quality also fit in either simple or complex interlinking models.

Complex interlinking models try to define the quantitative relationships in terms of strength and direction among many internal and external performance measures. Typical methods of analysis for complex interlinking models include path and factor analysis, covariance structure, conjoint, econometric, mathematical programming, and analysis of variance models.[15] Taguchi methods and design-of-experiment methods are also a part of complex interlinking methods.[16]

Complex interlinking models are best suited for trying to quantitatively define complex cause-and-effect relationships, whereas a data envelopment approach to benchmarking is more of a performance comparison and goal (standard) setting tool. Both methods complement each other and can be applied to the same set of data with slightly different objectives. All complex interlinking methods try to model and evaluate the multiple criteria problem.

APPROACHES TO SERVICE/QUALITY MONITORING AND CONTROL

Monitoring and controlling service/quality performance requires a variety of approaches, on-the-spot-action, a reliance on human performance, and an interdisciplinary viewpoint. Many reasons that control is more difficult for services than for products are founded in the basic ideas and premises of service management described here. Example ways to monitor and control service/quality performance are summarized in Table 11–2. We have described many approaches noted in Table 11–2 in previous chapters. Each approach cited in Table 11–2 can be the subject of a full discussion. Here we shall briefly examine only two approaches to monitoring and controlling service/quality performance. They are: (1) service guarantees and recovery actions, and (2) smart schedules.

Service Guarantees and Recovery Actions

Cooker Restaurant of Columbus, Ohio, says "if we fail to make you happy, then we don't expect you to pay." As described in Chapter 8, service guarantees and immediate service recovery actions by employees are cornerstones of Cooker's competitive strategy. Employees at Cooker's can authorize free menu items or meals—due to service breakdowns or unhappy customers. In fact, Cooker's main constraint to growth is the limited supply of qualified people who can execute their service guarantee and service recovery policies.

TABLE 11–2
Example Ways to Monitor and Control Service/Quality Performance

I. Quality by Design

- Excel at consumer benefit package definition and design.
- Excel at process definition and design.
- Design the service facility to accommodate world-class performance and customer and information movement.
- Standardize the service facility, process, and job designs.
- Develop a comprehensive customer contact (3C) plan.
- Use more technology (automation) and less employee discretion.
- Have continuous electronic monitoring of equipment and employee performance.

II. Quality by Measurement and Analysis

- Use internal historical measures such as cost per unit of output, errors per unit of output, and processing and waiting time.
- Use external historical measures such as customer surveys, focus group interviews, and customer comment cards.
- Use quality control techniques such as statistical process control, fishbone diagrams, Pareto analysis, acceptance sampling, etc.
- Develop predictive interlinking models based on history.
- Develop predictive interlinking models based on customer's future needs and perceptions.
- Benchmark relative performance, using smart data analysis methods such as data envelopment analysis.

III. Quality by People

Quality by Education and Career Progression

- Cross-selling.
- Training.
- Script dialogue training.
- Service management-based job rotation and career paths.
- Informate the employees about the importance of quality performance and competitive pressures via multiple communication channels.

Quality by Empowerment

- Employee empowerment training.
- Customer and process ownership.
- Immediate service recovery policies and actions.

Quality by Leadership, Rewards, and Grievance Procedures

- Employee incentive, gain, or profit-sharing programs.
- Employee recognition and reward programs.

continued

TABLE 11–2 *(concluded)*

- Behavioral management.
- Subordinate and peer performance evaluations.
- Management educational program participation and resource commitment.
- Formal employee grievance and counseling procedures.
- Coupling manager's performance appraisal to service/quality performance.
- Top management leadership and involvement by actual participation and commitment.

IV.   *Quality by Systems and Standards*

- Do quality and performance audits.
- Design professional peer- and standards-review processes and certification.
- Excel at time-based competitive strategies and capabilities as a form of control.
- Implement statistical process control methods and improvement cycles.
- Create detailed procedure manuals and job checklists at the process and service encounter levels.
- Develop and implement smart staff and equipment schedules that maximize service levels and minimize costs.
- Incorporate the value of a loyal customer and cost of poor quality into economic analyses.
- Use the judicial system to protect service concepts, and facility equipment, job, and process designs.
- Maintain safety capacity in the form of extra service channels, standby labor pools, and service recovery plans.
- Develop profit and loss (income) statements by consumer benefit package and process.
- Establish strong franchise agreements.
- Use yield management techniques to maximize revenues and service levels.

V.   *Quality by External Communication*

- Influence and set customer expectations by advertising world class performance levels (promises).
- Influence employee performance by public advertising so employees must live up to or exceed what the ads promise (commitments).
- Establish service guarantees using smart data analysis.
- Differentiate consumer benefit package features from competitors' through advertising.

Service guarantees can be used to achieve many objectives. For example, they can be used to (1) set customer expectation levels, (2) set employee performance standards, (3) build customer loyalty and increase customer retention, and (4) differentiate your CBP from competitors. Other possible objectives include (5) establishing in the minds of the customer a new or different company image, (6) generating reliable data and customer feedback, and (7) emphasizing improved performance and execution by the service delivery system. When all parts of the organization are coordinated and help design the service guarantees, these objectives are attainable. There are many fine points that must be examined to design a truly successful service guarantee such as what is the best payout for a service encounter upset.

Service guarantees, employee empowerment, and service recovery strategies are all interdependent. As the service-content of the CBP increases, employee empowerment, training, and service recovery strategies become more important. They must be coordinated and complement one another. Poor design or execution in any one of these areas can result in customer or employee confusion and dissatisfaction, poor organizational performance, and higher costs. When service guarantees are poorly designed and executed they can be viewed by employees and even customers as just another quality fad. Service guarantee failures are seldom publicized or documented like so many other quality improvement initiatives.

Cooker's Restaurants and Federal Express coordinate their service guarantee design, with other parts of the service delivery system. They use integrative, interdisciplinary teams early in the design of these programs. They match organizational capability to what they promise their customers. For example, the billing center at Federal Express authorizes its employees to resolve customer billing problems up to a $2,000 credit or refund level without management approval.[17] Federal Express also has in place procedures and higher-level organizational units to quickly resolve more expensive or complex service guarantee problems and customer complaints.

Smart Schedules

Good resource schedules are necessary to maximize customer satisfaction and minimize provider costs. The closer resource capacity tracks (matches) customer demand the better the schedule. For service organizations, smart scheduling is a key to controlling service/quality performance and costs. For example, how long you wait for service is dependent on scheduling.

The following service scheduling situations give you some idea about the structure, complexity, and benefits of smart scheduling. Each example gives you a glimpse of how important smart scheduling is to service/quality performance.

1. A major hotel books large and small convention, conference groups, and travel groups over a five-year planning horizon by day. Each group has certain booking and revenue spending behaviors based on historical analysis. Example booking parameters include no-show and double occupancy rates, room rates, departure patterns, food and beverage revenue per room night, stayover rates, length of stay, and the cost of overbooking and underbooking. Smart scheduling and booking methods increase room sales efficiency (actual total room sales divided by the

sum of maximum revenues at full room rates) by 10 percent compared to past performance the first year it is used. Smart scheduling and yield management help manage this perishable asset—hotel rooms.[18]

2. A dentist uses 15-minute booking intervals in his patient appointment and scheduling system. Appointments are determined based on standard time estimates per dental procedure and some multiple of the 15-minute booking interval. An analysis of patient and procedure mix, standard times, and the appointment system led to several recommendations. One recommendation is to reduce the booking interval to multiples of 10 minutes. After six months of use, the revised appointment system increased patient throughput and revenue by 5 percent with no increase in working hours or patient complaints.

3. The dietary department at a major hospital has 10 teams of patient tray (meal) delivery aides. Each team consists of four aides delivering hospital meals three times a day. Delivery aide schedules and team size were determined by trial and error. The labor utilization rate for these 40 delivery aides given generous standard time estimates is 57 percent. Patient complaints concerning tray delivery and pickup are collected and reported. Smart scheduling sets the team size at three delivery aides and a total of 10 teams. Ten delivery aides are reassigned or leave via attrition. Total dollar savings per year is over $200,000 of which $20,000 is used to improve the technical and customer service skills of the remaining delivery aides. Hospital patient customer complaints concerning tray delivery and pickup are reduced.

4. A major hospital accommodates 40 patients in its kidney dialysis unit. The waiting list to get into the unit for treatment is long, and many patients complain. Some patients drive long distances to other kidney treatment centers. The hospital has a request in for 15 more kidney dialysis machines. Smart scheduling allows the dialysis unit to accommodate a total of 50 patients with the same number of machines. The request for 15 more machines is withdrawn.

5. A small bank must reduce operating costs and finds that its branch bank tellers are overstaffed. The mix of full-time to part-time tellers is approximately 80 to 20 percent, respectively. Smart scheduling reduces the number of bank tellers, saves $130,000 per year, and changes the mix of full- to part-time tellers to 60 to 40 percent, respectively. Even with these teller staff reductions, there is a moderate decrease in the number of customer complaints. The reduction in customer complaints is partially explained by a new teller training program financed by smart scheduling.

Smart scheduling is a means to control service/quality performance, maximize customer satisfaction, and minimize provider costs.

For goods-producing firms, smart service scheduling is found in a host of support services as noted in Chapter 3. Example support services in goods-producing firms where smart scheduling is necessary include customer service centers linked to the customer by telephone, billing, waste management, repair, security and safety, legal and tax processes, and refund and recall services.

A good information system is a predecessor to smart scheduling. If the information system is lacking, smart scheduling and yield management cannot be done or its performance cannot be continuously evaluated. A schedule based on smart methods and poor data has little chance of producing world-class results. A schedule based on good data and poor methods also cannot produce world-class results. Management, and only management, is responsible for obtaining both—good data and smart methods.

CONCLUSION

"What gets measured, done well, and rewarded is what gets done," is an axiom that challenges everyone to measure and monitor performance. Information-intelligence (smart information) is the dominant asset of the future. It leads the organization into new markets and improvement cycles. It is embedded in the consumer and employee benefit packages of the business. It creates value for customers. To not actively pursue better service/quality data analysis is to ignore a tremendous source for gaining competitive advantage.

The original *seven* tools of quality control are not enough in today's information-rich and competitive environment. Data measurement and analysis skills within the organization must be upgraded to match the art they intend to serve—one of providing world-class service encounters in a complex multiple-criteria environment. That is why *nine* additional tools of service/quality management are highlighted and briefly discussed in this chapter. A basic requirement of doing business in the Servomation Age is super data collection, measurement, and analysis capabilities. Your organization should be building these capabilities now, especially the data analysis capabilities.

Chapter Twelve

Service/Quality Standards and Performance

A man in Spokane, Washington, became upset when his bank wouldn't validate his 50-cent parking ticket. He said that the bank teller and the branch manager told him that cashing a check wasn't a transaction that qualified a customer for free parking.[1] The bank teller said he was following the standard procedures of the bank.

The next day this upset customer took his $1 million dollars out of the bank and deposited it in another bank. To make matters worse, the original bank's weekly newsletter had identified this special bank customer by name and implied he should receive premium service. This service breakdown, service upset, or service encounter failure prompted the bank to review its policies, standards, empowerment and training programs, and ways of rewarding teller performance.

A service/quality standard defines a level of performance, an outcome or behavior for an organization, a consumer benefit package, a service process, a service provider or a service encounter. Standards of performance directly or indirectly imply certain levels of customer and employee satisfaction, revenues, and costs. Standards help you decide where and when to allocate the organization's resources to particular markets and processes. These metrics and standards of performance define your improvement strategy. Standards also must be understandable, measurable, meaningful, easy to calibrate, and traceable to lower- and higher-order standards of performance.

How to set good service/quality standards of performance is a task few organizations have mastered. Many organizations operate with token standards or none at all. Without standards, organizational resources are scattered, directions are vague, decisions are haphazard, and the organization drifts along. We have much to learn about setting service/quality standards of performance. For example, what are the best ways to relate service/quality standards to employee empowerment policies or pay for performance systems? How do you evaluate empowered service providers?

This chapter examines issues such as service/quality standards, the value of a loyal customer, the cost of poor service, and script dialogues. The cost of quality is one topic of this chapter that has received considerable attention. Good references on quality costs are available by authors such as Campanella, Harrington, and Rosander.[2] Let's begin by understanding the value of a loyal customer.

VALUE OF A LOYAL CUSTOMER

The bank customer in Spokane, Washington, might have deposited $10 million in this bank during his lifetime. This is the value of a loyal customer for this service upset. He also might have influenced his family and friends to do business with the bank. But the bank will never know because they did not validate his 50-cent parking ticket. Here, customer switching costs are low, so it was easy for the customer to move money to another bank.

The examples in Table 12–1 demonstrate the type of financial leverage derived from loyal employees and customers. The only way to develop numbers and relationships like those of Table 12–1 is by asking the right questions, collecting the right data, and analyzing the data the right way. Interlinking is a way to identify and quantify relationships like those in Table 12–1.

The value of a loyal customer raises the question, "Does improved quality and customer satisfaction pay off?" The answer is yes, in almost every case.[3] But to ensure you manage these decision variables properly, you must first define, quantify, and understand the relationships between process performance, customer satisfaction, revenues, and costs. Management by fact is the preferred decision making approach.

COST OF POOR SERVICE

Feigenbaum[4] in 1961 defined four categories of quality costs. They have since been improved and defined as follows.

Appraisal costs are those associated with determining actual quality levels for consumer benefit packages (CBPs), and their associated processes and service encounters. Example appraisal costs include inspection, audits, testing, statistical sampling, surveys, and quality-related data collection, storage, and analysis. These costs are measurable.

Prevention costs are those associated with preventing poor CBP and process quality from occurring. Example prevention costs include training programs, employee selection processes, quality planning, vendor selection and certification, continuous improvement costs, management time, employee empowerment training and costs of their decisions, and quality-related data collection, storage, and analysis. These are difficult costs to measure and cause considerable debate in cost of quality systems.

Internal failure costs are those associated with correcting a CBP and associated process and service encounter failure, before it is delivered to the customer. Example internal failure costs include backroom errors, downtime, rework, scrap, and waiting time. These costs are measurable.

External failure costs are those associated with correcting a CBP, and associated process and service encounter failure, once the customer experiences, pays for, or uses the CBP. Example external failure costs include service recovery

TABLE 12–1
Value of Loyal Customer Examples—The Revenue Side of Profits

A 2 percent reduction in employee turnover (or satisfaction) increases customer satisfaction by 1 percent.

Customers that are happy with their service encounter experiences will tell up to 10 people, whereas unhappy customers will tell up to 30 people.

A 2 percent increase in employee satisfaction results in a 5 percent decrease in customer complaints.

A loyal lifetime Brand W automobile buyer will spend $300,000.

A 2 percent increase in customer retention has the same effect on profits as a 10 percent decrease in costs.

A 5 percent increase in training costs increases employee satisfaction by 2 percent.

A one-day reduction in total processing time increases customer satisfaction by 0.5 percent and profits by 0.2 percent.

Ten-year customers generate 50 percent more profits than five-year customers.

Note: These generic examples are not applicable to all industries and situations, and are for illustration purposes only, but they do show the type of relationships interlinking methods can define.

actions, refund and return actions, fixing the problem or complaint, callbacks, warranty costs, loss of goodwill, and lawsuits. These costs are measurable although some numbers may be soft.

Perfect quality would have internal and external failure costs equal to zero, and prevention costs a higher percentage than appraisal costs. Here the quality management system is proactive and predicting future performance. A sound approach to evaluating these costs is to graph each cost category and work toward decreasing them and total costs. Performance goals can be set and the trends by cost category analyzed. Cost of Quality (COQ) improvement trends and attainment of goals can be reported in key performance documents, including the annual report. Crosby, in his first book *Quality Is Free*, noted that "A well run quality management program can get by with less than 2.5 percent of sales, which is spent on the prevention and appraisal activities necessary to make certain the company is maintaining its standards of excellence."[5]

Many books also graph (not shown) the cost of appraisal and prevention against the cost of internal and external failure. These graphs imply a trade-off between these quality costs, and therefore, an optimal level of quality and total costs. However, the functional form of these quality costs is far from proven and applicable to all situations. In fact, how these four quality cost categories are related is industry-, firm-, process- and CBP-specific.

In three service industries—telecommunications, transportation, and financial services—that I have studied, the functional forms of these cost categories were different, and sometimes no statistically significant relationships were found.

Key relationships that were specific for each firm were identified, but they did not necessarily follow ideal models.

John Groocock, the author of *The Chain of Quality* and a Vice President of Quality for TRW, Inc., concludes that "The so-called economics of quality have been examined. It was shown that the frequently published graphs of relationships between costs and quality that are supposedly applicable to all products, have no general validity. Unle⌐s the terms are carefully defined such graphs have no meaning. Even when the terms are defined, each product will have its own cost versus quality relationship which follows no general pattern."[6]

A cost for every service encounter upset can be estimated from (1) the customer's perspective, (2) the provider organization's perspective, and (3) society's perspective. Table 12–2 provides generic examples of the cost of poor service from all three perspectives.

The costs of not doing it right the first time are higher than we think. Phil Crosby in 1981 warned that "The only way to measure quality from a management standpoint is by calculating the price of nonconformance—how much does it cost you to make and overcome errors? In manufacturing companies, it usually runs about 23 percent of sales; in service companies, it is more than that."[7]

One strategic advantage of implementing a cost-of-quality information system is that it acts as an integrator of organizational systems and practices. It is best to develop a cost of quality system on a process-by-process basis so as not to overwhelm the organization and its people. Accounting systems, however, are not very compatible with collecting and using value-of-a-loyal-customer and cost-of-quality information. Some advances such as activity-based costing and activity analysis are being made. The ultimate goal of any value-of-a-loyal-customer and cost-of-quality initiatives is that they become a normal part of the organization's accounting, information, and financial systems. A cost of quality system should not stand apart from other information systems over the long term. It must become the normal way of measuring performance and running the business.

Millions of service encounter upsets occur every day with a wide range of nonproductive and negative costs. The cost of poor service ranges from a customer thinking a service-provider was rude, to the wrong medical diagnosis of a patient that results in a major lawsuit or the patient's death. Determining the cost of poor service requires a broad, interdisciplinary perspective—a service management perspective—both in terms of definition and measurement. Once you estimate the value of a loyal customer and the cost of poor service, justifying error removal systems and quality improvement initiatives are not so difficult.

In terms of continuous improvement cycles, cost of poor quality systems must be coupled with other improvement approaches. For example, when a bank customer closes his or her accounts, one bank has a *Service Encounter Debriefing* procedure. This systematic procedure finds out why the customer left the bank, where they took their business, and was there any way the bank could get them to return. MBNA America, for example, asks every customer who drops their

TABLE 12–2
Cost of Poor-Service Examples—The Cost Side of Profits

Our organization requires a $1,000,000 increase in sales revenue to realize a 5 percent after-tax profit to equalize and recover from a $50,000 cost-of-poor quality problem.

Rework capacity is 11 percent of total capacity and every 1 percent of capacity costs $1,240,000.

The average full cost of a service/quality performance audit is $3,240, and our company performed 71 audits last year.

The average cost to society of catching, convicting, and keeping a person in prison for 20 years is $1,600,000.

A 1 percent increase in warranty claims costs the company $124,000 per year.

The pure variable cost of an avoidable telephone recall is $28.68 for our customer service representatives.

The average full cost per assembly line inspection station is $46,000 per year.

The cost of gaining a new customer is four times more expensive than retaining an existing customer.

Note: These generic examples are not applicable to all industries and situations, and are for illustration purposes only, but they do show the type of relationships interlinking methods can define.

credit card services why they left. About one-half of these customers reverse their decision and stay with MBNA America. Their service encounter debriefing practice greatly reduces customer turnover rates and improves profitability.

CBP, PROCESS, OR SERVICE ENCOUNTER RETURN ON INVESTMENT

Return-on-investment computations for improvements to the consumer benefit package (CBP) or the process and service encounters that deliver it can be done several ways. One way is to build into traditional capital budgeting models the benefits and costs of a specific service/quality improvement initiative. The idea is to compute a return on investment over a specific planning horizon as shown by the following general relationship.

$$\text{Return on investment for improvement initiative} = \frac{\text{Benefits of improved performance}}{\text{Total costs of improvement initiative}}$$

Return on investment can be computed at several different levels of aggregation such as at the organization, CBP, process, or service encounter level.

Benefits can include the dollar value of shorter cycle times and time to market, improved productivity, increased market share, the ability to increase prices, increased customer retention, and lower costs. The examples in Tables

12–1 and 12–2 provide ideas on what types of dollar benefits and costs can be incorporated into capital budgeting models. Once these streams of benefits and costs are netted out, they can be discounted back to current time by methods such as net present value.

In the past, the difficult part of this approach is getting everyone to agree on the numbers used to describe the value of a loyal customer and the cost of poor service. But, today, interlinking can help define the quantitative relationships between these variables. Interlinking, sometimes, can validate relationships and turn soft numbers into hard numbers. *If you don't interlink, a soft number argument will always lose.* You must come to the meeting armed with interlinked data that define the relationships in your organization.

For example, when trying to justify a computerized system for a retail pharmacy on the basis of better quality, reduced inventory, staff reductions, and better accounts receivable recapture, the "hardest" (i.e., ease of quantification and soundness) benefit categories were used first. Then the "next hardest" benefit category was used, and so on, with the "softest" set of benefit numbers used last. The cost side of this financial analysis used hard numbers and was very concise.

Here, accounts receivable recapture and inventory savings resulted in a positive net present value (NPV) of $93,000 and an internal rate of return (IRR) of 28 percent over the planning horizon. Staff reductions and better quality benefits were icing-on-the-cake if these benefits happened, raising the NPV to $337,000 and IRR to 57 percent. Also, a long list of benefits from improved service/quality performance, such as better screening of patient prescriptions, were presented in the strategic section of the financial justification report.

The point of this pharmacy example (without showing you all the financial spreadsheets) is that we must use what we know about the value of a loyal customer, the cost of poor quality, labor and computer productivity, and general organizational performance measures. Quality and customer satisfaction performance must be built into the financial and decision-making systems of the organization. We do not have to change the methods and formats of traditional financial analysis to do this. We simply need to use interlinking methods and turn soft numbers into hard numbers.

One study by Ernst & Young, titled "American Competitiveness Study," surveyed 277 top executives of US manufacturing companies. The insights from this study are not directly transferrable to US service companies.[8] But the results do give a sense of the state of the art of cost of quality practices. It is easy to argue that if the huge US service sector was similarly surveyed, those results would be worse.

The Ernst & Young survey asked participants to estimate the cost of quality for their businesses. Forty percent of the survey participants could not provide an estimate. "The average cost of quality as a percent of cost of goods was 11 percent and ranged from a low of 0.4 percent to a high of 90 percent. By way of comparison, firsthand measurement of this cost category (by Ernst & Young) typically ranges between 8 percent and 35 percent. When these results were compared with business performance, no relationship was found. However, when only those responses that fell within the more realistic range of 8 percent to 35 percent were analyzed, lower cost of quality was closely tied to better relative cost position and, to a lesser degree, higher relative price and profitability."[9]

The high cost of poor quality shocks most managers and many simply do not believe it. As one consultant recently noted, "I have found cost of quality to be as high as 85 percent in some government services, and related to this, nonvalue-added costs to be almost uniformly 50 percent of public service operations."[10] Likewise, once I visited a football-field-sized claims processing center for a major trucking firm. Over 300 people worked in this center. In the first 30 minutes of our conversation, a manager asked me what I thought the cost of poor quality was in their firm. I said, "Well, I think you are standing in it."

SETTING SERVICE/QUALITY STANDARDS OF PERFORMANCE

Service/quality standards of performance are elusive, especially those used on the frontstage. For example, consider the challenge of developing service/quality standards of performance for a theatrical play—the CBP, and its associated process and service encounters. One internal service/quality standard of performance is how close the actors place themselves to a mark on the floor at a certain point during the play. Is an actor on-target, one foot, or four feet away from the mark? If the actor is more than one foot off-target, a star (stage prop) will hit the actor as it falls from the sky. Since the play director does not want a service upset during the live performance, the director coaches and trains the actor to meet this internal service/quality standard of performance. During the first night of the play before an audience, the actor misses the mark by two feet and the star bounces off the actor's shoulder. The audience gasps as the actor slightly amends the play's script to accommodate this new situation—the service recovery. The actor smoothly continues with the play. The audience is not aware the actor missed the mark—the internal service/quality standard of performance. The audience thinks the play scene was planned and exciting—the unplanned service encounter executed by an empowered service provider. The audience leaves the play highly satisfied and delighted—the external service/quality standard of performance.

Should the actor be rewarded by the play director? The actor missed the internal standard of performance but hit the external standard of performance by executing a clever service recovery strategy. Should the internal service/quality standard be dropped or changed? Should the script of the play be changed? These are the types of questions service managers face daily when service is a performance.

The following are other examples of service/quality standards of performance. For a bank teller the performance standards include smiling frequently, knowing the technical part of the job, and showing empathy toward the customer's problems. For a hotel restaurant waiter, the one and only way to set the customer's table, and set up the waiters' service station are key standards of performance. A prosthodontist must be licensed in the state where he or she practices dentistry. A franchise agreement is a way to set service/quality performance standards. For a building security officer, certain customer interaction skills and physical abilities are clearly specified. For a day care center there shall be a minimum of 10 square feet of activity area for each child two years or older.

These examples show the diversity and challenge of setting service/quality standards. (Table 10–1 on page 167 also defined service/quality and standards of performance.) Table 12–3 is a list of example service/quality standards of performance. The standards of performance frequently focus on the process because, most often, the process is the service.

Many issues surround the setting of service/quality performance standards. These will be briefly examined here:

1. Setting good service/quality standards.
2. Measurement scales, perspectives, and plateaus.
3. Balancing organizational capabilities to customer promises.
4. Script dialogues as standards of performance.
5. Service/quality standards and cost of errors.

Setting Good Service/Quality Standards

American Airlines, Federal Express, MBNA America, and Otis Elevator, for example, provide their employees with multiple sources of internal and external performance data. These data are timely and accurate and become the fuel that drives the world-class service organizations and helps them set their standards of performance. Standards of service/quality performance must be linked back to customer requirements defined by the CBP. Good data analysis is a prerequisite for setting good service/quality standards.

Once you collect mountains of data, you must know how to analyze the data, quickly turn it into smart information, communicate it clearly to the users, and act upon it. Here the 16 tools defined in Chapter 11 provide the means of analysis. Some organizations spend millions of dollars on hardware and software to collect data and then analyze it with eighth-grade levels of analysis, or let it sit in storage with only causal attention by management. The data analysis capabilities of the organization must complement and match the complexity of service processes and encounters.

World-class organizations use their information systems to help them determine cause and effect. They know what CBP and service encounter attributes are

TABLE 12–3
Service/Quality Standards-of-Performance Examples

- 96 percent of our customer (employee) survey respondents must be satisfied, very satisfied, or delighted.
- No more than 5 percent of all customer service transactions will be stored on paper.
- At least 95 percent of hospital patients must complete the admissions process within 20 minutes of their arrival time.
- Each telephone customer service representative (CSR) will be evaluated quarterly in a random "listening in" audit and scored on 10 performance measures as defined in the CSR Operating Manual. Audit results constitute 33.3 percent of the weight for the CSR's annual performance review.
- All credit card allowance increases will be processed in one hour or less.
- All passenger baggage must reach the airline baggage carousel within 15 minutes of the airplane's gate arrival time.
- The target employee turnover goal for this year is 8 percent, and after that, decreases by 1 percent point per year.
- The dinner table should be set exactly as shown in the restaurant operating manual. Four random audits per waiter per year will be performed by the waiter's immediate supervisor, with audit results documented in the waiter's personnel file.
- 100 percent on-line computer availability is the goal.
- The postoperative wound infection rate goal at this hospital will be 14 cases per 1,000 patients next year, and after that, decrease by 2 cases per 1,000 patients per year.

Note: These generic examples are not applicable to all industries and situations, and are for illustration purposes only, but they do show the type of relationships interlinking methods can define.

most and least important to their customers. They know the range of performance outcomes. They know why results are caused by approach. In these world-class organizations, insightful information replaces assets, and adds value to (informates) consumer benefit packages, processes, and service encounters.

One example of setting good service/quality standards of performance is Ford Motor Company's sales and service customer satisfaction standards for their dealerships. There are standards for sales personnel such as "using a checklist, the Sales Consultant delivers vehicle in perfect condition when promised" or "customers courteously acknowledged within two minutes of arrival and advised that a Sales Consultant is available upon request." Example customer satisfaction standards for automobile repair service include "service status provided within one minute of customer inquiry" or "appointment available within one day of customer's requested service day."[11] These standards are clearly defined in plain English so everyone can understand them. The full set of seven service and six sales standards is a good mix between quantitative and qualitative standards of performance. They give direction to everyone involved in the sales and service processes. They also require the automobile dealership to make good capacity and scheduling decisions, otherwise the standards of performance will not be achieved.

Measurement Scales, Perspectives, and Plateaus

Performance measures are made on one of four scales:

1. *Nominal* scales such as street addresses, words to describe service encounter performance, or brand names serve as labels or tags to identify things, events, properties, outcomes, and places. Nominal scales are the least restrictive scales but cannot be used to compute basic statistical measures such as means and variances.

2. *Ordinal* scales are ranking scales, say, 1, 2, 3, 4, and 5. They establish the order of things but the differences between, say, 1, 2, 3, 4, and 5 are not necessarily equal and linear. Here statistical measures such as rank, median, quartile, and percentile have meaning.

3. *Interval* scales allow one to interpret the ranking and differences between two measures. But the origin of the measure is arbitrary. Fahrenheit and centigrade temperature scales are good examples of interval scales. Most basic statistical measures such as means, variances, and correlations can be computed for interval scales. Also, many statistical tests such as t-test can be used on interval-measured data.

4. *Ratio* scales, such as processing time ranging from zero to infinity possess a zero point and the measurement properties of order and distance. Examples include measures of length, weight, loudness, and waiting time.

Interval scales have order and distance properties, while ordinal scales have only order properties. Nominal scales have none of the measurement properties of order, distance, or origin. It is important to figure out what you expect from the data collection and analysis effort before selecting a measurement scale and perspective. What is it we need to know? How will these data be analyzed? How should the questions be structured and organized for best results? Dillman's book on survey design is one of many that focus on questionnaire design and analysis.[12]

Should service/quality performance be measured from a positive or negative perspective? The positive perspective accents the things that go correctly. Here the goal is 100 percent. The adverse or negative perspective accents the things that go wrong. Here the goal is zero defects. The Malcolm Baldrige National Quality Award identifies customer satisfaction and dissatisfaction criteria. Examples of adverse performance indicators include callbacks, complaints, claims, customer retention rates, refunds, recalls, returns, litigation, replacements, losing market share, downgrades, repairs, and warranty work and costs.

Measuring performance from a positive perspective highlights the successes, instills a positive attitude in people and organizational culture, and challenges the organization to deliver 100 percent customer satisfaction. For these reasons, most organizations select the positive perspective measurement approach.

Adverse or negative performance measures can balance out the remaining indicators depending on the specific objectives of the work unit. Federal Express, for example, uses adverse performance indicators to describe operational and logistical system performance. Twelve adverse indicators are used in Federal Express's Service/Quality Indicator, such as lost packages, abandoned calls, missed pickups, damaged packages and complaints reopened.

Balancing Organizational Capabilities to Customer Promises

Consider Figure 12–1 where the two axes are (1) over- and underprovides and (2) over- and underpromises. Here both axes must be based on comparable measures and scales. In terms of revenues, costs, customer satisfaction, and profits, where on this two-dimensional solution space do you want to play out your Service/Quality Solution? Where do you place each of your CBPs and those of your competitors? How long can an organization stay in each box before bankruptcy?

What happens when the organization promises too little and provides too little (lower left quadrant)? In this case, revenues and market share are depressed or decreasing. The cost to provide service is unpredictable. Profits decrease under these circumstances with a high risk of going out of business. *Customer disgust* is warranted because of poorly defined or executed CBPs, processes, and service encounters.

When the service-providing organization promises too much and provides too little (upper left quadrant), customers become dissatisfied. Customer expectations are seldom fulfilled. *Customer dissatisfaction* dominates this arena of unbalanced marketing and operational capabilities. Revenues decrease and costs are again unpredictable. Profits decrease and the organization struggles to coordinate its marketing and operational areas.

When the organization promises too much and provides too much (upper right quadrant), it is difficult to predict the direction of revenues or costs. Revenues may temporarily increase but costs are likely to be higher than competitors'. When your CBP and associated service encounters perform in this quadrant there is a high risk of *customer confusion*. Customer expectations and perceptions are unstable. A key issue is how long can an overpromising and overproviding organization stay in the market? For an entrepreneurial company trying to create a new market or enter an old one, overpromising and overproviding may be a necessary service strategy to differentiate itself. But over the long term, an organization that promises and provides too much will not survive.

When the organization promises too little and provides too much (lower right quadrant), *customer satisfaction* is highest. Here customers are delighted when perceptions of actual service exceed what was expected. Revenues and repeat business increase while costs are kept under control. Profits increase and market share grows.

FIGURE 12–1

The Problem of Balancing Organization Capabilities to Promises Made to Customers

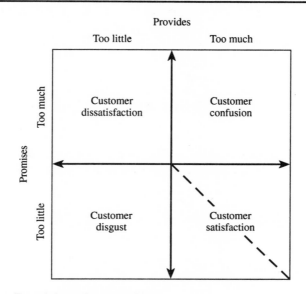

Example issues for an organization:
1. Where is each CBP, and those of competitors, on this grid?
2. How long can we (they) stay in each box?
3. Can we (they) make a profit, given the time horizon?
4. How should we enter a new market or business?
5. How to balance operational capability and marketing promises?
6. How do we move each CBP or CBP family to the customer satisfaction box?

In the world defined by the paradigm of Figure 12–1, the best place to be is in the customer satisfaction quadrant. There marketing and operations have coordinated their plans and actions into one harmonious effort. The marketing area is promising exactly what or slightly less than the operational system can provide. Ideally, costs are minimized while customers are satisfied or delighted. There marketing and operations are coordinated, and their capabilities hover around the dashed diagonal line within the customer satisfaction quadrant.

Script Dialogues as Standards of Performance

Script dialogues to train service providers are good examples of America's service expertise. Telephone customer service representatives of all types use script dialogues to learn how to respond to customer inquiries and complaints. Hotels, for example, use script dialogues to train security guards, check-in and check-out service-counter employees, maintenance workers, bartenders, and baggage handlers.

Elsewhere, many Japanese companies are intensely studying Disneyland in Tokyo. They are in awe of the precision of Disneyland's training programs for thousands of different types of service encounters executed on any given day at Disneyland. Script dialogues are of particular interest to the Japanese. They are studying America's script dialogues as they once did Dr. Deming's statistical methods. They recognize that standards of performance take many different forms in a service business. If the Japanese do with script dialogues what they did with Dr. Deming's statistical control ideas, American service industries are in for a severe challenge.

"The Disneyland manuals, for example, try to anticipate every conceivable situation and tell employees exactly how they should respond. The result, says SpaResort's Susumu Yamada, is quality far higher than his company could accomplish with total quality control."[13]

Service/Quality Standards and Cost of Errors

The United States's annual medical bill is approaching $1 trillion dollars. In 1993, the US cumulative federal deficit was about $4.1 trillion, or $16,500 for every man, woman and child in the nation. If ever standards of service/quality performance needed to be linked to revenues, costs, and customer satisfaction, the time is now. Interlinking is imperative if these types of mammoth costs are to be controlled, key relationships understood, and service/quality standards set.

Consider the diagram in Figure 12–2 that shows the degree of service/quality control and the number of errors or service upsets per million service encounters. The vertical axis also shows the cost of an error or service upset. By multiplying the cost of an error times the number of errors, the total cost of poor service can be computed. The same total cost of poor service can be attained by a low cost-per-error times many errors or a high cost-per-error times a few errors.

The horizontal axis uses the definition of total process capability over the range of -3 to $+3$ standard deviations, or 6 sigma capability.[14] A normal probability distribution is assumed here. Process capability refers to the degree of variation in the process about a specific target value. "In Motorola's view, 6 sigma initially allows the distribution to shift by 1.5 sigma, resulting in a 4.5 sigma performance, or 3.4 parts per million (ppm). Ultimately, this shift in average will be eliminated, resulting in a process capability of producing nonconforming levels of 1 part per billion."[15] By the end of 1991, Motorola had reduced its defects from 6,000 per million in 1986 to 40 per million in 1991.[16]

The functional form of how the total cost of poor service is related to 1 to 6 sigma process capability in Figure 12–2 is not known for these generic examples. Therefore, the solution space is shown as an envelope defined by two arbitrary curves. Figure 12–2 implies that 6 sigma standards of service/quality

FIGURE 12–2
Service/Quality Standards of Performance—When Is Enough, Enough?

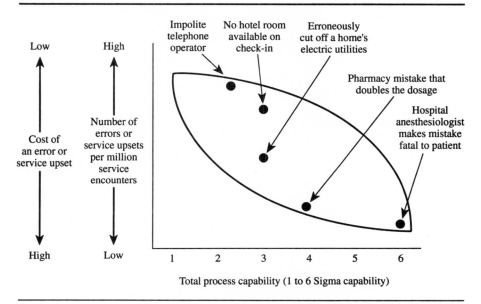

performance are not necessary for service upsets such as an impolite telephone operator or the erroneous cut-off of electric utilities or the unavailability of a hotel room for a booked hotel guest. Yet, a standard of 3 sigma would result in 1,350 service upsets per million. Given the cost of further improvement, management must decide if 135 service upsets per 100,000 customers is an appropriate standard of performance, and then work to get there.

For dispensing certain prescription drugs with harmful health consequences, at least a 4 sigma standard of performance is required. Here CBP, process, and service encounter control must be capable of providing 32 ppm or 3.2 service upsets per 100,000 patients. At 5 sigma, we are talking about 287 service upsets per billion, or 0.0287 upsets per 100,000. The process capability for a hospital's anesthesiologist making a fatal procedural mistake in the operating room (if it could be set as in a manufacturing process) could be set at 6 sigma capability. If the anesthesiologist can hit the ideal target rates continuously throughout the operation, there will be only one fatality due to an anesthesiologist error per billion surgeries.

Goods-producing firms, such as Motorola, will ultimately achieve 6 sigma performance goals for their processes and products. But when the customer is in your factory, as in a service business, and knowing human nature and the complexity of service encounters, 5 and 6 sigma standards of performance goals are difficult to achieve. We might like to think that some medical services achieve these 5 and 6 sigma standards of performance, but the vast majority do not. When humans are involved in the service process, standards of performance of 3 (1,350 ppm), 3.5 (232 ppm), and 4 (32 ppm) sigma are appropriate service/quality standards of performance. For highly automated service systems such as electronic funds-transfer performance or purchasing systems for goods, 5 or 6 sigma performance standards are attainable.

CONCLUSION

When is good, good enough? When is bad, bad enough? Only internal and external standards of performance based on smart data analysis provide the baseline to answer these questions. Standards are the basis for improvement strategies and management action. Setting good performance standards requires good data, good methods of analysis, good mechanisms to get this information into the organization's decision cycles, good communications, good managerial judgment, and skilled analysis people. Without standards of performance, it is a guess as to what action to take or when to take it or how good/bad we are doing.

More research and field studies are needed to help figure out the best approaches for setting service/quality standards of performance. It is one of the more challenging areas of service management. Once you determine what standards of performance to set, the next question is how to achieve these standards? Here we begin to think about implementation, the subject of Chapter 13.

But before we examine a service management approach to implementation, please be aware that there are two basic ways to continuously improve. They are either by (1) breakthrough improvement initiatives or (2) continuous improvement initiatives. Breakthrough improvement initiatives may achieve 20 percent to 1,000 percent annual improvements in performance. Breakthrough improvement initiatives are radical changes in the process, technology, organizational architecture, or the way things get done. Continuous improvement initiatives normally try to achieve a 1 percent to 20 percent improvement in performance per year. Here people assume much of the technology and structure are fixed, and work toward improvement within these constraints.

Management must decide when no amount of small continuous improvements are going to keep the organization competitive over the long term. The signals are typically not clear and management must balance the benefits and risks of using continuous improvement too long, versus committing monies for a breakthrough approach. Interlinking can help management search for these signals, define relationships among key performance variables, and benchmark themselves against competitors.

Chapter Thirteen

A Service Management
Approach to Implementation

P lans mean nothing unless they are implemented successfully. Plans are sometimes stopped or stymied by bothersome details, narrow viewpoints, and organizational barriers. Unfortunately, service/quality excellence requires everyone to master the details, broaden viewpoints, and ignore organization boundaries.

This gap between talk and action is wide for most organizations. For example, a Gallup Survey sponsored by the American Society for Quality Control revealed there is much room for improvement in American companies when it comes to successfully implementing quality programs.[1] One finding of the Gallup survey was that "More than a third (36 percent) of employees in companies where quality improvement activities are in place do not participate in these activities. Failure to involve the workforce in quality improvement activities is a serious stumbling block to growth and prosperity in the new era of international competition."[2] Another finding of the survey was that 36 percent of employees surveyed say the company could increase their job performance if management would "let them do more to put their ideas into action." Also, only 14 percent of employees surveyed feel completely empowered to make on-the-spot decisions.[3]

A joint survey by the American Quality Foundation and Ernst & Young found the following percent of North American and German bank employees currently participating in these quality improvement activities: outside training and conferences (14 percent), small group activities (25 percent), membership on teams (17 percent), problem solving training (14 percent), and suggestion programs (28 percent). Although these findings are disappointing, these same banks plan to increase these percentages in the next three years to the 20 percent to 40 percent range.[4]

And as noted in Chapter 1, even though American Fortune 500 service companies are embracing service/quality improvement as a way to define and run the business, the overall degree of effort in service industries is low. For example, the Gunneson Group International, Inc., a quality consulting company reports that only 10 percent of American service companies have any kind of quality program. The Gunneson Group predicts that by the year 2000, perhaps 70 percent of those with more than 500 employees will adopt a formal quality improvement initiative.[5] These example survey results illustrate the gap between reality and the hoopla that sometimes surrounds quality improvement.

Philip Crosby, W. Edward Deming, and Joseph Juran[6] all contributed greatly to our understanding of how to implement quality improvement within organizations. Deming and Crosby both propose 14 steps for their quality improvement implementation plans. Their implementation guidelines include ideas such as commitment from management, quality teams, employee participation, eliminating workplace barriers and driving out fear, cost of quality analysis, quality councils, education and training, using statistical methods, employee recognition programs, and the like. Juran recommends a quality breakthrough sequence that employs major changes in company culture and employee attitudes, focusing on the vital few, and overcoming resistance to change.

Historically, service firm managers have been in the uncomfortable position of trying to adapt goods-producing-based implementation approaches to organizations that provide services. Yet, if we truly understand the ideas of service management, we see that goods-producing approaches are not 100 percent transferable to service-providing organizations.

New approaches are needed. We all should have done more to help make this transformation from a product-producing to a service-providing management style. Remember that jobs in the US economy were about equally divided between goods-producing industries and service-providing industries in the mid-1950s! Only with the arrival in the 1980s of service marketing, service operations, and human resource management applied to service organizations did we begin to address service issues. Now their integration is called service management and it is beginning to address the needs of practicing service firm managers.

Here, I have outlined an implementation plan with services in mind. Table 13–1 defines 16 action steps to implement continuous improvement with a focus on services. The 16 action steps provide a framework, but sub-steps must be tailored to each organization's industry structure, markets, culture, financial position, strategy, risk profile, competitor actions, capabilities, and so on. Examples of these sub-steps were shown for Action Step #7 in Tables 7–2 and 7–3. To help understand the details of each step, I have referenced related chapters and ideas.

Once success is achieved, improvement and nurturing cycles keep the approach revitalized and fresh. It is a continuous cycle of self-renewal and improvement. Benchmarking can help drive the continuous improvement initiatives. The 16-step implementation plan defined in Table 13–1 is never finished.

A SIXTEEN-STEP IMPLEMENTATION APPROACH TO SERVICE/QUALITY IMPROVEMENT

Is your quality management system equal in status and capability to other company systems? Or better yet, is your quality management system so integrated with other organizational systems that you cannot tell where it starts and ends—it

TABLE 13–1

A Sixteen-Step Implementation Approach to Service/Quality Improvement

Action Step	Implementation Approach
#1	Learn to "think service management"
#2	Gain top-management commitment and participation
#3	Restructure "the service management way"
#4	Define the organization's service management vision and objectives
#5	Excel at consumer and employee benefit package management
#6	Excel at facility design and location
#7	Design the service process and its performance system
#8	Set service/quality standards of performance
#9	Measure and evaluate consumer (employee) benefit package, service process, and service encounter performance
#10	Develop a Comprehensive Customer Contact plan for critical service encounters
#11	Excel at interlinking and informate CBPs, service processes, service encounters, and people
#12	Integrate service/quality performance into all organizational systems and decision making
#13	Evaluate everyone frequently on service/quality performance
#14	Use benchmarking to drive and build continuous improvement and nurturing cycles into all aspects of the organization
#15	For Action Steps #1 through #14, establish multiple communication channels to disseminate plans, status, and actions
#16	Repeat Action Steps #1 through #15 for each consumer or employee benefit package provided by the organization

permeates every facet of the organization? If your answer to either of these questions is no, the implementation approach defined here can help your organization move toward these goals.

The 16 action steps defined in Table 13–1 are best described as an approach rather than a system or program.[7] The term *program* implies a temporary endeavor. The term *system* denotes a long-term commitment and permanence in the quality endeavor, but one that might stand alone. This book uses the word *approach* to describe the integrative, holistic, and systematic quality journey defined in Table 13–1.

Action Step #1
Learn to "think service management."

Education and training on the ideas of service management are the basis for successfully implementing this approach. A coordinated training plan for all levels and areas of the organization must be developed. It should be taught from a service-providing, service encounter, and service management perspective. The old approach of teaching from a goods-producing, customer and factory order, and functional perspective must be discarded.

Everyone in the organization must understand early in the implementation plan why things should be done the service management way. Why do we need a service management approach to organizational architecture? Why is the consumer and employee benefit package idea and format a better way to define the business, and conceptualize what the customer buys? Why is the service often the process? Why do customers evaluate services differently than they do goods? Why is product quality becoming an order qualifier and service quality an order winner? Why do we need a comprehensive customer contact plan (3C Plan) for critical service encounters?

Paradigm shifts and all the human behaviors that accompany them catch organizations and their people in mental traps. Making the transition from a goods-dominated economy to a service- and information-dominated economy is one of those traps. If you adapt, you have a chance of survival. If not, you die one way or another. Learning to think service management is a first step in changing the mindset of everyone in the organization. Until everyone understands why, there will be doubts and mistrust, and the quality vision and agenda for action will be lost.

Action Step #2
Gain top-management commitment and participation.

The 1993 Malcolm Baldrige National Quality Award (MBNQA) places 9.5 percent of its total points squarely on the shoulders of senior management. In reality, the importance of senior executive commitment and participation is much more important than the weighting scheme of the MBNQA. Roger Milliken, the Chair and CEO of Milliken & Company, a 1989 MBNQA Winner, stated, "We have learned that there are only three barriers to executing a successful quality improvement process. The first is top management. The second is middle management. The third is first-line management."[8]

Recent surveys show that top management is beginning to get the message. Ernst & Young's 1992 International Quality Study found that "In all four countries studied (Canada, Germany, Japan and the United States), quality performance of the organization is dramatically rising in importance as an assessment criterion for senior management compensation."[9] This study also found that "over half of all businesses in all four countries frequently (i.e., monthly or more frequently) evaluate the impact of quality on financial performance."[10]

One way for quality improvement efforts to capture top managements' attention is to state the benefits of quality improvement in terms of financial performance. Interlinking is a way to help achieve this objective. Interlinking sometimes can change soft numbers into hard numbers. Top management may not understand the significance of a 10 percent reduction in processing time or a 2 percent improvement in the customer's satisfaction rating. But if you can relate these improvements to financial performance, top management will listen. Several examples of quantifying the relationships between revenues, costs, and customer satisfaction are given in Chapters 12, 14, and 15. Action Step #11 in Table 13–1 incorporates interlinking into the implementation procedure.

The problem with an organization's having to convince senior management about the benefits of quality improvement is that it takes up valuable time. As discussed in Chapter 6 on time-based competitive strategies, competition can butcher a company if it takes several years just to gain top management commitment.

Action Step #3
Restructure "the service management way."

Chapter 8 outlined a service management approach to organizational design. Some of these ideas are summarized in Figures 8–1 and 8–2, and Table 8–1. In Chapter 16, Table 16–1 also shows how a service management philosophy is put to work in a service-providing organization.

The infrastructure must change before tactical issues can be taken up. For service-management-designed organizations, the three basic levels of the organization are: (1) consumer and employee benefit package management, (2) process management, and (3) service encounter management. Horizontal relationships are dominated by processes and process managers. Electronic networks as discussed in Chapter 9 glue all organizational entities together and enhance communication. In a service-management-designed organization, we organize around information and service, not products and locations.

Action Step #4
Define the organization's service management vision and objectives.

In Chapter 9 on service innovation, we described the challenges facing Eastman Kodak as their business shifts from paper and film to electronic pictures on high definition telecomputers transmitted directly to and from the home or office. A basic challenge for Eastman Kodak is to shift its thinking and decision making from a product-perspective to a service management and process perspective.

Eastman Kodak management must define their vision from a service management perspective. The service management vision directs and encourages people—it gives them direction, a sense of purpose, and confidence to meet the future head-on. What is important now—goods or services? What is important in 10 or 20 years? How will we get there as an organization? What principles and values will guide the organization? What capabilities must we develop?

Example service management statements of vision and values might include the following:

1. Our organization's goal is getting and keeping the right customers for life.

2. Our organization believes in making a profit by exceeding customer expectations and anticipating customers' future CBP, process, and service encounter wants and needs. We will be the first to recognize and adapt to changing customer wants and needs, technical capabilities, and new delivery structures.

3. Our organization recruits the best people and continuously trains and supports them to provide world class service encounters to our customers at home, at retail outlets, and the workplace.

4. One of our organization's core values is to constantly strive to create, leverage, and protect our service innovations so as to build competitive advantage.

Mistakes in defining the organization's vision and objectives can cause the entire organization to misallocate precious resources, set vague or conflicting priorities, try to achieve too many world-class performance goals, and ultimately fail. Decisions at this strategic step set immediate guidelines for all subsequent steps. It is better to achieve concentrated success than comprehensive failure.

Action Step #5
Excel at consumer and employee benefit package management.

Consumer and employee benefit package (CBP/EBP) management includes definition, design, and strategy. Chapter 4 described CBP/EBP definition and design. Chapters 5 and 6 described key ideas of service strategy. Figures 2–3 and 2–4 graphically depicted how CBP management fits into the overall approach to build quality and competitive advantage. CBP management is where specific strategies and objectives are set at the CBP family and individual CBP level. A CBP/Process Oversight Committee or Council must keep CBP and work unit plans aligned, evaluate performance, and act as a key mechanism of communication (i.e., Action Step #15).

Action Steps #5 through #7 in Table 13–1 are usually done sequentially. But they should be done almost simultaneously, especially in service businesses. In a service-providing business, these steps must also be imagineered. Service processes must support the CBP; facilities must enhance and fit the service process; and performance systems must support CBP and process objectives.

Service organizations can also learn from their goods-producing partners about Action Steps #5 through #7. These processes and approaches are not, in general, as well defined in service organizations as are goods-producing firms. The interfaces between CBP, facility, process, equipment, and service encounter design are key failure points in many service businesses. These interfaces are not well managed or even recognized in many service-providing organizations.

CBP management and service process design (Action Steps #5 and #7, respectively) also can become incongruent due to regulatory actions. For example, consider a US telecommunications manager's explanation to me in 1985.

My main problem is managing 50 people who must explain to the customer an increasingly complex set of options, prices, and services associated with getting a telephone installed. People used to call one number, before deregulation, and we did it all from A to Z. Now the customer and my phone service representatives get very frustrated. The customers get upset because they don't understand why the phone company can't answer all their questions in five minutes. We now confront the customer with a host of very complicated decisions. This creates great stress in trying to grasp all options and reach a decision.

My customer service representatives now spend up to an hour explaining all this to the customer. The expansion of services we provide has increased my standard time per call, and now I plan to hire more people to maintain my service levels. Also, we have had to spend a lot more time training and retraining my customer service representatives to keep up with the expanded set of services we provide. Costs are rising.

My workers see the gap every day between the public's expectations and the reality, at least up to now, of deregulation. This gap creates stress for my people. They sincerely want to help each customer but can't spend a full work day talking to eight customers.

Here consumer benefit package proliferation is partially in the control of federal and state regulatory agencies and courts. Obviously, process capability is inadequate to handle the number and diversity of CBP options offered to the public for sale. In this example, CBP management (Action Step #5) and service process design (Action Step #7) were not coordinated and aligned. Operational capability did not match the marketplace requirements required by regulatory agencies.

Action Step #6
Excel at facility design and location.

Chapter 7 provided examples of how facility and process design fit or don't fit together. These examples included Broadway Pizza, LensCrafters, an insurance company's policy approval process, Burger King and Amoco's combined fast food restaurant and gas station, Disney World's Main Street design, and an airport's baggage processes. These examples highlight the desperate need in all businesses, especially service businesses, for the synchronized design of CBPs, facilities, processes, and service encounters.

Convenience, distance traveled to and from a service facility, average time traveled, and multiple locations to enhance synergistic sales are also important in service organizations. Part of what the customer buys includes these types of location-dependent CBP attributes. Health clinics, rental car firms, health clubs, fast-food restaurants, emergency service facilities, branch banks, libraries, hotels, and many other types of service facilities depend on good location decisions. A good location can partially overcome poor facility design, but a good facility design can seldom overcome a poor location.

Many service locations, as noted in Chapter 9 on Service Innovations, are now mobile or in temporary locations, using portable service centers and electronic offices. Other services are dependent on electronic networks, with a super-centralized backroom and a completely decentralized frontroom connected to the individual's office, home, or person. Technology, in some cases, is making service facility location less important.

Action Step #7
Design the service process and its performance system.

The process of creating and delivering the CBPs and associated service encounters must be precisely defined. Service system design begins by meticulously defining process work elements, scripts for ideal service-provider behavior and style, and flowcharting the service process—ignoring organizational boundaries. The process flowchart must be drawn from the customer's point of view.

Many traditional tools of operations management are applicable here, such as work measurement techniques, process output and input definitions, Pareto analysis, person-machine activity charts, process capability analysis, waiting-line analysis, layout methods, reliability analysis, and various issues related to the social-technical aspects of job and process design. Process flow analysis and process flowcharting have been popularized in service businesses, most notably by G. Lynn Shostack, now the chair and CEO of Joyce International, Inc. She was the first to call it *service blueprinting*, and many of her works are referenced in Chapter 7. Table 7–3 summarized key sub-steps of Action Step #7. At the sub-step level we begin to tailor the implementation plan to the unique characteristics of the organization.

Once service processes are designed and flowcharted, many sub-plans are needed. Plans for reward and recognition, training, standards, script dialogues, performance evaluation, communication, and continuous improvement and nurturing must support Action Step #7. Some organizations develop a Comprehensive Customer Contact Plan (3C Plan), as highlighted by Action Step #10 in Table 13–1 and by Table 7–2. For each service process, it defines *ideal* customer contact performance requirements, training requirements, the degree of empowerment, service recovery policies and guidelines, and so on, for critical service encounters.

Action Step #8
Set service/quality standards of performance.

Part IV of this book on service/quality management has described the challenge of setting service/quality standards of performance. Internal and external service/quality standards of excellence must, over time, become congruent. Otherwise, costs are high and service is less than it could be. Managers practicing service management should be required to explain and correct the discrepancy between internal and external standards of performance. They must direct resources to the appropriate area to meet and balance target internal and external quality standards.

An airline, for example, may be meeting its internal service/quality standard of no more than a 15-minute wait for baggage after the plane arrives at the gate, but the customer may perceive a much longer wait. The reason(s) for this discrepancy must be determined and the inconsistency between these internal and external measures of performance resolved. Likewise, an airline telephone reservation clerk may meet calls per hour standards, yet departmental managers listening in on the conversations with customers may judge the airline employee's tone of voice and script dialogue to be impolite and abrupt.

If Action Steps #1 through #8 are done well, the service firm manager gains new freedoms and capabilities other competitors don't enjoy. Outrageous performance standards compared to industry standards can now be set and attained. For example, Federal Express provides all customers with a 30-minute answer guarantee. If they cannot answer a customer's inquiry within 30 minutes, the package is free of charge. At the time this service/quality standard of performance was set, no one else in the industry could promise such a standard.

Action Step #9
Measure and evaluate consumer (employee) benefit package, service process, and service encounter performance.

The performance of the consumer or employee benefit package, and its delivery process and service encounters, must be constantly evaluated to see if actual performance (perceptions) meets the standards of performance (expectations). Chapter 11 examined service/quality measurement and control. Table 11–1 defined reactive and proactive approaches to performance measurement. Table 11–2 outlined ways to monitor and control service/quality performance, and the chapter described other ways of control such as service guarantees and smart schedules. Sixteen methods of quality measurement and analysis are also described, each with an appropriate user. Other chapters, such as Chapters 8 and 12, also discuss topics such as performance measurement, script dialogues, service management career paths, and service encounter ownership.

Action Step #10
Develop a Comprehensive Customer Contact Plan for critical service encounters.

A Comprehensive Customer Contact Plan (a 3C Plan) first identifies all points within the process where the customer interacts with backstage or frontstage service providers. For each of these customer contact points, what (outcome quality) and how (process quality) to accomplish world-class performance objectives must be specified. Job performance must be directly tied to service encounter performance. Each point of customer contact must be assigned an owner. Many other requirements must be specified such as training requirements and the degree of empowerment. For each process, a 3C Plan must define performance requirements at least at critical customer contact points.

Many of the ideas of this book can help develop a 3C Plan. Remember, it is at customer contact points that the customer has the greatest opportunity and expertise to evaluate service/quality performance. Customer satisfaction is a function of good or bad performance at these customer contact points. Customer contact points in a service business are analogous to setting the tolerances correctly on a machine tool in a manufacturing process. This is the reason why developing a 3C Plan for each service process is so important. For high contact and professional service systems, the 3C Plan must be flexible (loose), whereas for low contact and routine service situations, the 3C Plan can be more exact (tight).

Action Step #11
Excel at interlinking and informate CBPs, service processes, service encounters, and people.

A major trucking firm asked for help in quantifying the cost of poor quality. The first thing we asked to see was their claims processing center. It was a football field size building with over 200 leased computer terminals, lots of file cabinets, and about 300 employees. We asked for the full costs associated with the claims processing center including retirement, medical, insurance, and day care related expenses.

What would happen to the claims processing center if this trucking firm achieved zero claims every year? You could eliminate the processing center and all its associated costs! On a more realistic level, what are the relationships between cost and service for the claims processing center? The answers were found in an interlinking study. As in any interlinking study, there were surprises and disappointments. Some of these quantitative relationships stunned management and triggered immediate actions. Continuous improvement had begun!

Sometimes the data did not support long-held beliefs about how things are related and what should be done. These results could be due to bad data or not clever enough data analysis. Or it could be exposing a myth about how things are supposed to be related. Even disappointing results can have value. We then discussed questions such as, "Wouldn't it be better to put these resources into doing it right the first time and use the extra funds to grow the business?" Subsequently, they launched a series of service/quality improvement efforts that over the next 14 months saw expenses increase, not decrease. But eventually service/quality costs began to decrease and service levels (claims processed) improved.

Today, this trucking firm has the same building but only 100 leased computer terminals and about 160 employees. The sales department now occupies part of this building. Also, a small office was added and housed in the claims building that provides a customer telephone hot line service to handle customer complaints. Service/quality improvement allowed them to free up resources, add a new peripheral service, and reach a new service/quality performance plateau. Without improved claims performance, the firm might have had to build a new building. Here service/quality improvement benefits funded future growth. Sales are increasing and profits are growing.

Interlinking gives managers power—the power of transforming data into information, knowledge and action. Interlinking helps document performance relationships and turn soft data into hard numbers. It helps improve people's intuition. It adds value (i.e, informates) to the consumer or employee benefit package. Interlinking is also a first step toward a companywide decision support system. And finally, it can help coordinate and align the operations (internal) and marketing (external) functions of the organization. Interlinking is discussed in Chapters 1, 11, 12, 14, 15, and 16.

Action Step #12
Integrate service/quality performance into all organizational systems and decision making.

Collection, evaluation, and the use of service/quality performance data are typically fragmented in the organization. Marketing has its survey and focus group results. The operations area has its internal process performance measures. Research and development and engineering are armed with reams of CBP and process performance data few understand. Personnel has its recruiting and training performance data. Accounting has its budgeting and standard cost data. Sales has its sales reporting data. Finance has its balance sheet and income statement performance data with a focus on what Wall Street thinks.

These guarded islands of knowledge can defeat the general objectives of the firm. Who's focusing on the customers in this fragmented organizational design? It is so easy to suboptimize organizational objectives for the sake of functional, or work unit, goals. Action Step #3 in Table 13–1 reorganizes the service management way to try to deal with this problem.

But even with a service management designed organization, everybody needs to know the relationships and relative importance of customer satisfaction, revenues, costs, and service/quality in an organization. These performance measures must be linked to consumer or employee benefit package definition and design. If customer satisfaction and quality-related performance are top priorities, they should be reported in the firm's annual report, just like revenues, costs, and profits. Think about the signal that top management sends to customers, suppliers, employees, and stockholders with a section on quality performance in the annual report. Of course, this can only be done if Action Steps #1 through #16 are implemented and organizational capabilities are firmly established.

Action Step #13
Evaluate everyone frequently on service/quality performance.

One service/quality challenge is to translate CBP, service process, and service encounter performance standards into individual performance standards. The more the individual values and goals are aligned with organizational values and goals, the better able the organization is to create and deliver world-class service encounters.

At Federal Express, for example, the Supertracker is a hand-held computer with keyboard used to enter and transmit package information to the van's computer and then to the system's computers in Memphis. It took about seven years to develop the Supertracker and the systems that accompany it. The Supertracker allows the organization to track the "anxiety relief" CBP through the service process. Process and employee performance are monitored at service encounter milestones along the way. Here individual performance is linked to CBP, process, and service encounter performance. Up to 40 percent of a manager's annual salary is based on the Service/Quality Indicator as described in Chapter 11.

One financial service company that spends millions of hours a year talking to customers over telephone lines, has a cost-of-poor-service entry on each manager's budget. There are several categories of service/quality costs and one is the cost of an avoidable recall. If a customer service representative (CSR) must call a customer back to obtain information that should have been obtained the first time or because of an error in previous input despite who was at fault, the cost of the avoidable recall is charged to that manager's budget. How often do you think the CSRs must call the customer to get them back on the telephone? It averages over four calls per customer, so the total cost of correcting incomplete or inaccurate information is higher than you might think. This cost of poor service/quality performance is reported with other monthly budget cost categories to all CSRs, their supervisors, and middle management. Although these avoidable recall costs per month were very small as a percent of the total budget, the fact they were on the budget and visible to everyone greatly reduced these service upsets. Today, this CSR operation sets world class service/quality standards of performance and does it right the first time.

Action Step #14
Use benchmarking to drive and build continuous improvement and nurturing cycles into all aspects of the organization.

Nurturing is how you keep continuous improvement initiatives fresh, energetic, innovative, and on top of things. Benchmarking is one nurturing approach that helps drive continuous improvement. After initial successes and failures, the novelty of continuous improvement can result in a reduction in achievements. A nurturing plan such as top management leadership, or the results of a benchmarking study, can revitalize continuous improvement initiatives. Action Step #14 also requires continuous improvement processes to be integrated into the management of primary processes. The design of the primary process is not complete until benchmarking and continuous improvement cycles are built in.

Continuous improvement initiatives also require employees, managers, staff, and sometimes customers to use the 16 tools of service/quality measurement and analysis defined in Chapter 11. Implementing continuous improvement also requires changes in management style as discussed in previous chapters. Continuous improvement is driven by educated and skilled people at all levels of the organization. Sometimes continuous improvement initiatives are not an adequate response to changes in the marketplace and competitor capabilities. Here, management must establish breakthrough improvement teams to achieve revised performance goals as discussed in Chapter 12.

Continuous improvement efforts are viewed by some as just more work outside their primary duties. Extra meetings, problem-solving training, teams' personality conflicts, and implementing good improvement ideas trouble the already overloaded workforce. But the days of managing any process with a *once-in-a-while* approach are gone. Continuous and breakthrough improvement initiatives are part of every job description, whether you like it or not. A continuous improvement and nurturing cycle is one way to keep the organization competitive, and jobs secure.

Action Step #15
For Action Steps #1 through #14, establish multiple communication channels to disseminate plans, status, and actions.

My favorite all-time implementation guideline is Dr. W. Edward Deming's point #8: *drive out fear*. This timeless piece of advice is at the heart of a successful implementation initiative. But how do you drive out fear, and keep it out? Fear can be put to sleep but it can awaken anytime.

To drive fear out of the organization, top management's commitment is one of the two required capabilities. The second capability is to support top management's commitment by a variety of effective communication mechanisms/channels.

There are many forms of communication mechanisms or channels. Examples include: company television channels, frequent video updates of company and work unit performance and trends, recognition and reward activities and programs, face-to-face meetings of all types, newsletters, speeches and presentations, annual reports, competitor updates, training and seminar classes, operating manuals, reporting results (using the 16 quality analysis tools), well designed and well-managed grievance procedures, visuals in the workplace, individual and team performance reviews; wide dissemination of consulting, competitive analysis, and internal report results; regularly scheduled telephone conference calls, interviews with the press and other external groups; facility tours, being host to conferences, and employee, supplier, and customer surveys.

The Communication Approach, as discussed in Chapter 10, is critical to successfully implementing a quality improvement system. *Quality Progress*, for example, has several good articles on how good communication in an organization must be established before behavioral change or cultural change can occur.[11] These articles document the role of good communication in a quality improvement initiative.

Action Step #16
Repeat Action Steps #1 through #15 for each consumer or employee benefit package provided by the organization.

Employee benefit packages (EBPs) must be designed and managed with the same vigor as consumer benefit packages (CBPs). Employee benefit packages consume vast amounts of resources, so each EBP should follow Action Steps #1 through #16 just like the CBPs. With employee health, insurance, retirement, and well-being programs making up a significant portion of total costs, the consumer and employee benefit packages should follow the same steps of the service management implementation process, as defined here. If you understand the ideas of this book, it makes no difference whether we are designing and managing an employee or a consumer benefit package. This approach speeds up the organization's learning process—a necessity in today's world economy.

After these 16 steps are well executed for each consumer and employee benefit package, and associated processes and set of service encounters, improvement must be ongoing. Action Step #14 requires that benchmarking and continuous improvement be built into all aspects of the CBP to service encounter process. This step tries to ensure that self-renewal capability is inherent in the design. In practice, all 16 of these steps are continuously being redone and improved to meet revised customer requirements and fresh organizational capabilities. Adopting the approach advocated here is hard work and much of it must be done by the employees themselves.

WHO OVERSEES IMPLEMENTATION?

Crosby, Deming, and Juran provide ideas on how to implement a successful quality improvement program. A top-level committee usually oversees a company-wide quality initiative. Typical committee names include the Quality Council, Quality Oversight Committee, the Quality Advisory Board, Quality Board of Directors, Total Quality Management Forum, and the Quality Steering

Team. The term *improvement* can be added to these names or substituted for the *quality* term.

An organization needs three or four types of coordinating committees to implement their service/quality improvement initiatives. They include: (1) an organizationwide quality improvement oversight committee, (2) CBP, or CBP family, committees, (3) process committees, and (4) service encounter committees. CBP and process committees often can be combined in a service business, resulting in three levels and types of committees. For a given organization, there might be one Quality Improvement Executive Committee, 5 CBP/Process Committees, and 30 Service Encounter Committees. This structure for implementation assumes the organization is organized the service management way as described in Chapter 8.

Another step in this implementation plan is to list all EBPs and CBPs and associated processes—primary, business, supplier, and support. Then all CBP and EBP processes are rank-ordered in terms of relative priority on performance criteria that the organization deems most important to achieve overall goals. The top ranked EBP/CBPs are selected first and Action Steps #1 through #16 are followed. Again, the focus here is on concentrated success for the most important CBP/EBPs first, then we can shift to lower priority work.

Time-based competitive strategies also include the amount of time it takes to implement a comprehensive quality improvement and management system. If you're slow, it hinders you from growing profits and becoming competitive. For example, Globe Metallurgical won the 1988 MBNQA. When sales were about $100 million they estimated that their quality efforts were saving (this is net savings!) them about $10 million a year. What if they took three years versus seven years to turn the business around? So, move briskly with well-defined, focused, and communicated implementation plans that eventually cover every part of the organization.

CONCLUSION

Four distinct approaches to service/quality improvement initiatives each with a dominant means of execution were described in Chapter 10. They are (1) the communication approach, (2) the people approach, (3) the systems and standards approach, and (4) the service management approach. World-class organizations integrate all four approaches and do it better than competitors do.

Approaches to implementing quality improvement vary greatly and each has a record of successes, outright failures, and hidden failures. The problem is we don't have perfect information about what works in situation A, B or C, and many failures are concealed. But even if we did have perfect information, few situations are identical. Implementation plans must be customized to organization nuances, people capabilities, and marketplace characteristics.

The *Best Practices Report*[12] jointly done by the American Quality Foundation and Ernst & Young is one of the few studies that tries to match improvement initiative do's and don'ts to the current performance and characteristics of the organization. In general, their study provides many useful insights. But you must make sure you fit the general characterizations in the study. If your chosen approach and pace of improvement are too slow or fast, you put the survival of the organization at risk.

The 16-step implementation approach outlined in Table 13–1 is most applicable to business with a modest to high degree of service-, entertainment-, and information-content in their consumer and employee benefit packages. This situation probably includes 70 to 90 percent of the world's consumer and employee benefit packages. So, the opportunity for improvement is gigantic. This 16-step service management approach to implementation is a long-term commitment to the organization's internal and external customers.

V

INTERLINKING

We must move to higher forms of data analysis that model and evaluate multiple performance measures interrelated in complex ways. In the Servomation Age, interlinking is a business necessity.

The Author

Chapter Fourteen

Introduction to Interlinking

A stronomers examine huge volumes of data, sometimes studying the same data many times, in many different ways. Many of their great discoveries were *right before their eyes* but they didn't see them the first time. The second time they used a different paradigm or method of analysis or reconfigured the data a certain way. Business can learn a lot about smart data analysis from astronomers.

In the past, management didn't have timely performance data. But hard technology and electronic networks now give the organization the capability to collect vast amounts of data. Sometimes the data just sits or is only partially analyzed. Timely data reporting is not the same as finding relationships in the data. Soft technology now provides the capability to analyze these data, and find the relationships quickly. The key to building quality and gaining competitive advantage frequently lies *right before your eyes*.

Interlinking was defined in Chapter 1. Typical interlinking questions are:

1. How are operational (internal) and marketing (external) measures of performance related?
2. What are the best (and worst) internal and external measures of performance?
3. Can we predict customer satisfaction based on process/operational performance measures?

Interlinking can be viewed as part of an organization's decision support system. It can enhance management and organizational learning and decision making. Objectives and benefits of interlinking include:

- Screening out weak or misleading performance measures.
- Focusing management attention on key performance measures that do make a difference.
- Helping management predict performance such as customer satisfaction levels.
- Helping management in setting target standards for performance.
- Requiring areas such as marketing and operations to coordinate their data analysis efforts.

- Helping management make wise decisions faster than competitors do.
- Seeing relationships among performance variables that competitors miss.
- Enhancing communication within the organization based on good data analysis and management by fact.

Organizations constantly reposition their resources of people, equipment, know-how, facilities, and network architecture to gain competitive advantage. Smart data analysis methods can help people understand the causal relationships between this huge array of internal and external performance criteria. Managers, employees, and regulators typically confront hundreds of performance measures daily with inadequate analysis as to what measures are important or unimportant. Information-rich service companies such as financial, telecommunication, and transportation services are exploring how to gain competitive advantage by doing interlinking studies.[1]

Collecting *matching* internal and external performance data is itself a challenge. So beware, interlinking studies will create many new requirements on how performance data is collected, organized, analyzed, and used. Marketing, for example, cannot collect customer satisfaction and external performance data in isolation. They must work very closely with all other areas of the organization. Their data must *match up* well with corresponding operational or financial data. Once this capability is established, the power of interlinking becomes a core organizational capability. This smart data analysis capability is a necessity in the service and information (Servomation) Age.

Interlinking also can quantify the cause and effect performance relationships between strategic and tactical decisions. For example, performance at the CBP management level can be linked to external market, financial, and regulatory results, and have strategic implications. Or customer satisfaction measured for specific service encounters can be linked back through the organization to process performance, and have tactical implications. Good interlinking capability can link external performance to CBP management, process management, and service encounter management decisions and performance. Tables 12–1 to 12–3 listed examples of interlinking relationships.

SIMPLE AND COMPLEX INTERLINKING

Chapter 11 defined 16 tools of service/quality measurement and analysis. Our focus here is the last two methods—simple or complex interlinking. As noted in Chapter 11, example methods most appropriate for simple interlinking models include scatter plots, histograms, correlations, gap analysis, parametric statistical tests, nonparametric statistical tests,[2] learning curves, and linear and nonlinear regression models.

Simple interlinking models are usually trying to define the relationship between two performance variables or two-way criteria linkages. This pairwise modeling approach is characterized in Figure 14–1A. Here, the relationship

FIGURE 14–1
Results Caused by Approach

A. Two-way criteria linkages—Simple interlinking

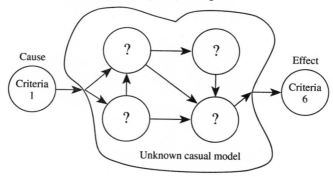

B. Multiple criteria linkages—Complex interlinking

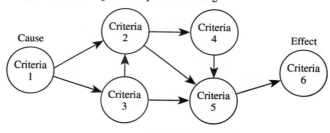

between performance criteria #1 and #6 is modeled and estimated. The number, type, and causal relationships between the four possible intervening variables (shown by the four question marks in Figure 14–1A) are not known. We do not know, for example, exactly why Criterion #6 increases as Criterion #1 decreases.

Complex interlinking models try to define the quantitative relationships among many internal and external performance measures. The key difference between simple and complex interlinking models is how many variables the approach is capable of modeling. Simple interlinking models try to define relationships between no more than two performance variables. Complex interlinking models are capable of modeling performance between more than two variables.

Typical methods of analysis for complex interlinking models include linear and nonlinear programming, path analysis covariance structure,[3] conjoint,[4] econometric,[5] simulation, and factor analysis[6] models. Taguchi methods[7] and design-of-experiments are a subset of complex interlinking methods. Some parts of quality functional deployment and the house of quality approach also can be categorized as simple or complex interlinking. A data envelopment analysis approach to benchmarking, as described in Chapter 11, is also a complex interlinking model.

Complex interlinking tries to define the number, type, and causal relationships among a large set of explanatory performance variables. Therefore, Figure 14–1B hypothesizes a more complex causal (cause and effect) structure denoted by Criteria #1 to #6. Statistical tests help determine the significance of the causal model. If you are fortunate enough to develop a good model, your organization can quantitatively show that *results are caused by approach*. You now know "why" Criterion #6 increases as Criterion #1 decreases. Moreover, you can predict the performance of Criterion #6 based on changes in Criteria #1 to #5. Or you can set the target value of Criterion #6 and work the interlinking model backwards to derive the target operating value for, say, Criterion #3. Smart data analysis becomes the source of competitive advantage.

INTERLINKING SKILL REQUIREMENTS

As noted throughout this book, there is no substitute for an educated and skilled workforce throughout the organization. People do continuous or breakthrough improvement, correct service encounter mistakes on the spot, and design new CBPs. Interlinking is another building block for creating a learning and improving organization. Self-renewal is driven by good data analysis capabilities. Here, we briefly address the people skill requirements of interlinking.

Interlinking can be done on four general levels of expertise. Each level of expertise has its own place in the organization. Some of these quality assessment tools are appropriate for front-line employees while others are appropriate for management, corporate staff, or internal consulting units.

The first level of interlinking is on the front-line where products and services are created and delivered. The first 10 of the 16 tools of service/quality measurement and analysis, listed previously, are appropriate here. This includes methods such as cause-and-effect analysis, line and bar graphs analysis, Pareto analysis, quality improvement teams, and statistical process control analysis. The main advantage of these approaches is they can be understood and implemented by a wide audience. The main disadvantage is that these methods consider only one- and two-way variable relationships. Organizational performance and their processes are seldom accurately described by one- and two-way criteria linkages.

The second level of interlinking expertise uses university bachelor's and master's degree levels of expertise. Skill levels here include all the previous first-level skills plus other more advanced skills. These more advanced skills might include queuing analysis, statistical sampling plans and testing, linear regressions, mathematical programming, and many parametric and nonparametric statistical tests.

The third level of interlinking expertise requires people to major in certain areas of expertise at the bachelor's and master's degree level. University graduates who major in statistics, quality, management science, or engineering fit into this specialized skill category. Here we are talking about all the previous skills but with a more in-depth level of understanding. Other data analysis skills at this level might include multiple linear and nonlinear regressions, queuing analysis, learning curves, simulation, certain experimental designs using analysis of variance statistical tests, and statistical analysis of survey results.

People with this third level of expertise can do interlinking projects using these techniques, train other people, and effectively communicate the results to appropriate audiences. These skills can be found with engineers, on-staff statisticians, specialized MBAs, and other specialists. The advantage of this level of analysis is that more complex performance relationships can be studied. The disadvantage is finding the talented people who can do these types of data analyses well, focus on practical results, and know how to communicate the results in formats everyone can understand.

The fourth level of interlinking expertise uses advanced master's and PhD skills. Techniques at this level might include covariance structure modeling, data envelopment analysis, advanced experimental design methods, econometric modeling, simulation, and conjoint analysis. These approaches can model most consumer or employee benefit packages, and their associated processes and service encounters.

In large organizations, interlinking skills are frequently available in-house. But even in large organizations, the data analysis skills of these talented people are mostly focused on work unit or functional area issues and problems. Interlinking simply asks that some of these data analysis resources be reallocated to determine the relationships between internal and external performance, and focus more on interdisciplinary work.

INTERLINKING AND THE MBNQA

If you were to read and score 10 Malcolm Baldrige National Quality Award (MBNQA) applications you would quickly see how important data definition, collection, and analysis are for world-class performance. The 1993 MBNQA Category 2.0 is on Information and Analysis. Here 75 of 1,000 points are directly related to managing data and information at least as well as you manage your people, equipment, and facility resources.

Although there are many key points in the 1993 MBNQA Category 2.0 on data analysis, consider Item 2.3 on Analysis and Uses of Company-Level Data. Note 3 for Item 2.3 is quoted below:

Analysis appropriate for inclusion in 2.3a could include *relationships* between and among the following: the company's product and service quality improvement and key customer satisfaction indicators such as customer satisfaction, customer retention, and market share; *relationship* between customer relationship management strategies and changes in customer satisfaction, customer retention, and market share; *cross-comparisons* of data from complaints, post-transaction follow-up, and won/lost analyses to identify improvement priorities; *relationship* between employee satisfaction and customer satisfaction; cost/revenue implications of customer-related problems; and *rates of improvement* in customer indicators.[8]

The key words in Note 3 are *relationships* and *rates of improvement*. Interlinking can help determine if these relationships exist in your organization, and if so, the strength of the relationship. If you look closely at Note 3, or the other four notes (not shown here), you see that it also implies interlinking performance between MBNQA Category 6 (Quality and Operational Results) and Category 7 (Customer Focus and Satisfaction).

The MBNQA is based on several core values such as customer-driven quality, continuous improvement, fast response, design quality and prevention, and *management by fact*. World-class data analysis is the basis for achieving these core values and associated performance levels. An organization cannot win the MBNQA without world-class data analysis and management by fact.

Let's now present example results of an interlinking study done for a telecommunication firm. Before we examine these results, let's briefly apply some service management thinking to telephone service.

DEFINING TELEPHONE SERVICE/QUALITY PERFORMANCE

Telephone service is a primary service complemented by peripheral goods and services. The primary service is communication between humans (i.e., talking) or machines (i.e., electronic data flows). Peripheral or facilitating goods include telephone lines and switching machines, monthly telephone bills, telephone repair trucks and equipment, and telephone credit cards. Peripheral services include well-trained telephone customer service representatives who handle a customer problem with knowledge and skill, hot line customer inquiry telephone numbers, polite and technically competent repair persons, and home inside wiring maintenance programs.

The ideas of technical and functional quality first defined by Gronroos[9] are applied here to the telephone repair business. Technical or outcome quality is "what" the customer receives, pays for, experiences, or uses because of interacting with the service delivery system. For telephone repair service, the technical or outcome quality may be that the customer's telephone now works—they can communicate with other people or machines. An automatic system test or a repair person may have to fix the telephone. The customer judges the technical outcome—it works or it does not, the dial tone is loud and clear, the call goes through fast, there is no static on the line, etc.

Process or functional quality is "how" the customer receives, pays for, experiences, or uses the service. This includes all aspects of how the service was delivered to the customer. It includes procedural steps and the style of service. This notion recognizes the service delivery process is at least as important as the service outcome.

For telephone repair service, process quality includes how knowledgeable and polite the customer service representative was to the customer when the customer reported a problem, not missing a scheduled repair visit to the customer's site, steps in the service delivery process, polite and skilled repair persons, and the like. Process quality includes how the process worked and how the people in the process interact. Deficiencies in process quality can negate excellent technical (outcome) quality.

As a telecommunication's analyst with Shearson Lehman Hutton, Inc., remarked, "Service and price have become especially important for users of long-distance services because system (technical) quality among the vendors is evening out." Litel's Marketing Director Thomas S. Kohlbry, Jr., also reinforced these ideas when he said, "You can't get better than fiber optics. Then it becomes a question of customer service." Mr. Warren Ellis, a manager of Online Computer Library Center, Inc., and customer of a major telephone company stated, "For me, service is most important with cost a close second."[10]

As the three example quotes suggest, service/quality performance is frequently cited as the most important performance criterion, closely followed by price. In addition, technical (outcome) quality seems to have reached parity among the major US telecommunications providers, or at least most telephone customers cannot perceive a substantial difference. When technical (outcome) parity exists, process quality is the key to marketplace differentiation and gaining competitive advantage.

THE TELEPHONE REPAIR SERVICE DATABASE

The data used in this study covers a period in the late 1980s for one telephone provider. The proprietary nature of the data requires that the telephone company remain anonymous, as well as the key results. The medley of telephone repair performance measures reflects the company's response to regulators over the years and management's desire *not to miss anything*. The result is information overload for management and regulators, without a comprehensive framework for performance analysis. Historically, financial performance in the telecommunications industry dominated all other performance categories, with certain thresholds of performance for other customer service related measures. Today, customer service and price have become the top two competitive priorities.

Many duplicate or worthless performance measures also become established in the company and regulator's systems. The data analysis challenge is to sort out measures that are useful for management decision making and discard poor or outdated measures.

SIMPLE INTERLINKING MODELS (TWO-WAY CRITERIA LINKAGES)

How is one variable related to another variable? Preliminary data analysis on this question resulted in many interesting findings for the telephone company. The results presented are not necessarily the best relationships found but do show the idea of interlinking models.

Repair Service Performance and Company Operating Revenue

Telephone repair service performance is measured internally by "the percent of total trouble reports received before 5 PM, classified as out-of-service, and not fixed until the following day or later (percent out-of-service)." How is percent out-of-service related to company financial performance?

Figure 14–2 shows an example of how percent out-of-service is related to company operating revenue. The correlation coefficient is minus (–) 0.468. Therefore, as percent out-of-service increases, operating revenue decreases. Better telephone repair service generates more revenue for this telephone company. Figure 14–2 is similar to the modeling situation of Figure 14–1A.

Figure 14–2 is an excellent way for managers to visualize the correlation between variables. The correlation between any two pair of variables is seen by the collapsing of the enlongated ellipse along the diagonal axis. If the ellipse is somewhat round and is not diagonally oriented, the variables are uncorrelated. The direction of the ellipse reflects either a positive or negative correlation. The modeling challenge, of course, is to move to higher levels of analysis. Our goal is to develop a set of causal relationships, similar to Figure 14–1B, that predict the company's operating revenue based on operational performance.

Repair Service Performance—A Multiple Criteria View

Knowing which operational or internal service/quality measures track other performance measures well and which do not is of value to the management decision-making process. This benefit of interlinking is often considered the most important by practicing managers. There is great risk if management or regulators concentrate on the wrong performance indicator, as some do. Resources can be misallocated and the very goals everyone is trying to achieve may be hindered by using misleading performance criteria.

FIGURE 14–2

Company Operating Revenue and Percent of Telephones Out of Service

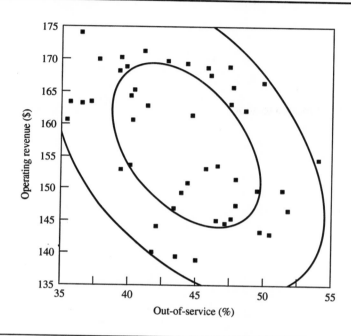

Consider the service/quality relationship diagram shown in Figure 14–3. It shows how percent out-of-service is related to other internal and external performance measures. Definitions of each of these other performance measures are not presented here to save space. In Figure 14–3, the number of complaints to higher management, residence and business customer satisfaction, and the state regulatory rating all focus on external organizational performance. Special services maintenance, repair hours per access line, customer service expense, and plant-specific wages per access line are internal measures of performance.

Any performance measure inside the inner circle is negatively correlated with percent out-of-service. Any performance measure between the inner and outer circles is positively correlated with out-of-service percentage. The center of the circles represents a negative correlation of −1.0, while any performance measure on the boundary of the outer circle is a positive correlation of +1.0. The key at the bottom of Figure 14–3 helps define these relationships.

External performance, as measured by residence and business customer satisfaction ratings is negatively correlated with percent out-of-service in Figure

FIGURE 14–3

Relationship of Percent of Telephones Out of Service to Other Performance Measures

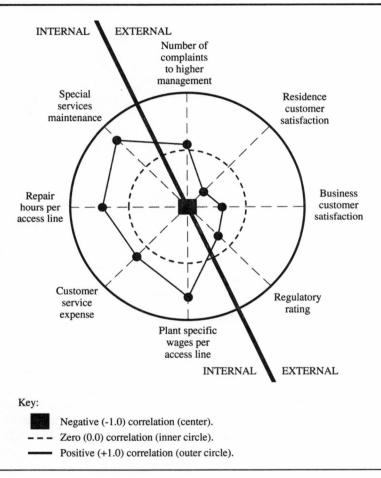

Key:

■ Negative (-1.0) correlation (center).

– – – Zero (0.0) correlation (inner circle).

—— Positive (+1.0) correlation (outer circle).

14–3. The correlation between percent out-of-service and residential customer satisfaction ratings is −0.68; with business customer satisfaction ratings it is −0.41. The regulatory rating, another external measure of performance, is also negatively correlated with percent out-of-service, with a coefficient of −0.24. As percent out-of-service increases, the regulatory rating gets worse (decreases). Finally, the correlation between the number of complaints to higher management and percent out-of-service is +0.13. Here, internal operational performance (percent out-of-service) does not seem strongly related to the company's customer complaint system.

Some of these relationships are strong while others are not. In all cases the data analysis does support the logical direction of the relationship between these pairs of variables. It does give management some hard evidence and simple insights into the relationship between decision variables. Management by fact begins to take its place in the management of the company.

Internal service/quality performance is measured by percent out-of-service and special services maintenance. The correlation between these two operational performance measures is $+0.66$. Variable costs are tracked by customer service expense and plant-specific wages per access line. The correlation between percent out-of-service and customer service expense is $+0.29$ and plant specific wages is $+0.62$. Poor repair service performance seems to be costing this company money. And, capacity measured in repair hours per telephone access line, a surrogate measure for costs, is also positively correlated with percent out-of-service. The correlation coefficient is $+0.43$. Each simple correlation shown in Figure 14–3 is backed up with other statistical analysis and models.

The important point is that this type of data analysis requires management to think about and try to explain what the data analysis shows. Sometimes the management discussion disregards the results of the data analysis, but other times new insights are gained. Interlinking focuses management's attention on improving performance measurement systems, a cornerstone of any world-class service/quality improvement effort. Companies are only beginning to interlink performance measures from diverse parts of the firm, such as engineering, marketing, operations, training, and finance.

COMPLEX INTERLINKING MODELS

Complex interlinking models can describe the cause and effect relationships among a set of variables. Statistical tests can determine the validity of the hypothesized model. The four-variable interlinking model presented in Figure 14–4 is relatively naive and it ignores many key intervening relationships. But it does illustrate the general notion of modeling complex cause-and-effect networks, which is our purpose here. If the order of the cause-and-effect relationships are important (i.e., the arrows are undirectional) among these four variables, then there are 12 ways to structure the relationship between any two performance variables. The chance that you will miss a key relationship or ignore a direct or indirect relationship is high. But the simple cause-and-effect relationships shown in Figure 14–4 capture some simple truths about how things are related. Complex interlinking takes advantage of process flow structures and managerial insights into how things are related.

Figure 14–4 is a diagram of a simple hypothesized causal model. Note the direct and indirect ways (paths) to influence customer satisfaction shown in Figure 14–4. By using various statistical tests we can determine how well the actual performance data fits this causal model. The complex interlinking model

FIGURE 14–4
Four-Variable Cause-and-Effect Interlinking Model for Telephone Repair
Service

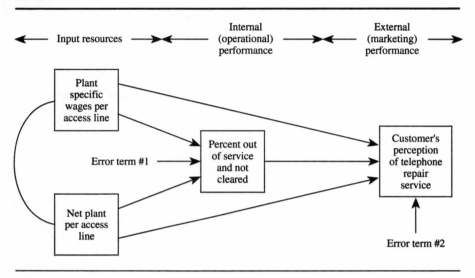

describing the relationships denoted by Figure 14–4 can be written in word form
as shown by Equations 1 and 2.

Percent out-of-service $= a$(Plant-specific wages per access line)   [1]
$\qquad\qquad\qquad + \, b$(Net plant per access line)
$\qquad\qquad\qquad + \,$ Error term #1

Customer satisfaction $= c$(Plant-specific wages per access line)   [2]
$\qquad\qquad\qquad + \, d$(Net plant per Access line)
$\qquad\qquad\qquad + \, e$(Percent out-of-service)
$\qquad\qquad\qquad + \,$ Error term #2

Statistical methods can estimate the model parameters *a* to *e* and *error terms*,
and overall model performance and fit. The causal relationships shown in Figure
14–4 accounted for 50.4 percent of the variance in the customer's perception
(satisfaction) of telephone repair service performance. Statistically, the model is
sound though we would like to explain a higher percent of the variance in residence customer satisfaction ratings. Also, alternative models not yet hypothesized might do better or worse than the model shown here.

The estimates of model parameters using Equations 1 and 2 can be placed on a
manager's personal computer and electronic spreadsheet. Many ''what if'' analyses can be done using these equations. For example, how much would percent
out-of-service have to improve (decrease) for customer satisfaction to improve

(increase) to 94 percent? The answer is percent out-of-service must improve (decrease) to 37.4 percent from a current mean performance of 44.3 percent.

The naive causal model described in Figure 14–4 and Equations 1 and 2 are based on a four-variable cause-and-effect model. We know that many intervening variables and relationships are left out of the model described by Figure 14–4 and Equations 1 and 2. Also, the naive model explains only 50.4 percent of the variance in customer satisfaction. Clearly, a more detailed, comprehensive, and statistically significant model is desirable. But the model helps demonstrate the basics of a causal modeling approach.

The four-variable interlinking model in Figure 14–4 is the beginning of a decision support system for improving customer satisfaction based on smart data analysis methods. Even in this simple example we are beginning to model a service process and define relationships between internal and external performance measures.

CONCLUSION

Data is analogous to blood and nerves in the human body. If blood and nerves are isolated and stand alone, they do little good. But the circulation and nervous systems of the human body interlinks these biological components into a complex network with the human brain as the central processor. It is only when smart data analysis occurs that data is turned into information, and becomes the basis for action.

Humankind created organizations and the information systems that drive them. Humankind also has the power to upgrade the data analysis skills of the organization and integrate this information into the decision making processes. Interlinking can make a contribution here by quantifying relationships, turning data into information-intelligence, and helping people set priorities and allocate resources wisely. Interlinking becomes a part of an organization's decision support system—its central processor.

Interlinking helps the organization learn, and the wiser its decisions are, the more capable the organization is in gaining competitive advantage. Data and its analysis must be managed at least as well as the organization manages its people, equipment and facilities. Many barriers must be overcome to install a successful interlinking program. Resistance to change did not vanish with the onset of total quality management, or interlinking, or continuous improvement initiatives.

But in the Servomation Age where information-intelligence is king, part of the Service/Quality Solution is to use information better than competitors do to allocate resources wisely and build market share and grow profits. You really have no choice—either become good at interlinking or your interlinking-driven competitor will eventually drive you out of business. It is not enough anymore to just collect mountains of data and do one variable analysis at a time or a few two-way criteria comparisons. In the Servomation Age, you must be able to model complex performance relationships, and take action based on the relationships you find.

Chapter Fifteen

Interlinking: Service/Quality Process Maps

S ervice/quality management is a key factor in gaining competitive advantage in the marketplace. For example, one survey found that one of every five customers had switched some of their financial service business from one provider to another during the past year.[1] Also, the desire to get better service ranked first, ahead of higher rates, increased convenience of location, lower fees, and changes in residence. Another study concluded that "service, service, and more service" is the most critical element of marketplace success in the 1990s."[2] But how is service or customer satisfaction related to process performance? Where in the service process is overachievement unnecessary? These are the type of questions a service/quality process map[3] can help answer.

A service/quality process map (S/QPM) is a complex interlinking model. There are many other types of complex interlinking models, as previously described. The interlinking example used in this chapter concentrates on defining the relationships between customer satisfaction (external) and process (internal) performance. Its focus is on interlinking marketing-based and operations-based performance data for a bank's credit card processing center. Other service/quality process maps, for example, can interlink training costs to operational (process) performance. As described in Chapter 3, the Malcolm Baldrige National Quality Award identifies many other types of performance relationships that help people manage their business.

Most marketing and operation functions in the same organization go about defining and evaluating service/quality performance "their way." These two diverse sets of service/quality data seldom are coordinated and comparable. The marketing function evaluates the customer's perception of service/quality performance via external measurement techniques, such as customer surveys, interviews, focus groups, and comment cards. The corresponding operations function evaluates service/quality performance based on many internal (in-house) standards of performance, such as average item (customer) processing time, error rates, conformance to script dialogues, number of things processed (checks, rooms cleaned, customers, etc.) per unit of time, average wait/response time, etc.

Marketing and operations managers' interpretation of what the data means are frequently in disagreement. This management problem contributes to extra meetings, poor decision making or inaction, and encourages each functional area to protect their interests. This adverse behavior ultimately affects organizational capability, customer retention, market share and profitability.

Another complication of developing internal and external performance systems is, "Who is (are) the customer(s)?" For example, a hospital has many customers—the patient and his or her family, the physicians, third party payers, hospital employees, and the community the hospital services. Thus, the performance of a hospital process can have several ultimate customers. External surveys for each customer category must be quantitatively linked to the performance of a single process. Complex interlinking models can handle this degree of complexity. Of course, much restructuring of survey designs and procedures, and internal performance measurement systems must take place before interlinking can begin.

The chapter begins by defining a service/quality process map. Next, descriptive statistics for a credit card processing center that provide insights into marketing and operations service/quality performance are presented. Then a complex interlinking model is described for this credit card processing center, and we explore what is possible using a service/quality process map approach. Finally, suggestions are made for collecting, coordinating, and evaluating service/quality data using the service/quality process map approach.

WHAT IS A SERVICE/QUALITY PROCESS MAP?

A service/quality process map exhibits the following characteristics:

1. It combines the insights of flowcharting the process, a popular improvement tool, with the power of interlinking data analysis techniques.

2. It recognizes that "the process is often the service" for many organizations.

3. It defines (and connects in a network) quantitatively the causal relationships between internal and external performance measures.

4. It is organization- and process-specific.

5. It is capable of modeling goods-producing or service-providing processes, and business-to-ultimate-customer or business-to-business processes and performance,

6. One service/quality process map can be a subset of a more comprehensive service/quality process map.

7. It must be statistically valid and, therefore, have reasonable capability to make predictions and define key relationships between performance variables.

Figure 15–1 presents a flowchart of the customer service function for one large credit card processing center. The network of relationships documented in Figure 15–1 identifies the major causal relationships between (1) operations (internal) service/quality performance measures denoted with an "*o*" subscript, (2) marketing (customer's evaluation via surveys) service/quality performance measures denoted with a "*m*" subscript, and (3) hypothesized *links* between operations and marketing's service/quality performance relationships. The service process and its cause and effect relationships are stable and duplicate process flows. The process is interlinked to the market-based performance criteria by the two hypothesized links shown in Figure 15–1.

Please note that Figure 15–1 is a flowchart of the process and how management thinks process performance is related to customer satisfaction. It is not a service/quality process map yet. To be a service/quality process map, the performance data must support the validity of the hypothesized causal model based on statistical testing. If the statistical tests show that no significant relationships exist then, the model is not a service/quality process map. To be called a service/quality process map, the model must be statistically valid.

Actual performance data is used to estimate interlinking model parameters and the strength of the overall model using various statistical techniques. An example that uses the network defined by Figure 15–1 will be presented later in this chapter.

The primary objective in developing a service/quality process map for this bank's credit card system is to:

1. Quantitatively define how customer satisfaction relates to process performance.

Other general objectives of service/quality process maps are to:

2. Motivate marketing and operations managers to define service/quality for each service they provide on a comparable basis.
3. Formalize numerically how well the marketing and operations service/quality performance data match up and, therefore, reduce the subjective judgments of the meaning of these two sets of service/quality data.
4. Add a new idea and supporting data analysis technique to the repertoire of traditional quality tools and methods, especially for service processes.
5. Encourage management to coordinate and integrate the marketing and operations functions.

Ultimately, interlinking models and development efforts can help managers reduce costs, retain customers, and increase customer satisfaction, market share, gross margins, and profits. Improved service/quality performance works on both the revenue and cost sides of the profit equation. Other studies have documented the causal relationships between improved service/quality performance and market share, profits, and so on.[4]

FIGURE 15–1
Interlinking Customer Satisfaction and Process Service/Quality Performance

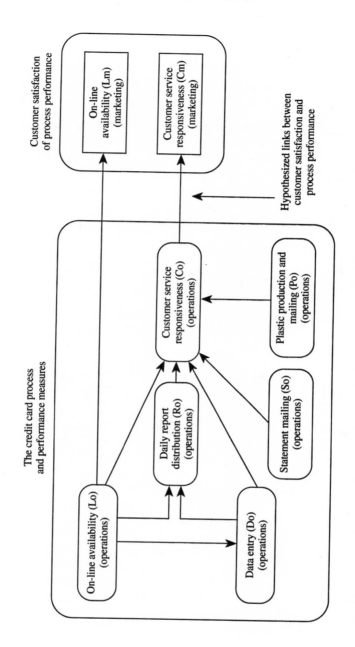

A few words of caution concerning service/quality process maps are necessary. Developing service/quality process maps include these potential problems:

- They assume marketing customer survey questions are an accurate measure of service/quality performance from the customer's perspective, and operations in-house service/quality related statistics accurately measure how well the service delivery process performed.
- They are myopic models based on historical relationships and may ignore a "new or hidden" variable as conditions change.
- Actual marketing and operations service/quality performance data may not "fit the model" based on statistical analyses.
- Differences in sample size, and timing of marketing versus operations data, can eliminate the possibility of doing a service/quality process map or reduce the statistical validity of the final model(s).
- Development of these maps requires that diverse functions and work units cooperate closely, which may be atypical of current practices.

A STUDY OF SERVICE/QUALITY PERFORMANCE FOR A CREDIT CARD PROCESSING CENTER

The credit card division of a major bank provided marketing and operations data for this study. The source of the marketing data was customer surveys that were done frequently and electronically. Figure 15–1 depicts part of their credit card delivery process. The analysis of the credit card processing center's service/quality performance begins by addressing the nature of the marketing and operations data they provided. The data comes close to meeting the ideal criteria (to be discussed later) of service/quality performance data.

The service/quality data available from this credit card processing center was complete. First, customer survey questions and scores could be matched with operations performance statistics. The center's managers were well aware of the potential power and usefulness of comparable internal and external performance data. These data were available for years 1985 to 1987, resulting in 36 observations per criterion. (The author's "A Service Quality Map for Credit Card Processing" provides a detailed discussion of the appropriate sample size, given the nature of the interlinking model and other preliminary data screening and testing methods.) Finally, because of the electronic survey method used to administer the customer survey data, there was no need to lag any of the variables in Figure 15–1.

Insights Gained by Basic Descriptive Statistics

One important measure of service/quality performance for an organization that processes credit cards is on-line availability. Customers either call the credit card processing center to ask about the status of various accounts, or retail/corporate customers have direct lines to the center's computer for immediate electronic inquiry. In both cases, on-line system availability (denoted by L_o and L_m in Figure 15–1) is critical to providing excellent service. The operation's function measured on-line availability (L_o) as the percent of total prime-time hours the system was available for customer use and inquiries. The customer service department also administered a customer survey that contained a question concerning on-line availability (L_m).

Descriptive statistics about on-line availability are summarized in Table 15–1. For example, when the operations function measures on-line availability with a 99.7 percent score, the customer also perceived the excellent service and responded with its highest average rating of 97 points. The customer's reaction to lesser degrees of service was immediate and followed the operations-based statistics as shown by the positive 0.715 correlation factor. Other statistical tests support the significance of these results. Even these simple statistics take much of the human interpretation of data out of evaluating service/quality performance from these two diverse sources.

Managers recognized intuitively that on-line availability was an important service/quality performance measure to the customer. More importantly, this analysis supported their notion with facts and allowed them to define the relationship through simple regressions, graphs, and statistics. Knowing these relationships became a powerful tool to help them justify process improvements.

What accounts for the gap or difference in the average of on-line availability in Table 15–1 as measured by operations (98.6 percent) versus the customer's perception of on-line availability (84.4 percent)? The answer to this question can be found in the customer surveys and human behavior. When customers experienced customer service problems because the credit card processing center's computer network was "down" during the reporting period, they would rate on-line availability performance at 60 to 80 percent, though they received much higher average on-line availability. For example, one bad experience—a disruption in on-line availability lasting minutes during the reporting period—resulted in a disproportionate (negative) jump in the customers' perception of service. The ratio of the coefficient of variation (standard deviation/mean performance) for the marketing versus operations data reveals that the customer's perception of on-line availability (L_m) was 12.9 times more variable than operational performance (L_o). One lesson for management from this basic analysis is the importance of perfect (100 percent) on-line availability from the customer's perspective. Customers did not want the system to be down at any time, and when it was, they quickly rated performance much lower.

Operations measured the responsiveness of customer service (C_o) with a mean of 84.1 as shown in Table 15–1, while the corresponding customers' marketing survey rating (C_m) was 83.6. Why no difference (gap) between these two measures (C_o and C_m) of service/quality performance? The customer service responsiveness measure reflects a variety of activities such as handling customer complaints, responding and writing letters, and special requests. The 84 percent performance level means that 84 percent of customer inquiries were handled sat-

TABLE 15–1
Basic Statistics on On-Line Availability and Customer Service Responsiveness Performance for a Credit Card Processing Center

On-Line Availability	Minimum	Maximum	Mean	Standard Deviation
Operations (L_o)	96.4%	99.7%	98.6%	0.95%
Marketing (L_m)	60	97	84.4	10.5

Correlation coefficient between marketing (L_m) and operations (L_o) data = +0.715.

Customer Service Responsiveness	Minimum	Maximum	Mean	Standard Deviation
Operations (C_o)	68%	97%	84.1%	7.5%
Marketing (C_m)	56	95	83.6	10.6

Correlation coefficient between marketing (C_m) and operations (C_o) data = +0.838.

isfactorily within a three day standard time. With a variety of tasks to do each month, the marketing (C_m) and operations measures of customer service responsiveness (C_o) tend to converge. The ratio of the coefficient of variation (standard deviation/mean performance) for the marketing versus operations data reveals that the customer's perception of customer service responsiveness (C_m) was 1.4 times more variable than operational performance (C_o). The correlation coefficient between C_o and C_m was +0.838.

The credit card processing center's internal measure of customer service responsiveness (C_o) was a close reflection of how the customer perceived service/quality performance (C_m). Here, internal performance (C_o) is a good predictor of external performance (C_m). Managers who focus at doing better on this internal performance criterion (C_o) were also emphasizing what's important to the customer (C_m).

Much can be learned about service/quality performance from these basic statistical comparisons. However, the relationships among all the variables in Figure 15–1 are still not understood. A service/quality process map must be developed and statistically validated to help us understand these relationships.

A Service/Quality Process Map Example

The basic question we are addressing is as follows: Does the service/quality performance data support the cause-and-effect structure as defined by Figure 15–1?'' The four structural equations that characterize the causal relationships of Figure 15–1 are as follows:

Data entry (D_o)	$= a(L_o) +$ Error term #1	[1]
Daily report distribution (R_o)	$= b(D_o) + c(L_o) +$ Error term #2	[2]
Customer service responsiveness (C_o)	$= d(D_o) + e(R_o) + f(L_o) + g(S_o) + h(P_o)$ $+$ Error term #3	[3]
Customer service responsiveness (C_m)	$= i(C_o) +$ error Term #4	[4]

where:

D_o is data entry performance

L_o is on-line availability performance

R_o is daily report distribution performance

S_o is statement mailing performance

P_o is plastic production and mailing performance

C_o is customer service responsiveness as measured internally by the operations function

C_m is customer satisfaction of credit card process performance as measured externally by marketing customer surveys

Examine the logic of Equations 1 to 4 and relate them to the relationships (arrows) shown in Figure 15–1. At this point in the service/quality process map development effort, there is a network of the relationships between operations- and marketing-based service/quality performance criteria. The operational relationships are moderately stable since they are a function of the service process and change only if the process changes. These relationships also tend to mimic the process flow and thus are often predictable and recursive. The links between operations- and marketing-based criteria correspond closely to how management thinks they are related. These marketing-operation links (i.e., C_o to C_m and L_o to L_m in Figure 15–1) represent the hypothesized feature(s) of the service/quality process map.

Overall model performance statistics for the causal relationships documented by Figure 15–1 were developed. Estimates of model parameters, a to i and the four error terms, were computed using interlinking techniques.[5] Based on statistical tests, the interlinking model in Figure 15–1 and defined by Equations 1 to 4 is a plausible model.

The overall model's coefficient of determination of 0.64 also shows that the strength of the relationships was adequate. The model's coefficient of determination is a measure of the strength of all model causal relationships jointly. If the interlinking model defined here was a perfect predictor of customer satisfaction (C_m), the overall model's coefficient of determination would be 1.0.

S/QPM as a Basis for an Expert System for Service/Quality Management

The final interlinking model describes the credit card service delivery process and relates its performance to the customer's evaluation of service/quality. This is the essence of a service/quality process map. The structural equations for these models can be placed in an electronic spreadsheet model for use on a manager's personal computer.

For example, consider the management decision as to where to gain the most improvement in the customer's perception of customer service responsiveness (C_m in Figure 15–1) for two alternative projects, each costing \$50,000. Project A provides the main computers with a more reliable backup electrical power source in cases of temporary disruptions in power and more backup computer systems and procedures. Project A is expected to increase on-line availability (L_o in Figure 15–1) by 1 percent (or 1.01 average on-line availability). Project B improves the systems, procedures, and training of personnel responsible for plastic production and mailing (P_o) in Figure 15–1. Project B is expected to improve operational performance by 3 percent (or 1.03 average plastic production and mailing performance).

Using Equations 1 to 4 in an electronic spreadsheet, the interlinking model predicts that the \$50,000 is best spent by improving on-line availability (L_o). That is, C_m will increase by 5.5 points on a 0 to 100 point customer survey scale if Project A is done. For Project B, C_m is predicted to increase by only 1.5 points.

This example illustrates the power of service/quality process maps to aid management decision making. For this example, the following "what if" question was answered. Where in the operation process can we get the most improvement (benefit) with respect to customer satisfaction for the same cost? The answer is Project A.

SUGGESTIONS FOR THE DEVELOPMENT OF A SERVICE/QUALITY PROCESS MAP

All work units involved in an interlinking study should simultaneously do the following 10 steps when developing a service/quality process map. The most practical benefit of developing a service/quality process map is usually to get the different departments and functions to coordinate their efforts. When an interlinking model is developed many benefits of interlinking have already been attained.

The *first step* is to define service/quality and service/quality performance goals for the entire organization and for each consumer or employee benefit package provided by the organization. The *second step* is to define each consumer benefit package the organization provides and clearly determine its attributes. These attributes form the basis for internal (operations-based) and external (marketing-based) measures of service/quality performance. A *third step* requires measuring each attribute as accurately as possible by using wise choices of criteria, measurement scales, data collection techniques, and customer survey designs. In practice, most marketing and operations service/quality collection and evaluation efforts are independent projects.

Once the consumer benefit package is clearly defined and its attributes accurately measured (step three), management must define these service/quality measures in *comparable ways* for both the marketing (external) and operations (internal) measurement systems (step four). The service/quality performance questions (and criteria) from the marketing surveys must correspond closely with the operations service/quality performance statistics. Another way these data must *match up* is ensuring they are over the same planning horizon and time periods.

The *fifth step* is to determine the number of observations. The objective here is to ensure a large enough sample size to result in at least robust estimates of interlinking model parameters. This is a major obstacle when the marketing surveys are administered less frequently than the operations data collection period. The solution here is to change what and how marketing collects performance data. It must match up well with process performance data. If it does, the power of interlinking can help the organization achieve performance goals far beyond modeling performance within a single functional area. Also, since a service/quality process map is organization- and process-specific, only data from that company can be used and this limits sample sizes.

Step six is to flowchart the service process, noting all points in the process where operations-based performance statistics are collected regularly. This step recognizes that "the process is the service" for most service-providing organizations. The *seventh step* is to ask managers how they think the service delivery process relates to external performance measures such as revenues or customer satisfaction. The objective here is to gain management consensus about what operational activities affect the customer's perception of service—that is, how process performance (i.e., the operational network of activities) is connected to specific questions on the customer survey.

Step eight is to select the appropriate interlinking data analysis technique(s) based on the nature of the network and data. In this step, we determine how well or poorly the data fits the hypothesized model. If the model and its equations are deemed a good model based on statistical analyses, the model becomes a service/quality process map.

Also, the model's structural equations can be placed in an electronic spreadsheet model for use by managers on their personal computers. Many interesting "what if" questions can be asked, such as:

1. Where in the process can we obtain the most improvement (benefit) with respect to customer satisfaction for the least cost?

2. What will happen to customer satisfaction if process performance on criterion X deteriorates by Y percent?

3. Where in the service delivery process is overachievement of service/quality unnecessary?

4. Can we tie a manager's performance appraisal into downstream departments' performance?

5. Can we improve customer survey design based on the insights gained from a service/quality process map analysis?

6. What standards of service/quality performance make the most sense?

7. What is the relative importance of key operational activities from the customer's viewpoint?

The *ninth step* in the development of a service/quality process map is to use the predictive capabilities of the map (model) to help management allocate resources to gain the most benefit, in terms of improved customers' perceptions, for each dollar spent. In this way, a firm can gain competitive advantage by using service/quality as a competitive weapon.

The *final step* is to continually work to improve service/quality process map procedures and models. In most cases, organizations do not collect internal and external performance data that match up well by time period and by type of questions and criteria used. But those data collection habits can be changed. Until these data match up better, few organizations can do internal versus external gap analysis or interlinking.

Interlinking models show you what is possible by better data collection and analysis procedures. And the scary part is that some organizations are developing interlinking ideas and methods now. It could be your competitor!

Envision a service/quality performance evaluation system that electronically surveys customers frequently and uses this information and internal process (operational) performance to build a service/quality process map every week or month. The revised model aids management decision making. The final interlinking model equations, such as Equations 1 to 4 here, are loaded automatically into a manager's Lotus or Excel personal computer spreadsheet. "What if" questions like the seven example questions given here are posed often in this *interlinking-driven organization*. Interlinking models are now a part of the organization's decision support system.

Organizations have control of the nature of and the methods by which they collect operational data and marketing survey information. Thus, the responsibility for improving and coordinating the quality of their performance data falls on the organization itself. Once these data are coordinated, basic statistical analyses, gap analysis and the service/quality process map provide alternative tools of analysis. The data and models shown here are not perfect but they demonstrate what can be accomplished once better data are available. Example issues about building an organization's interlinking capabilities are outlined in Table 15–2.

TABLE 15–2
Interlinking Action-Starter Questions

1. When is good, good enough? When is bad, bad enough? How do you know when the organization is over- or under-promising and over- or under-providing per consumer benefit package? How can interlinking help answer these questions?

2. What is the dollar value of a loyal customer for each key consumer benefit package in your organization? What service encounters result in the most service upsets per service process? What is the cost per service upset? How can interlinking help answer these questions?

3. Define the organization's plans to build its interlinking data analysis capabilities and use it as a key way to gain competitive advantage at the consumer benefit package, process, and service encounter levels.

4. How many of the 16 tools of service/quality measurement and analysis (Chapter 11) is your organization using? How many should it be using? Where? What plans does your organization have to acquire and train people to do a better job of data analysis at all levels of the organization?

5. To what degree does your organization rely on reactive versus proactive approaches for service/quality measurement, control, and evaluation? What reactive and proactive approaches should (could) you be using?

6. What does it mean to "empower employees in your organization"? What is the role of timely and smart data analysis?

CONCLUSION

Service/quality process maps provide the manager with a visual road map of how excellent service/quality is created and delivered, and is seen through the eyes of the customer. This conceptual map is supported by equations and parameter estimates that define the relationships between many performance criteria. These interlinking ideas try to define the vision of what is possible, and the tools to do the job. Service/quality process maps, described in this chapter, tie the performance of the marketing and operations functions together; but other functions, processes, and cost centers can be interlinked. Management by fact begins to take its rightful place in the Servomation Age.

Service/quality process maps give services and service processes a new tool capable of modeling complex processes and performance relationships. Services and service processes are in need of new modeling approaches if their performance is to be improved. This interlinking and map approach takes advantage of process flowchart knowledge and uses it as a basis for modeling. Service/quality process maps and a data envelopment analysis approach to benchmarking may eventually be to service processes what the original statistical quality control models were to manufacturing organizations. Service processes need better ways to model their performance, and these two data analysis tools can help fill this need. More development efforts are needed, but the basic ideas and methods are established.

All the hardware, software, and knowledge necessary to build a service/quality process map and an interlinked decision-support system exist today in many information-intensive industries. Customers can be electronically surveyed and these data matched up to process performance data. Process flowcharting is a popular tool in business. Methods to do complex interlinking exist and are ready for the challenge. It is now a matter of management commitment—to make it happen. Interlinking is part of the Service/Quality Solution.

THE SERVICE ENCOUNTER

"We cannot direct the wind . . . But we can adjust the sails."

Unknown

Chapter Sixteen

Service Encounter Management

W inning or losing the service/quality challenge depends on design expertise and execution capabilities. Consumer benefit package and service delivery system design define the infrastructure for acting out service encounters. Given a well-designed structure, people's behavior, decisions, and skills are the other major ingredients of executing world-class service encounters.

Design is the rigid (structural) part of the service encounter playing field. It does not change in the short term. Service-provider skills are the fluid (behavioral) part of the service encounter. These human skills are critical in creating value and consistently making customers happy. Determining the right combination of the rigid and fluid parts of the service delivery system is where the art and science of service management meet. It is a challenge to get it right!

Service encounters include a vast number of structural, technical, and behavioral requirements. If you could define every requirement and knew how to model it, it would take a super computer to solve it at the service encounter level. The computer solution would have to be instantaneous, and resolved as new information became available. Process procedures, service recovery actions, and a host of behaviors would have to be programmed into the software logic. The issue here is what employee behaviors increase sales? Even Commander Data of Star Trek fame could not duplicate every ideal human behavior. Yet, we ask frontstage people every day to execute thousands of complex service encounters. Only a handful of world-class organizations have mastered the mix of rigid and fluid resources that creates and delivers world-class service encounters.

Everything in the organization, as shown earlier in Figures 2–3 and 2–4, including the Chief Executive Officer, exists to support service encounter execution. As Mr. C. Lee Johnson, President of The Limited Distribution Services, said, "The Limited's distribution theory of success is: think small. Think small, because no one today is able to think large enough. Think small enough, however, to serve one customer on any one day, one item that he or she wants, and a company is able to serve all customers. If it can't serve one, it can't serve any."[1]

A service encounter was defined in Chapter 2 as one or more moments of truth. *Service Encounter Management* involves the design and management of service encounters. It concentrates on the third and lowest level in the service management organizational hierarchy as shown by Figure 8–2. There, strategies and plans are executed to create service encounters between service providers and customers. Strategies and plans by themselves accomplish nothing, whereas service encounters create consumer and employee benefit packages. These consumer and employee benefit packages create value in the marketplace and generate sales and profits for the firm.

This chapter begins by examining service encounters in the luxury versus super-budget US lodging industry. Then we embark on a mental trip to see what it might be like to buy celery in the Servomation Age. The Servomation Age is when the information-, entertainment-, and service-content of the consumer benefit package dominates goods-content. It is a convergence of the Service Revolution and the Information Age with the remnants of the Industrial Age. The chapter ends by summarizing and recommending 18 solutions to the service/quality challenge(s).

SERVICE ENCOUNTERS AT LUXURY AND SUPER-BUDGET HOTELS

Consider the range of service encounters, for example, in the US lodging industry segmented into, say, six categories:

1. Luxury hotels at premium prices, such as the Four Seasons and the Ritz-Carlton.
2. Deluxe hotels at high prices such as Omni and Hyatt.
3. Upscale hotels at moderate prices such as Hilton and Embassy Suites.
4. Hotels at moderate to low prices such as Marriott Courtyard and Ramada Inns.
5. Budget hotels at low prices such as Cross Country Inns and LaQuinta Inns.
6. Super-budget hotels such as Motel 6 and Econo Lodge.

What are service encounters like at the high and low ends of the US lodging industry? Luxury hotels create and deliver very specialized and personal service encounters. Peripheral service- and information-content are bundled to the core service, which is a clean and safe place to sleep. The luxury hotel is designed to be convenient, with intimate places for conversation, comfortable lobby chairs, and elegant restaurants and lounges. The physical hotel design features are the rigid part of the service delivery system. They support many fluid consumer benefit package attributes such as a guest's need for security, privacy, and an intimate place in which to talk.

Job design is another part of service encounter excellence. The training program for luxury hotel telephone operators, for example, includes a segment on being upbeat and responding to customer requests by saying "certainly" and "at your convenience." Operators are also instructed to protect the privacy of their VIP guests. Employee recruiting also differs for the luxury hotel segment. People are screened for caring, personal and service-oriented behavior attributes. Communication skills, manners, appearance, and willingness to serve luxury hotel guests are part of the hiring criteria.

Luxury hotel service providers are trained to anticipate hotel guests needs and wants even before the guest asks for such service. Every effort is made to remember the guest's name. Guest recognition is given high priority in information system design, employee reward and recognition programs, and employee empowerment training. The rigid part of the service system supports a proactive approach for the fluid part of the system. Some luxury and deluxe hotels keep an automated guest profile of past hotel stays. Guest preferences are documented, such as Mr. Thomas likes white chocolate chip cookies left on the bed at evening turn-down service.

All luxury hotel service providers have immediate access to each guest's profile through a computer network. Here the hotel's guest information system supports the memory of service providers to help them deliver highly personalized service. The guest information profile system increases service-provider behavior capabilities—nothing is left to chance.

Employee empowerment at a luxury hotel takes many forms, such as "whoever receives a customer complaint, owns the complaint until it is resolved, and the customer is delighted with the actions taken by the employee." The employee, and others who may need to help, are authorized to stop whatever they are doing to resolve the customer complaint. Employee empowerment at the service encounter level is part of a service/quality/time-based competitive strategy for the luxury hotel. After the complaint is resolved, a *service encounter upset report* is filed in the hotel's guest information system. This report also is maintained in the guest's profile records. This type of guest profile information is immediately accessible to all hotels in the luxury hotel chain.

Service/quality standards for the rigid part of the luxury hotel's service delivery system can be clearly specified and audited. The standards of performance for the fluid parts of the service encounter are more difficult to define, measure, and evaluate. Educated and well-trained employees must be given the latitude and incentives to adapt to each guest's unique behaviors and requests. Every service encounter must be seen by hotel employees as a precious opportunity to build customer loyalty and retention, and thereby, increase job security and profits.

Super-budget hotels are more interested in throughput, efficiency, and multisite standardization. Here, the hotel room is more of a commodity. The consumer benefit package for super-budget motels is dominated by low price and fulfilling basic customer needs such as a safe, clean place to sleep. Its consumer benefit package has a more standardized degree of service- and information-content than the luxury hotel.

The super-budget hotel is designed to have fewer points of contact with its guests per visit than a luxury hotel. The rigid/structural part of the service delivery system dominates the fluid/behavioral part of the system. Drive-thru check-in and check-out, adjacent but off-site restaurants, no room service, automated wake up service, few special services, and no lounge, lobby, or meeting rooms are example design characteristics of a super-budget hotel. The motel room and facility design, as well as job design, are standardized. Employee training, and recognition and reward programs, are also highly standardized. This way, consistent service/quality performance is maintained at all motel locations. Employee recruiting for super-budget motels places more emphasis on operational skills than on marketing or personal skills.

Employee empowerment is not quite as critical in a super-budget motel because the motel guest does not have as high expectations as the luxury hotel guest. Service/quality standards for the super-budget motel are more standardized and measurable than for luxury hotels. The super-budget hotel can be run more like a factory flowshop.

Service encounter requirements for these two extremes in the US lodging industry are dramatically different. If either the rigid or fluid parts of these service delivery systems are out-of-sync, the result is confusion. And service encounter confusion leads to service upsets that lead to higher costs, less repeat business and revenue, and ultimately, decreasing profits. Once this cycle of service encounter failure gets started, it is difficult to stop it and win back customer loyalty.

For luxury hotels, the consumer benefit package and associated service encounters are customized and personalized to the individual. The consumer benefit package for super-budget hotels is standardized for the average hotel guest in that particular market segment. In both cases, people are being processed through the service delivery system—in the one, more like a commodity; in the other, like a speciality. As defined in Chapters 1 and 4, a commodity is analogous to a universal consumer benefit package, while a speciality is like a focused consumer benefit package. For these two extremely different consumer benefit packages, service encounter design and management are also very different.

BUYING CELERY IN THE SERVOMATION AGE

America's General Motors (GM), for example, was founded in 1908 and dominated the industrial revolution of the 1900s. Today, its share of worldwide automobile sales continues to decline. There are bright spots within its infrastructure, such as the Cadillac Motor Car or Saturn Divisions and GM's venture into the credit card business. But General Motors is slowly losing its world-class status. The stories of American companies with similar bylines are growing longer.[2] As noted in the first paragraph of this book, the students of capitalism have caught up, and sometimes, surpassed the performance of the teacher—America. General Motors symbolizes the American Century of goods-producing dominance.

What is next? Many futurists have their vision of what's next, so I'll try. There are two parallel and major developments in the world of economic enterprise that are converging. *The first is the developing and converging capabilities of communication and information technology.* This capability creates mass customization, virtual corporations, and electronic cottages with access to everybody anywhere in the world. One consequence of this capability is to *fragment the future.* Super and/or temporary niche markets, smaller companies, compressed consumer benefit package life cycles, self-employment, automated service encounters, teleworkers, and many types of big and small alliances that come and go quickly will play a much larger role in future business transactions. Together, they help make up this fragmented, flexible, and time-sensitive market and business structure.

The second major and parallel development in the world of economic enterprise is the rising dominance of information-, entertainment- and service-content over goods-content (product) for any given consumer or employee benefit package configuration. Nongoods- or service-content will increasingly dominate business transactions of the future. America finds itself as the author of this service expertise, much like its past dominance in goods-producing industries.

These two business developments are converging and creating (1) a new economic age and (2) a new type of business transaction. I call this new age the *Servomation Age.* It is the confluence of the Service Revolution and the Information Age with the remnants of past Industrial Ages. In the Servomation Age, the nongoods-content of the consumer benefit package will almost always dominate the goods-content. The Servomation Age begins in the 1990s.

In the Servomation Age, goods, information, entertainment, and service are tightly intermingled, bundled, imbedded, and blurred together *in the customer's mind.* Figure 4–4 is representative of consumer benefit package configurations in the Servomation Age. But even Figure 4–4 delineates too much between primary and peripheral goods, services, and information in the Servomation Age. Customers, especially your kids and grandchildren, will slowly forget the notion that products should dominate consumer benefit packages.

For example, the new smart video recorders that can read bar codes or allow the user to input numerical codes, and then the television show is automatically taped is an example of a Servomation consumer benefit package. Everyone expects the actual video box and tape (products) to work. And these products create new markets for services. But the thing that differentiates smart video recorders in the marketplace is information- and service-features. Services will piggyback onto these products and generate many new revenue-generating opportunities. Service-related revenue over the long term will far outpace revenue generated by the products themselves. That is why Sony bought Columbia Pictures and Matsushita Electric Industrial Company bought MCA, Inc.

Another example centers around the definition of money and whether it is a good or a service? In the past the concept of money included trading lumps of metal in 1,000 BC, gold and silver during the Roman and Greek empires, paper money in China in AD 800 and still used today, and electronic impulses in the Servomation Age. The idea of money has evolved from lumps of heavy metal to electronic impulses where service is the dominant performance criterion.

The point is, we are in the midst of a colossal paradigm shift about how to define and do work, how to use smart data analysis best, and what it is we buy, sell, and value in the marketplace. It is time for the idea of what we buy and sell to evolve from products to something broader and much less tangible. So, I have defined in this book the terms *consumer or employee benefit package* to fit the new economic reality of the Servomation Age.

Products in the Servomation Age will be of the same status as celery is today in a modern supermarket. The following service management vision of buying celery in the Servomation Age helps us see this paradigm shift. We don't think much about the quality of celery because it is usually fresh, crisp, and beautifully green or else it's thrown away. Product quality is perfect or very close to it. If product parity exists between competing celery producers and supermarkets, then how will they differentiate their celery-based consumer benefit packages?

Consider this vision of how information- and service-content define the purchase of celery in the Servomation Age. First, high-quality celery that is sparkling clean, fresh, crisp, tasty, and well packaged is the qualifier to be in the business. Genetic engineering also will help produce perfect celery. Just-in-time distribution will get it to the customer quickly. The world consumer will demand and get the goods-portion of the consumer benefit package with little variance in product quality. The information- and service-content of the consumer benefit package will distinguish market leaders from all others. Information- and service-content become the consumer benefit package attributes that win customer orders in the frontroom (supermarket) and differentiate suppliers in the backroom. Here, the core (see Figures 4–1 and 4–2) of the consumer benefit package will be fuzzy between goods and services.

For celery, it might include a customer scanning a bar code on the celery package or searching the telecomputer at home to immediately (remember Service/Quality Challenge #4 on instantaneous service in Chapter 1) see a menu of 30 ways to use celery in a meal, party, and picnic. Of course, up-to-date nutrition information about celery or the history of celery or the genetic structure of celery or step-by-step video cooking lessons can quickly be brought to your home by the telecomputer screen. Information and peripheral services are bundled with the core good to define the consumer benefit package.

Cooking schools that can teach you how to prepare celery can quickly be accessed for your local area or, for that matter, anywhere in the world. Hot line telephone numbers for answers to the customer's most perplexing questions about celery are readily available on the telecomputer. Quick home delivery of your groceries, including that colorful picture of celery on the high-definition telecomputer, is as convenient as pushing a button. These peripheral services complement the purchase of an information-enriched good. And who knows what other intriguing consumer benefit package configurations humankind will come up with to sell celery.

If you were born of an earlier age you might still have a product-perspective and "see" your celery transaction as buying a pure product. But if you were born in the Servomation Age, product quality and performance are not your primary concerns. Product quality is seldom an order winner in the Servomation Age. How well information, entertainment, and services are bundled to the consumer benefit package is what differentiates one consumer benefit package from another. What have you done for me lately in terms of service-content is the attitude of the consumers of the Servomation Age.

The Servomation Age is as different from the service-sector revolution as the service-sector revolution is from the industrial revolution. Or the industrial revolution was from the agrarian revolution. Or the agrarian revolution was from the hunting age. Each time, mammoth paradigm shifts in how we think about work and economic life were required. And we must once again restructure our notions of work, value, and management.

The Servomation Age also must deal with many other climatic shifts. Some we cannot even guess but others are barely visible. For example, dramatic increases in the average life expectancy of humankind are close at hand. It is estimated based on anthropological studies that the average life expectancy of a newborn baby in 3000 BC was 18 years, in 275 BC it was 26 years, in AD 1900 it was 76 years, in AD 2000 it will be 85 years, AD 2010 it will be 100 years, AD 2040 it will be 200 years, and AD 2200 230 years. By 2040, human genetic engineering will not be a fantasy but a set of realistic life choices.[3] What type of consumer or employee benefit package(s) will century-plus people need?

This is my brief venture into the world of a futurist. Celery is my surrogate for any product in the Servomation Age. The future of products is to informate (add information content) and servomate (add service and entertainment content) them, perhaps like my off-beat celery example. Let's now get back to more immediate concerns: (1) How do you win the service/quality challenge? and (2) What are the solutions?

SERVICE/QUALITY SOLUTIONS

The three service/quality premises and eight service/quality challenges described in Chapter 1 define the environment in which solutions must be found. The following 18 summary solution approaches are intended as a basis for discussion, learning, and change. Each solution approach must be tailored to the specific application. These summary points do not encompass every idea in this book, and are in random order. They tend to aggregate many ideas and details discussed in this book. These 18 solution approaches represent suggestions and a starting point as to how to use service management to gain competitive advantage for your organization.

Solution Approach #1
A service management perspective and style must replace a product- and functional-management perspective and style.

A product or functional perspective limits service encounter capability and creativity. Consumer benefit package, processes, and jobs are defined too narrowly when a product and functional perspective is at work. A product or functional perspective ignores many basic tenets of service management, and where they lead us. Table 16–1 compares a service management philosophy and management style to a product approach. Managing a service-providing business is more like coaching a competitive sports team or directing a theatrical play. Table 8–1 also made similar comparisons on a career-path basis.

Some people recognize this mismatch of applying product approaches to a service business. For example, Frederick F. Reichheld, founder and director of consultant Bain & Co.'s customer retention practice noted, "Indeed, a big mistake some service companies make is approaching quality with a manufacturing perspective. Traditional MBA programs and accounting systems don't cut it in the service game."[4]

Solution Approach #2
Services are increasingly dominating goods as the key marketplace differentiator and order winner, and therefore, think services first.

Product quality is or soon will be the qualifier to be in your business. Service/quality performance is the order winner in the majority of consumer and employee benefit package transactions. It is the marketplace differentiator. And when it is, a service management perspective frees everyone to think like the customer. For example, do we make yard fertilizer or beautiful lawns? Many people in an organization have a difficult time thinking like the customer. This is due to several reasons such as the organization's structure and functional silo mentality, internal-performance-based recognition and reward systems, the product-perspective education and training that employees receive, and many other remnants of previous industrial revolutions.

The term *product* is obsolete in today's marketplace. It should be eliminated from all organizational documents and ways of communicating inside and outside the organization. *Pure products* are such a small percent of total worldwide consumer and employee benefit package activity that the continual use of this term does a great disservice to how we should design and manage today's business enterprises. Consumer and employee benefit packages, as described in Chapter 4, offer a new way to think about what we buy, sell, and value in the marketplace.

Products and the industrial revolutions of the past were a good match. But today and in the Servomation Age, what you call a business transaction is important because it sets the stage for how you think about it, and all subsequent activi-

TABLE 16–1

Making the Shift to a Service Management Philosophy and Style

Producing a Product	*A Theatrical Performance*	*Service Management*
Products	A play	Consumer/employee benefit packages (CBP/EBPs) and associated service encounters
Research and development in the lab	Script writing, revisions, and rehearsal onstage	Service innovations sometimes onstage with the customer
Product strategy	Play theme and strategy	CBP/EBP management
Product, process, and job design	Play script and actor lines	CBP, process and service encounter design
Manufacturing facility design	Stage set and props designed	Service facility design
Factory manager	The director	The process manager
Salespersons	Salespersons and actors	Customer solution representatives
Factory workers	Actors	Service providers
Engineering	Directing	Imagineering
Production capabilities	Acting skills	Behavioral capabilities
Product conforms to specifications	Standing ovation and customer retention	Standing ovation and customer retention
Employee suggestion systems	Rehearsal and ongoing revisions	Continuous improvement driven by employee empowerment
Best product value	Best entertainment value	Best consumer or employee benefit package value

ties. Using the terms *consumer* and *employee benefit package* are first steps in adopting a service management approach to defining and running the business. It signals everyone that the organization is changing its perspective.

Solution Approach #3
Consumer and employee benefit package (CBP and EBP) management must be done well, and it is the driver of all subsequent plans and actions.

To be world-class, consumer and employee benefit package definition, design, and strategy, as described in Chapters 4 to 6, must be done well. For example, consumer benefit package attribute definition is what drives process design and performance measurement. Figure 16–1 shows how CBP definition

FIGURE 16–1
How Consumer/Employee Benefit Package (CBP/EBP) Managment DRIVES
Service/Quality Performance

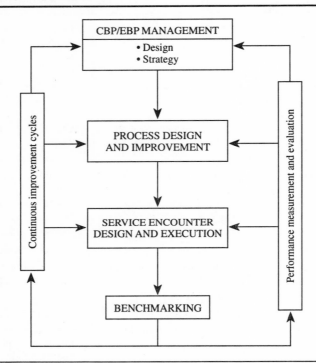

drives all subsequent design and people programs. Here, the detailed attributes of the CBP are the basis for a service/quality measurement and performance system.

Many corollaries and suggestions have been made in this book about how to excel at consumer benefit package management. For example, use the seven P's of service management as a framework for analysis. Also, developing a Comprehensive Customer Contact Plan (3C Plan) helps you see how to unbundle CBP/EBP attributes successfully.

The more practice you have with CBP/EBP definition, especially when the service- and information-content are high, the better you get at doing it. Follow your CBP/EBP definition and strategy through the entire process defined by Figures 2–3, 2–4, 16–1, and Table 13–1. Use the formats shown in Chapter 4 to practice defining your consumer and employee benefit packages. Consumer benefit package management is fun, exciting, and challenges you to take a fresh look at defining and managing the business.

Solution Approach #4

Time-based capabilities reside at the consumer benefit package, process, and service encounter levels, and must be the targets of continuous improvement and sources of competitive advantage. A time-based competitive strategy, especially in a service process, is not complete until it reaches the service encounter level.

Time-based competition exists at three levels in the organization. The first level is where the consumer benefit package is designed. Consumer benefit package life cycles are being compressed at an amazing rate, as discussed in Chapter 6. The benefit of being "first to market" has been well documented in terms of increased market share and profits.

The second level where time-based competition occurs is at the process level. Hard and soft technology are providing the capability to compress months into seconds. Value is added to the consumer benefit package by quick delivery to the customer. Chapters 7, 8, and 9 examined how process management is related to facility, organization, and information network designs. The process management mosaic is an interesting challenge, especially for service processes.

The third and most demanding level of time-based competition is at the service encounter level. Here, everything is real-time, with direct contact between a service provider and the customer. The service encounter can move very fast with many subtle human behaviors going on that only humans can recognize and respond to. Service failures or upsets must be corrected on-the-spot by the service provider. Service recovery demands much from employees and their immediate supervisors.

Solution Approach #5

Service/quality excellence is in the details, and therefore, reward those people who know how to take details and turn them into a difficult-to-replicate competitive advantage.

"Show me someone who's not in the detail business and I'll show you someone who's not in a service business," is a comment attributed to J W Marriott, Jr. In business schools we have a name for managing the practical details of the manufacturing or service delivery system—it's called *operations management*. Here, how the organization works and creates value, and how all areas of the organization converge to create world-class service encounters are studied. Operations management demands attention to details. A process flowchart and a complete understanding of how it works are its most important tools. Operations management demands an interdisciplinary perspective.

To some people, the details of a manufacturing or service delivery process are seen as boring or too messy. Meanwhile, his or her foreign counterpart sees these details as opportunities for continuous improvement and a better life. Execution creates value, wins customers, earns profits, and enhances the standard of living. The Service/Quality Solution is based on mastering details and their execution. Often, mastering the details is not glamorous work. American business seldom rewards, to the extent they should, the people who actually know how to create and manage the details of providing world-class service encounters.

The challenge to boards of directors, senior management, and government officials is to promote through the highest salaries, and the most organizational respect, service management career paths. Usually a service management career path includes line management experience in several areas such as marketing, operations, personnel, field service, and engineering. Reward these knowledgeable, experienced, and talented people who know how to take details and turn them into a difficult-to-replicate competitive advantage. The masters of execution reap the long-term rewards—they are the core capability of any Service/Quality Solution.

Solution Approach #6
Process technologies and capabilities will increasingly dominate product technologies and capabilities, especially as services increase in importance in consumer and employee benefit packages. Organizations must build in-house service process improvement capabilities and use this expertise to improve performance of all processes. Service process capabilities are the true source of competitive advantage in the Servomation Age.

Process management is not widely used in service businesses today. For example, one study on the North American and German banking industry in 1992 by Ernst & Young and the American Quality Foundation found these percentages of banks usually or always used the following practices: process capability studies (28 percent), process value analysis (22 percent), process simplification (34 percent), process cycle-time analysis (20 percent), and statistical process control (18 percent).[5] But these percentages will increase because service/quality performance is created by service process capabilities. *How* the consumer or employee benefit package is delivered is as important as *what* is delivered.

Another study done in 1991 by the same parties, but with a manufacturing-based sample, found a much higher percentage of process management approaches in use. Here the percent of businesses by country show the frequency of usually or always using process simplification. For the survey question, "How often do you use process simplification to improve business processes?" the results were as follows: Canada (71 percent), Germany (34 percent), Japan (82 percent), and the United States (47 percent).[6]

Service businesses, as these example survey results show, are in the early stages of using process management approaches. The potential benefits of improved service process performance in goods-producing and service-providing businesses are immense. For example, more people in the United States are working in federal, state, and local governments in 1993 than in manufacturing.

Consider the comments of Dr. H James Harrington, the author of *Business Process Improvement*. He stated in 1992 that, "If service and support areas had kept pace with manufacturing in the 1980s, America would have a positive net revenue in government that is greater than its debt today. Service industries and support functions made America a debtor nation. They are the villains . . . The manufacturing quality gap between US and Japanese auto manufacturers has narrowed to such an extent," he goes on to say, "that a US car maker has a better chance of losing an order to poor service than to poor product. There were huge gains in manufacturing, yes, but the charge now is to focus the same determination in the service area. If we can't do that in the next year or two, there is no sense in talking about what business can do to meet the challenges of the 21st century. Without an immediate focus on business processes, American businesses will not have the option of competing in the 21st century."[7]

Solution Approach #7
A service management approach to organizational design is a necessity for long term service/quality success.

A service management approach to organizational design includes three organizational levels, as previously depicted in Figure 8–2. These levels are consumer benefit package, process, and service encounter management. A service management-based organizational design is also characterized by functional areas of expertise at the corporate level, much more reliance on empowered employees to run the business, and an electronic information and communication network to instantaneously couple people and information together and support service encounter execution. The instantaneous service, Service/Quality Challenge #4, requires an agile and fast organization, as shown in Figure 8–2.

The implications of the organizational design depicted in Figure 8–2 are great. For example, process management and service encounter management have no need for independent marketing and operations areas. Marketing strategy becomes a customer service strategy. Operations strategy focuses on process and service encounter efficiency and effectiveness. Service management skills replace functional expertise at all three levels of the organization. Service process and organizational design are inherently tied together. Employee empowerment with all its implications becomes a necessity. Organizational architecture is now based on service, time, and information capabilities, not the movement of physical products. The paradigm shifts noted in this paragraph illustrate the restructuring required to compete in the Servomation Age.

Solution Approach #8
Smart data analysis or interlinking is not a "wish we had" capability—it is an absolute necessity to compete effectively in the Servomation Age. Interlinking metrics are most meaningful when tied to a process and its results.

Interlinking, as described in Chapters 11, 12, 14, and 15, can help identify opportunities to differentiate your consumer benefit packages from those of competitors. It elevates data and information analysis to the same status as the other key assets of the firm, such as equipment and people. Changes in customer preferences, predicting customer satisfaction based on process performance, adjustments in advertising programs, identification of new market and service innovation opportunities, and informating consumer benefit packages are examples of how interlinking can help the organization attain world-class performance. Interlinking is also a substitute for service prototyping. Clever data analysis can predict performance and be a form of service research and development. It helps define the relationships between the drivers of performance. Finally, interlinking is capable of modeling goods-producing or service-providing processes, and business-to-ultimate customer or business-to-business processes.

Only so much can be accomplished by analyzing one or two performance variables at a time. For example, the seven tools of quality management usually include (1) cause-and-effect (fishbone) diagrams, (2) checklists, (3) histograms, (4) Pareto charts, (5) scatter charts, (6) trend charts, and (7) process flowcharting. These methods are dominated by one- or two-criteria comparisons. They were primarily intended for frontline employees who are making the product or providing the service. They are frequently the tools of quality improvement teams. They are the drivers of many continuous improvement initiatives and have been highly successful. They play a key role in any quality initiative and should be used by all people and levels of the organization.

But what about using methods of data analysis that can model complex cause-and-effect relationships involving more than two performance variables? Should management champion these more powerful multiple-criteria modeling methods? Or should they be complacent with the seven tools of quality management? The issue is what is possible versus what is done. We need to move to higher forms of data analysis, especially at the CBP and Process Management levels. Interlinking recognizes information as the key asset in the Servomation Age.

To overcome the deadly disease of too much dependence on one- and two-variable data analysis methods, the 16 tools of quality management must be more widely used in practice and taught in school. Large organizations frequently have these data analysis capabilities in-house, but most small organizations do not. Organizations lacking this data analysis and interlinking capability must start building it now.

As noted in Chapter 1, the Gunneson Group International, Inc., a quality consulting company, reports that only 10 percent of American service companies have any kind of quality program. The Gunneson Group predicts that by the year 2000, perhaps 70 percent of those with more than 500 employees will adopt a formal quality improvement initiative.[8] Organizations of all types can benefit from improving their data analysis skills.

Solution Approach #9
Overcome the deadly diseases, if you are diagnosed as having them, of too much dependence on (1) a product perspective, (2) functionalism, and (3) one- and two-variable data analysis methods. These diseases hinder the transition to service management, competing in the Servomation Age, and finding a tailor-made Service/Quality Solution for your organization.

In Chapter 5, we reviewed Dr. W. Edward Deming's seven deadly diseases. They are: (1) lack of constancy of purpose, (2) emphasis on short-term profits, (3) annual rating of performance of salaried employees, (4) mobility of management, (5) use of only visible figures for management, which ignores equally important figures that are often unknown or unknowable, (6) excessive medical costs, and (7) excessive costs of liability swelled by lawyers that work on contingency fees.

Three more diseases have been described in this book and are identified here. (They also represent a lack of management leadership more than anything else.) Chapter 1, and many other chapters, describe and give examples of the consequences of *relying too much on a product-perspective*. To combat this disease we must teach service management in our schools and practice it in our organizations. Chapter 8 discusses the *functionalism disease*, some of its dire consequences, and a service management solution for organizing work. Chapters 10 to 15 examine various methods of data analysis that move beyond the capabilities of the *one- and two-variable at-a-time approach*. In the Servomation Age, developing complex interlinking capabilities is a key part of any Service/Quality Solution.

Solution Approach #10
Service innovation management must be measured and managed as well or better than product research and development in goods-producing firms.

America leads the world in service innovation research and development achievements. Yet, as noted in Chapter 9, most service innovations are not recognized in any formal way in organizations, industry associations, or government statistics. Today, many service innovations are given away, free of charge.

Several actions can help define and manage service innovations better. First, the accounting and financial systems on the organizational level must do a better job of identifying and tracking service research and development work. Service innovation activity and reporting needs to be improved at the organization, association, industry, and government levels. Service innovations need to be recognized more in the press, as noted in Chapter 9 with the Service Innovation Design Excellence Awards. Second, service innovations must be protected as best they can through trade agreements and the worldwide legal system. Third, and most importantly, America's expertise and accomplishments in developing service innovations must be sustained. Service innovations must be recognized as a driver of economic development and competitiveness. Government and organizational policies must encourage continued service innovation success, measure it, and recognize and reward it.

Solution Approach #11
Convince your organization that service/quality performance is the best competitive weapon to build long-term economic success.

The vast majority of businesses sell *time, information, expertise, advice, plans, entertainment, place utility, and services*. If you are lucky enough to sell (provide) a consumer (employee) benefit package with a degree of goods-content of at least 95 percent (close to a pure product), you might be able to ignore service management, at least for now.

But for most businesses, service in all its forms is the great marketplace differentiator. When it comes to differentiating your consumer or employee benefit package(s) from those of competitors, you are either (1) a service business and you know it, or (2) a service business and you don't know it. Even goods-producing firms that produce commodities such as wheat and carbon-black or business-to-business product suppliers, rely more on information and service content than they may suspect. The greatest impact I have had in consulting engagements is with businesses that defined themselves from a product-first-perspective when a service-first-perspective is best.

Product specifications, genetic codes, formulas, building designs, uniforms, equipment, organizational architecture, and software codes can be copied. But the fluid/behavioral part of service processes and encounters is not easy to duplicate. Service/quality performance is so interdisciplinary and dependent on human skills that lesser competitors never quite get the world-class service/quality puzzle together. It takes time to build an organization whose primary competitive weapon is world-class service/quality performance and all the behaviors that accompany it. And time is the enemy of the copiers.

Solution Approach #12
You must measure and reward performance at the consumer benefit package, process, and service encounter levels in a service business. Employee empowerment becomes an organizational necessity

when service-content is high. The performance measurement and appraisal system must support employee empowerment, service encounter execution, and service recovery actions.

Performance measurement at the service encounter level is the most difficult type of performance to measure and evaluate. It must be very specific by service encounter type. Service encounter performance also must be readily aggregated to the process and consumer benefit package levels. Performance systems must be aligned at all three levels and become part of the process itself, and not a separate entity. It must be integrated into how things get done on a daily basis.

As the degree of service content increases in your consumer benefit packages, and associated processes and service encounters, plan for control to also shift more to the employees who create and deliver service encounters. Employee empowerment is part of a time-based competitive strategy at the service encounter level. Employee empowerment is *not* a gift from management to employees. It is a *necessity* if the service-providing organization is to survive.

The proper balance between empowered employees and the degree of organizational structure and measurement is a point of tension in any service/quality-related implementation plan. This balancing act is an ongoing process every manager must recognize and watch. A Comprehensive Customer Contact Plan (3C Plan) for each service process and key service encounters, as discussed in Chapter 7, is one way to plan and manage this delicate balance. A 3C Plan helps to focus attention on the service encounter level. Chapter 8 also describes eight minimal requirements of empowerment that give you some idea of what true employee empowerment means.

Solution Approach #13
A tight or loose Comprehensive Customer Contact Plan (3C Plan) is part of a service encounter design strategy for your consumer or employee benefit package(s). A 3C Plan is a prevention-based improvement strategy, a source of competitive advantage, and it must be designed into the service delivery system.

Service encounters are where execution takes place. A set of service encounters usually creates and delivers a consumer or employee benefit package that the internal or external customer uses, experiences, pays for, or works for. All prior plans and resource allocation decisions support service encounter execution. The entire business exists to design and execute world-class service encounters.

A 3C Plan is the script for ideal service performance at key points of contact with the customer. It makes certain that appropriate resources have been committed so that frontstage and backstage service providers can do an extraordinary job. At times, service upsets or unusual customer requests will require the empowered service providers to deviate from the ideal script. But the 3C Plan provides the baseline of performance expectations—what should happen, when, and how.

Sometimes a 3C Plan defines *tight* customer contact requirements and at other times rather *loose* requirements. In Chapter 7 and Table 7–2 tight customer contact requirements were presented for one contact point for shipping custom software to a customer. Routine services such as fast-food restaurant jobs and low-contact jobs such as check encoding operators are typical environments where tight 3C Plans are most appropriate.

Professional services, high-contact services, and certain consumer benefit package configurations require 3C Plans to be specified loosely. Medical, legal, and consulting services, for example, all demand loosely defined 3C Plans. The quality of the people and the skill they use to satisfy each customer's requirements is the key ingredient for professional service organizations. But loosely defined 3C Plans can also be found in the more routine processes such as buying shoes.

Consider the following example of a loose set of customer contact requirements for a 3C Plan. It shows how a 3C Plan is very much a part of facility and process design. A Nike shoe store in Portland, Oregon, defines its consumer benefit package and associated service encounter design as having significant entertainment and freedom dimensions. The store design includes an open town square complete with birds chirping, a basketball floor, aquariums, and much more. As store manager Mary Burns said, "Nike Town is a theatrical presentation, a glittering production number starring the customer. People love to shop here. It's kind of entertainment, a social thing.[9] Nike Town in Chicago also bundles entertainment with the shoe-buying experience, much like the Portland store. Uplifting videos of people worldwide buying and using Nike shoes heightens the shoe-buying experiences along with huge icons of National Basketball Association players such as Michael Jordan.

As the Servomation Age evolves, more and more information-, service-, and entertainment-content will be bundled to goods (in this case, shoes) to help differentiate them in the marketplace. Many examples of this were described in Chapters 4 and 9. Nike Town demonstrates summary Solution Approaches #1, 2, 3, 6, 10, 11, 13, 15, and 16.

At Nike Town, freedom, entertainment, color, fantasy, technical shoe performance information, videos, and music are part of the consumer benefit package definition. Facility- and process-design support this consumer benefit package definition. Here, service process and encounter design are left to the discretion of the shoe-buying customer. They set the pace, they define the route through the store and processing times per stage, when they want self-service versus help from a sales representative, and how and when they want to bundle music, trying the shoes out on a basketball court, entertainment, and fantasy with the buying of shoes.

Although some sales representative customer contact points can be scripted at Nike Town stores, *the customers have built-in freedom to design their shoe-buy-*

ing experience and set of service encounters. This design-yourself service encounter capability is a vision of what future economic competition will be like in the Servomation Age. Study Nike Town closely and figure out: How would you replicate this *service encounter design strategy* for your consumer or employee benefit packages?

Solution Approach #14
The strategic alliance between American education and American business must be strengthened and fully deployed.

Bricks and mortar don't execute the vast majority of routine and professional service encounters—people do. Bricks and mortar don't initiate continuous improvement cycles—people do. Bricks and mortar don't define new consumer benefit packages—people do. And yet, the most powerful American strategic alliance is not fully developed or deployed. It is an alliance between American education and business. It could shape the future of America's competitiveness and standard of living. It could recharge America's batteries and get America ready for the Servomation Age.

America's workforce skills are eroding when they should be developing new capabilities. The skills of the future are not based on past product-perspective and industrial revolution notions. The skills of the future are service-management-based. High performance people are needed at the (1) consumer and employee benefit package, (2) process, and (3) service encounter levels of any organization. Design and execution skills must be developed and plentiful. Jobs are at risk if you are great at design but weak at execution. Any service/quality solution absolutely requires people who can execute great designs at the process and service encounter levels.

To establish Education–Business Strategic Alliances (EBSAs), American business must view US educational systems as their top priority *vendor*. American business must get involved, define what skills they want, and help US educators excel at it. It must become a partnership of the highest national priority. For example, business must have permanent representatives on every school board who can encourage schools to develop student skills that support core organizational competencies. Government can help with the proper incentives to make these EBSAs happen quickly.

Selective, and narrowly defined, EBSAs are working today, but America needs a more extensive set of EBSAs. One educational initiative of the type needed has been suggested by the Southport Institute for Policy Analysis in Washington, DC. They recommended in 1992 that a $100 million federal program be launched to bring a better-educated workforce to US small businesses. It would be modeled after the highly successful US Department of Agriculture's Cooperative Extension Service.

Another EBSA initiative that could be a model for future EBSAs is the Total Quality Forum.[10] These forums initiated by David Kearns, then Chief Executive

Officer of Xerox Corporation, have aggressively pursued many initiatives, such as integrating quality-related topics into America's educational system, defining the body of knowledge we sometimes call total quality management (TQM), training faculty on what business needs and is doing concerning TQM, and encouraging research on TQM. This approach needs to be expanded to all universities, technical schools, and secondary schools.

The skills needed in the Servomation Age are mostly mental and behavioral service management skills—not physical, goods-producing skills. Some companies such as Marriott Corporation are putting 70,000 employees through empowerment training. Other companies, such as Arthur Anderson & Co. consulting, Disney World, and Four Seasons hotels, are finding it much harder to recruit people capable of providing quality service.

Business, government, unions, and educational institutions must all work together to ensure that skilled people are America's best competitive asset. All competitive strategies will fail if the organization's human capital is weak and underdeveloped. As Marc S. Tucker, president of the US National Center on Education and the Economy, states, "We have to rebuild the system, not simply improve it. If we don't get vastly improved education in a very few years, real wages in the US will go into a tailspin."[11]

Solution Approach #15
The pace of change in the Servomation Age is accelerating, and therefore, management must prepare their organization and its people by adopting a service management approach. Laggards and nonadapters will not survive the brutal competition of the Servomation Age.

Figure 16–2 is one view of the highly competitive Servomation Age that began in the 1990s. In Figure 16–2, a few world-class organizations, big and small, are on the leading edge of best practices in areas such as managing consumer benefit packages, interlinking, building communication networks, training and empowering service providers, controlling costs, organizing the service management way, and managing service processes. To prepare for the Servomation Age, many of these service management practices, as well as others noted in this book, must be adopted.

Middle-of-the-pack industry performers in Figure 16–2 are good at one or two key areas but do not have the overall expertise to lead their global industry. Middle-of-the-pack competitors are quick to follow the lead of world-class industry performers. But fast followers are always one step behind, and if this step is of a long duration, the fast follower can be out of business.

About one-half of today's industry competitors have a low probability of survival in the Servomation Age, as shown in Figure 16–2. Some of these organizations will die from the 10 deadly diseases previously mentioned. Some will

FIGURE 16–2
Chances of Surviving the Servomation Age

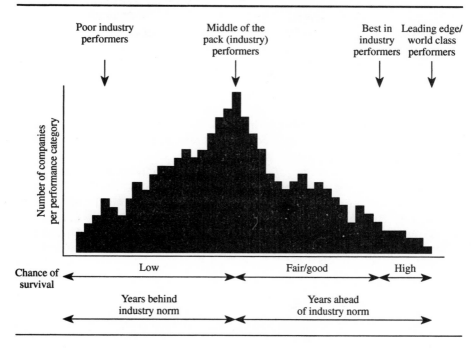

downsize too much and miss emerging market opportunities. Others will not master service encounter execution or learn how to bundle and unbundle information- and service-content like leading edge firms. Meanwhile, the Servomation Age will raise performance levels and the complexity of consumer and employee benefit packages. Big and small organizations that cannot cope with these changes fast enough or make the wrong strategic move will wither away.

Solution Approach #16
Organizations must define and adopt a long-term service management vision, when information, entertainment, and service play a key role in consumer and employee benefit package success.

If you don't have a vision of where you are going, the organization will waste valuable time and resources. Organizational goals and plans become vague. Work unit objectives become nonaligned and conflicting. Vision statements answer questions such as, "What business are we in?" Vision statements are the underlying premise for changing things. They also reduce the solution space for decisions to manageable proportions. Buying celery in the Servomation Age is one example of a service management vision. One objective of this book, in a way, is to define a service management vision of future business practices.

Consider these examples of a well-directed service management vision: Matsushita Electric Industrial Company buying MCA Inc or Sony buying Columbia Pictures. The Japanese companies built these empires based on product and manufacturing expertise. Their consumer electronics businesses are world-class, and particularly their television and video recorder capabilities. But they recognized that the consumer benefit package definition of tomorrow shows information-, service-, and entertainment-content as the core of the consumer benefit package. The actual hardware (product) is slowly becoming a peripheral and supporting good. That's right, within the consumer benefit package configuration framework, services are switching places with goods and becoming the dominant or core thing people buy.

What will consumers really buy in the Servomation Age when home telecomputers are electronically connected to world information and entertainment networks? What constitutes value in this marketplace? Goods? Services? These two giant goods-producing companies have a vision of the future, one that includes service management and service/quality performance. They have positioned themselves so they can try to dominate the electronic delivery of entertainment and information services to individual homes. Their strategic vision spans 20 plus years, not just a few years. Right now, Matsushita and Sony are treading water when it comes to combining and leveraging these consumer benefit package components of information-, service-, and entertainment-content. But when home telecomputers and worldwide electronic networks are more developed, they will be well positioned to dominate global markets. Their long-term service management vision is part of their service/quality solution.

Matsushita's and Sony's next step is to begin to adopt a service management approach within their organizations, and train everyone to *think service management*, as shown in Action Step #1 of Table 13–1. Over time everything in this book, and others like it, about service/quality must be imbedded into their people's thinking, decisions, behaviors, and actions. It all begins with a service management vision of the future and the will to stick to it.

Solution Approach #17
Federal, state, and local governments must adopt a service management vision and approach with the goal of improving service process efficiency and effectiveness.

Government agencies at all levels execute billions of service encounters everyday. They manage tens of thousands of service processes. They consume a growing portion of the resources of any nation. Government agencies must also have a vision of the future. Who are our customers? What should this service process look like in 3 to 10 years? Should it be paperless? How automated? Centralized? Decentralized? What does the service process and accompanying 3C Plan look like? Should we subcontract this service to for-profit companies? How should we measure and evaluate process performance? And so on.

Any plan to improve national productivity, competitiveness, and standard of living must include service/quality improvement at the federal, state, and local government levels. Government is too large a component of total economic activity to be ignored. To date, the Malcolm Baldrige National Quality Award, as described in Chapter 3, is probably the most significant action the US federal government has taken to encourage mega-gains in national productivity and competitiveness. Now this same federal government must look inward and dramatically improve its performance. Vice President Al Gore, for example, spent about one-half of his time in 1993 trying to champion the quality movement in US federal government offices. And there is evidence that service/quality improvement efforts are under way in US federal departments based on recent survey results.[12]

Solution Approach #18

A US national industrial policy is not a national growth policy. The huge US service sector must be included in any national growth policy.

Industrial Policy was the cover story of a 1992 issue of *Business Week*.[13] The article discusses the US economy as if much of the huge US service sector, except government's role, didn't exist. It notes, for example, that knowledge is king in a global economy and then ignores most information- and service-intensive industries. It views research and development (R&D) from a product perspective. As discussed in Chapter 9 on service innovations, service sector R&D is mostly ignored in reporting statistics. A product-perspective raises its aged head again—this time in defining a US national economic policy.

A US national growth policy should be focused on service industries and service processes. By some estimates, 95 percent of the jobs in the US are found in service processes. That is, about 80 percent of total US jobs are in service industries, with the remaining 20 percent in goods-producing industries. And with as much as 75 percent of all jobs in goods-producing industries actually being jobs in service processes, you end up with this 95 percent estimate. Services consume the vast majority of resources of the US economy. The real opportunities and leverage for improving US productivity and competitiveness are now in service processes, not in goods-producing processes.

After the restructuring of the 1980s, most of the US goods-producing capability is globally competitive. This is not so for service processes in either service-providing or goods-producing industries. Some of these US service industries are in disarray. Meanwhile, foreign competitors are building their service-management-based capabilities.[14] Table 1–2 showed who these formidable competitors might be. US service industry disarray gives foreign competitors time to study and learn service/quality expertise, and then *execute* it better than American firms do. Sound familiar?

FORGET PAST MISTAKES BUT REMEMBER THEIR LESSONS

During the turmoil of the 1970s and 1980s, some US manufacturers became stronger and their quality and productivity dramatically improved. Today, they do very well in the global marketplace. But many US manufacturers just closed their doors, and these jobs were lost. The remaining US manufacturing sector in the 1980s was said to have increased its productivity 25 to 40 percent, depending on the data used. The extraordinary growth in US service industry jobs during the 1970s and 80s softened the effect of what was happening in the restructured goods-producing sector of the US economy.

Now the job displacement and industry restructuring shock wave is moving through US service industries, including government. This economic shock wave is serious business. For example, Lester C. Thurow, Dean of the Sloan School of Management at the Massachusetts Institute of Technology, in a keynote address in 1993 to the National Retail Federation's annual convention noted that the average American worker saw a 19 percent decline in real wages between 1973 and 1992. He said, "Those are your customers. What are they going to buy from you if their income is slowing?" Because products or technology can be easily copied, Mr. Thurow suggests a skilled workforce "is the heart to the competitive advantage. There is nothing else you can be unique in."[15] And this is one reason why service management and service/quality performance move to centerstage. Service/quality expertise is America's ace in the hole.

Globalization of the world economy also requires other changes, such as effective and efficient government. It is time for governments to restructure their service processes and make them more effective and efficient. The taxpayer is also a stakeholder in the government finding a world-class service/quality solution.

After the Detroit Pistons won their first National Basketball Association championship after 32 years of frustration, guard Isiah Thomas said, "In order to win at anything, there has to be pressure." In manufacturing, America's pressure sensors did not pick up, or ignored, the signals of Japan's manufacturing and execution dominance until it was almost too late. The Japanese and other strong competitors will now begin to leverage this execution capability to providing world-class services. Educated and skilled workforces will help them do this. They are preparing for the Servomation Age. The question is whether America is ready? This time everyone in the United States can see over the hill. They feel the pressure. Will the champion of capitalism—America—respond to these pressures and find solutions or just fade away?

Final Thought

"Today's preparation determines tomorrow's achievement."

Unknown

Notes

Prologue

1. I wrote this prologue in July 1989 after attending a company presentation. I wrote the prologue, then, when it was fresh in my mind and I later decided not to change it or the companies I had listed. At the time, I had planned to write a book on service management and service/quality but I hadn't outlined its contents yet. Since then Columbia Pictures and Holiday Inns have been bought by global companies, Eastern Airlines is gone, and some of these other companies are struggling in the marketplace.

Chapter 1   The Service/Quality Challenge

1. Mr. Jan Carlzon, CEO of Scandinavian Airlines Systems first defined a moment of trust or truth. See T J Peters and N Austin, *A Passion for Excellence: The Leadership Difference* (New York: Warner Books, 1985), pp. 58, 78.
2. J B Quinn and C E Gagnon, "Will Services Follow Manufacturing into Decline," *Harvard Business Review*, November–December 1986, p. 7.
3. "U.S. Service Exports Are Growing Rapidly, But Almost Unnoticed," *The Wall Street Journal*, April 21, 1993, pp. A1, A6.
4. Ibid.
5. "Beyond May I Help You?," *Business Week*, October 25, 1991, p. 100.
6. "The Global 1,000," *Business Week*, July 13, 1992, pp. 50–108.
7. "America Still Reigns in Services," *Fortune*, June 5, 1989, pp. 64–68. © 1989 Time Inc. All rights reserved.
8. *The Wall Street Journal*, April 21, 1993, p. A1.
9. *International Quality Study—The Definitive Study of the Best International Quality Management Practices* (Cleveland, OH: Ernst & Young and the American Quality Foundation, 1991), pp. 16–17.
10. Ibid.
11. *1991 Shareholder Report* (Dublin, OH: Wendy's International, Inc., 1991), p. 5
12. *Annual Report 1991* (Washington, DC, 1991), Marriott Corporation, p. 18.
13. "An Open Letter: TQM on the Campus," *Harvard Business Review*, November–December 1991, pp. 94–95; "An Open Response to 'TQM on the Cam-

pus': We Need TQM . . . and More," *Harvard Business Review*, January–February 1992, pp. 148; and *An IBM Total Quality Management (TQM) Competition for Colleges and Universities in the USA*, IBM Corporation, 208 Harbor Drive, Stamford, CT, October 1991.

14. "Where Will the Jobs Come From?" *Fortune*, October 19, 1992, p.62.
15. "Gore Tackles Government Inefficiency," *USA Today*, May 25, 1993, p. 1B.

Chapter 2   Basic Service Management

1. A personal communication with Steven A. Clyburn, Senior Editor at Coopers & Lybrand, Washington, DC, December 28, 1992.
2. This three-part definition of service management is a revision of a prior definition found in D A Collier, *Service Management: Operating Decisions* (Englewood Cliffs, NJ: Prentice Hall, 1987), p. x.
3. C Gronroos, "A Service Quality Model and Its Marketing Implications," in *Managing Service Quality, an IFS Executive Briefing*, ed. Graham Clark (Kempston, Bedford, UK: IFS Publications, 1990), pp. 13–18.
4. V A Zeithaml, "How Consumer Evaluation Processes Differ between Goods and Services," in *Marketing in Services*, ed. J H Donnelly and W R George (Chicago: The American Marketing Association, 1981), pp. 186–99.
5. M R Solomon, C F Surprenant, J A Czepiel, and E G Gutman, "A Role Theory Perspective on Dyadic Interactions: The Service Encounter," *Journal of Marketing*, Winter 1985, vol. 49, p.100.
6. G L Shostack, "Planning the Service Encounter" in *The Service Encounter*, ed. J A Czepiel, M R Solomon, and C F Surprenant (New York: Lexington Books, 1985), p. 244.
7. T J Peters and N Austin, *A Passion for Excellence: The Leadership Difference* (New York: Warner Books, 1985), pp. 59 and 78.
8. R B Chase, and D E Bowen, "Service Quality and the Service Delivery System: A Diagnostic Framework." Paper presented at *Quality in Services Conference*, University of Karlstad, Karlstad, Sweden, August 1988. Also, published in *Service Quality: Multidisciplinary and Multinational Perspectives*, ed. S W Brown, E Gummesson, B Edvardsson, and B Gustavsson (Lexington Books, Lexington, MA, 1991), pp. 157–76.
9. R Normann, *Service Management: Strategy and Leadership in Service Businesses* (New York: John Wiley & Sons, 1984), pp. 7 and 10.
10. R B Chase, "Where Does the Customer Fit in a Service Operation?" *Harvard Business Review*, November–December 1978, pp. 137–42.
11. ———. "The Customer Contact Model for Organizational Design," *Management Science*, vol. 29 no. 9 (1983), pp. 1037–50.
12. Ibid.

13. D A Collier, ''Process Moments of Trust: Analysis and Strategy,'' *The Service Industry Journal*, vol. 9, no. 2, April 1989, pp. 205–22.

14. W E Sasser, R P Olsen, and D D Wyckoff, *Management of Service Operations* (Boston: Allyn & Bacon, 1978), pp. 8–21.

15. J A Fitzsimmons and R S Sullivan, *Service Operations Management* (New York: McGraw-Hill, 1982).

16. E M Johnson, ''The Selling of Services,'' in *Handbook of Modern Marketing*, ed. V B Buell (New York: McGraw-Hill, 1978), p. 112.

17. D A Collier, ''New Orleans Hilton & Hilton Towers,'' *Service Management: Operating Decisions* (Englewood Cliffs, NJ: Prentice Hall, 1987), p. 120.

18. ''Service 500/Rankings,'' *Fortune*, June 13, 1983, p. 152.

19. *Webster's New Collegiate Dictionary* (Springfield, MA: G.&C. Merriam Company, 1986), p. 236.

Chapter 3 The Malcolm Baldrige National Quality Award and the Service/Quality Perspective

1. Part of this chapter is based on my article titled ''Service, Please: The Malcolm Baldrige National Quality Award.'' Partially reprinted from *Business Horizons*, vol. 35, no. 4, July–August 1992, pp. 88–95. Copyright (1992) by the Foundation for the School of Business at Indiana University. Used with permission.

2. *1991 Application Guidelines*, Malcolm Baldrige National Quality Award, United States Department of Commerce, National Institute of Standards and Technology, Gaithersburg, MD, p. 1.

3. D A Garvin, ''How the Baldrige Award Really Works,'' *Harvard Business Review*, November–December 1991, pp. 80–93.

4. C E Lopez, ''The Malcolm Baldrige National Quality Award: It's Really Not Whether You Win or Lose,'' *The Quality Observer*, vol. 1, no. 1, Fairfax, VA, November 1991, p. 1.

5. *1993 Award Criteria*, Malcolm Baldrige National Quality Award, United States Department of Commerce, National Institute of Standards and Technology, Gaithersburg, MD, p. 24.

6. Ibid., p. 24.

7. Ibid., p. 27.

8. Ibid., p. 27.

9. Ibid., p. 29.

10. D E Bowen, R B Chase, and T G Cummings, *Service Management Effectiveness* (San Francisco, CA: Jossey-Bass Inc., 1990), pp. 388–89.

11. J B Quinn, and C E Gagnon, ''Will Services Follow Manufacturing into Decline,'' *Harvard Business Review*, November/December 1986, p. 7.

12. "Consumer Survey Reveals Cable-Bashing," *The Columbus (Ohio) Dispatch*, August 31, 1991, p. 5H.

13. "MAPI Survey on Quality," *Manufacturers' Alliance for Productivity and Innovation*, Economic Report-205, Washington, DC, June 1991, p. 17.

14. *1993 MBNQA Award Criteria*, p. 33.

15. "Frequent Flyer Gripes," *USA TODAY*, October 17, 1990, p. 10B.

16. "Absolutely, Positively Quality," *Quality Progress*, May 1990, pp. 25–26.

Chapter 4   Consumer Benefit Package Design

1. D A Collier, *Service Management: Operating Decisions* (Englewood Cliffs, NJ: Prentice Hall, 1987), p 19.

2. W E Sasser, R P Olsen, and D D Wyckoff, *Management of Service Operations* (Boston: Allyn & Bacon, 1978), p. 9; and J A Fitzsimmons, and R S Sullivan, *Service Operations Management* (New York: McGraw-Hill, 1982), pp. 16–20.

3. D A Collier, "The Customer Service and Quality Challenge," *The Service Industries Journal*, vol. 7, no. 1, January 1987, p. 79.

4. "Bonus Plans: 10 Years Old and Booming," *USA TODAY*, April 29, 1991, p. 1B.

5. "Car Dealer Floats Latest Idea in Auto Malls," *The Columbus Dispatch*, Columbus, OH, March 2, 1991, p. 2G.

6. Ibid.

7. T Levitt, "Production-Line Approach to Service," *Harvard Business Review*, September/October, 1972, pp. 41–52.

8. N S Kano, F Takashi, and S Tsuji, "Attractive Quality and Must-Be Quality" (Methuen, MA: Goal/QPC, January 1984), pp. 1–12.

9. For example, see J Engel, R Blackwell, and P Minard, *Consumer Behavior*, 5th ed. (Hinsdale, IL: Dryden Press, 1986); P E Green, D S Tull, and G Albaum, *Research for Marketing Decisions*, 5th ed. (Englewood Cliffs, NJ: Prentice Hall, 1988); and D R Lehmann, *Market Research and Analysis*, 3rd ed. (Homewood, IL: Richard D. Irwin, 1989).

10. D Clausing, and J R Hauser, "The House of Quality," *Harvard Business Review*, May/June 1988.

11. G L Urban, and J R Hauser, *Design and Marketing of New Products* (Englewood Cliffs, NJ: Prentice Hall, 1980).

12. For example, see "Implementing Internal Quality Improvement with the House of Quality," by K N Gopalakrishnan, B E McIntyre, and J C Sprague, *Quality Progress*, September 1992, pp. 57–60; and "Quality Function Deployment," by L P Sullivan, *Quality Progress*, June 1986, pp. 39–50.

13. T Peters, *Thriving on Chaos: Handbook for a Management Revolution* (New York: Harper & Row, 1987), pp. 67–70.

Chapter 5   The Service Strategy Whirlpool

1. See the following books on strategy to review a sample of this knowledge base:

  a. R H Hayes, and S C Wheelwright, *Restoring Our Competitive Edge: Competing through Manufacturing* (New York: John Wiley & Sons, 1984).

  b. J L Heskett, *Managing in the Service Economy* (Boston, MA: Harvard Business School Press, 1986).

  c. T Hill, *Manufacturing Strategy: Text and Cases*, (Homewood, IL: Richard D. Irwin, 1989).

  d. R Normann, *Service Management: Strategy and Leadership in Service Businesses* (New York: John Wiley & Sons, 1984).

  e. M E Porter, ed., *Competition in Global Industries* (Boston, MA: Harvard Business School Press, 1986).

  f. ———, ed., *Competitive Strategy: Techniques for Analyzing Industries and Competitors* (New York: The Free Press, A division of Macmillan Publishing Co., Inc., 1980).

  g. J B Quinn, H Mintzberg, and R M James, *The Strategy Process* (Englewood Cliffs, NJ: Prentice Hall, 1988).

  h. W E Sasser, Jr., C W L Hart, and J L Heskett, *The Service Management Course: Cases and Readings* (New York: The Free Press, 1991).

  i. J L Heskett; W E Sasser, Jr.; and C W L Hart, *Service Breakthroughs—Changing the Rules of the Game* (New York: The Free Press, 1990).

2. "Where Did They Go Wrong?," *Business Week*, October 25, 1991, p. 38.

3. Hayes and Wheelright, *Restoring Our Competitive Edge*, p. 12.

4. W E Deming, *Management's Five Deadly Diseases*, guide accompanying the videocassette (Chicago, IL: Encyclopaedia Britannica Educational Corporation, 1984), pp. 1–4.

5. Ibid.

6. W E Deming, *Out of the Crisis*, Cambridge, MA: Massachusetts Institute of Technology, Center for Advanced Engineering Study, 1986), p. 98.

7. Porter, *Competition in Global Indusries* and *Competitive Strategy*.

8. D A Collier, "Broadway Pizza," *Service Management: The Automation of Services* (Englewood Cliffs, NJ: Prentice Hall, 1985), pp. 174–83.

9. Sasser et al., *The Service Management Course*; and Heskett et al., *Service Breakthroughs*.

10. E Langeard and P Eiglier, "Strategic Management of Service Development," in *Emerging Perspectives on Services Marketing*, ed. L L Berry, G L Shostack, and G D Upah (Chicago: American Marketing Association, 1983), pp. 68–72.

11. Langeard and Eiglier, *Strategic Management*, p. 68.

12. Ibid.

13. D A Collier, "Best Hotels, Inc." *Service Management: Operating Decisions* (Englewood Cliffs, NJ: Prentice Hall, 1987), pp. 274–91.

14. Langeard and Eigler, *Strategic Management*.

Chapter 6   Recent Service Strategy Ideas

1. Bernard H Booms, and Mary J Bitner, "Marketing Strategies and Organizational Structures for Service Firms," in *Marketing of Services*, eds. James H. Donnelly and William R George (Chicago: American Marketing Association, 1981), pp. 47–52; A J Magrath, "When Marketing Services, 4 P's Are Not Enough," *Business Horizons*, vol. 29, no. 3, May–June 1986, pp. 44–50; and D A Collier, "New Marketing Mix Stresses Service," *The Journal of Business Strategy*, March/April 1991, pp. 42–45.

2. D A Collier, "Process Moments of Trust: Analysis and Strategy," *The Service Industries Journal*, vol. 9, no. 2, April 1989, pp. 205–22.

3. G Stalk, Jr., and T M Hout, *Competing Against Time* (New York: The Free Press, 1990).

4. "Western Union Faces Inglorious End. Stop.," *The Columbus Dispatch*, Columbus, OH, April 15, 1991, p. 3C.

5. J L Heskett, W E Sasser, Jr., and C W L Hart, *Service Breakthroughs—Changing the Rules of the Game* (New York: The Free Press, 1990).

6. T Levitt, "Exploit the Product Life Cycle," *Harvard Business Review*, November–December, 1965; and W E Sasser, R P Olsen, and D D Wyckoff, *Management of Service Operations: Text, Cases and Readings* (Boston, MA: Allyn & Bacon, 1978), pp. 534–66.

7. E Langeard, and P Eiglier, "Strategic Management of Service Development," in *Emerging Perspectives on Services Marketing*, ed. L L Berry, G L Shostack, and G D Upah (Chicago: American Marketing Association, 1983), pp. 68–72.

8. Refer to Booms and Bitner; Magarth; and Collier (see footnote 1 in this chapter).

9. Refer to Collier, "Process Moments of Trust" (see footnote 2).

10. Ibid.

Chapter 7   Facility, Process, and Job Design

1. J D Blackburn, "Time-Based Competition: White-Collar Activities, *Business Horizons* 35, no. 4, July–August 1992, pp. 97–98.

2. Adam Smith, *The Wealth of Nations* (New York: Random House, 1937).

3. W E Sasser, R P Olson, and D D Wyckoff, *Management of Service Operations: Text, Cases, and Readings* (Boston, MA: Allyn & Bacon, Inc., 1978).

4. D A Collier, "Process Moments of Trust: Analysis and Strategy," *The Service Industries Journal* 9, no. 2, April 1989, pp. 205–22.

5. L J Krajewski and L P Ritzman, *Operations Management: Strategy and Analysis* (Reading, MA: Addison-Wesley, 1990); and James H Harrington, *Business Process Improvement* (New York: McGraw-Hill, 1991).

6. Lynn G Shostack, "Designing Services That Deliver," *Harvard Business Review*, January–February 1984, pp. 133–39; "Service Positioning Through Structural Change," *Journal of Marketing*, January 1987, pp. 34–43; "The Sins of Alfred Sloan," Paper presented at *The Quality in Services Symposium (QUIS II)*, GTE Executive Development Center, Norwalk, CT, July 8–11, 1990; and Shostack and J Kingman-Brundage, "How to Design a Service," chap. 14 in *The American Management Association Handbook of Marketing for the Service Industries*, (New York: American Management Association, AMACOM, 1991), pp. 243–61.

7. Shostack, "The Sins of Alfred Sloan."

8. See the sources listed in footnotes 5 and 6.

9. D A Collier, "Broadway Pizza," *Service Management: The Automation of Services* (Englewood Cliffs, NJ: Prentice Hall, 1985), pp. 174–83.

10. M Irvine, "LensCrafters: Using a Unique Service Strategy to Compete in the Optical Market," student paper in an Ohio State University MBA course on service management, Winter Quarter, 1991.

11. D A Collier, *Service Management: Operating Decisions* (Englewood Cliffs, NJ: Prentice Hall, 1987), p. 43.

12. "Burger King Adds Unleaded to Menu," *The Columbus Dispatch*, Columbus, OH, August 31, 1991, p. 2B.

13. J E G Bateson, "The Self-Service Customer—Empirical Results," in *Emerging Perspectives on Service Marketing*, ed. L L Berry, G L Shostack, and G D Upah, (Chicago, IL: American Marketing Association, 1983), pp. 50–53.

14. R W Hall, *Queueing Methods: For Services and Manufacturing* (Englewood Cliffs, NJ: Prentice Hall, 1991).

15. "How Disneyland Works," *Quality Progress*, July 1991, pp. 17–30.

16. Ibid., p. 19.

17. "Those Who Wait," *The Columbus Dispatch*, Columbus, OH, June 19, 1989, p. 2B.

18. R B Chase and D A Garvin, "The Service Factory," *Harvard Business Review*, July–August 1989, pp. 61–69.

19. Ibid., p. 66.

20. "Quality," *Business Week*, November 30, 1992, pp. 66–67.

Chapter 8   Organization and Performance Design

1. Two books that cover many of these issues are J Clemmer, *Firing on All Cylinders* (Homewood, IL: Business One Irwin, 1992); and R Zemke and C R Bell, *Service Wisdom* (Minneapolis, MN: Lakewood Books, 1990).

2. L J Krajewski and L P Ritzman, *Operations Management: Strategy and Analysis* (Reading, MA: Addison-Wesley, 1990), p. 6.

3. For a more comprehensive treatment of the pros and cons of functional organizational designs, see for example, R L Daft, *Organizational Theory and Design*, 3rd ed. (New York: West Publishing, 3rd ed.) 1989.

4. This general idea of organizational design has been around for some time, but I first saw it in writing and coupled with service management ideas in a paper by Lynn G Shostack, "The Sins of Alfred Sloan," presented at *The Quality In Services Symposium (QUIS II)*, GTE Executive Development Center, Norwalk, CT, July 8–11, 1990. Figure 8–2 is my version of a service management approach to organizational design.

5. For example, see D E Bowen, R B Chase, T G Cummings, and Associates, *Service Management Effectiveness* (San Francisco: Jossey-Bass, 1990); or T S Bateman and C P Zeithaml *Management: Function and Strategy* (Homewood, IL: Richard D. Irwin, 1990).

6. R Zemke and D Schaaf "Beth Israel Hospital," *The Service Edge: 101 Companies That Profit from Customer Care* (New York: NAL Books, New American Library, 1989), p. 150.

7. "Absolutely, Positively Quality," *Quality Progress*, May 1990, p. 25.

8. B Schneider and D E Bowen, "New Services Design, Development, and Implementation and the Employee," in *Developing New Services*, ed. W R George and C E Marshall (Chicago: American Marketing Association, 1984), pp. 82–101.

9. Ibid., p. 86.

Chapter 9   Service Innovations

1. T Peters and N Austin, *A Passion for Excellence*, (New York: Warner Books, 1985), p. 4–5.

2. B R Guile and J B Quinn, *Technology in Services: Policies for Growth, Trade, and Employment* (Washington, DC: National Academy Press, 1988).

3. D A Collier, "The Service Sector Revolution: The Automation of Services," *Long Range Planning*, 16, no. 6, 1983, pp. 10–20.

4. D A Collier, *Service Management: The Automation of Services* (Englewood Cliffs, NJ: Prentice Hall, 1985).

5. *Webster's Third New International Dictionary* (Springfield, MA: G & C. Merriam Co., 1964), p. 148.·

6. Ibid., p. 2348.

7. Ibid., p. 1166.

8. J B Quinn, "Technological Innovation, Entrepreneurship, and Strategy," *Sloan Management Review*, Spring 1979, pp. 19–29.

9. "R&D Scoreboard—In the Labs, the Fight to Spend Less, Get More," *Business Week*, June 28, 1993, pp. 102–27.

10. C A Amatos, "Huntington Hopes Customers Get Smart," *The Columbus Dispatch*, Columbus, OH, October 2, 1991, p. 1F.

11. "Carla Hills, Trade Warrior," *Business Week*, January 22, 1990, p. 52.

12. S Shirley, "A Company Without Offices," *Harvard Business Review* 64, no. 1, January/February 1986, pp. 127.

13. Collier, "The Service Sector Revolution," and *Service Management*.

14. M Trust, "1000 Hours to Market," *A Summary of Proceedings at the Sixth Biennial W. Arthur Cullman Symposium on "Manufacturing Excellence: Strategies for the 21st Century"* (Columbus, OH: The Ohio State University, College of Business, May 20, 1992), p. 17.

15. S S Roach, "Technology and the Services Sector: America's Hidden Competitive Challenge," in *Technology in Services*, ed. B R Guile and J B Quinn (Washington, DC: National Academy Press, 1988), pp. 127–29.

16. Ibid., p. 133–34.

17. Ibid., p. 118.

18. D Wessel, "With Labor Scarce, Service Firms Strive to Raise Productivity," *The Wall Street Journal*, June 1, 1989, p. A22.

19. "The Technology Payoff," *Business Week*, June 14, 1993, p. 58.

20. Ibid.

21. "Winners: The Best Product Designs of the Year," *Business Week*, June 8, 1992, pp. 52–68.

Chapter 10   Service/Quality Definition, Design, and Approach

1. D A Garvin, *Managing Quality* (New York: The Free Press, 1988).

2. D A Collier, *Service Management: The Automation of Services* (Englewood Cliffs, NJ: Prentice Hall, 1985), pp. 1–15.

3. A Parasuraman, V A Zeithaml, and L L Berry, "A Conceptual Model of Service/Quality and Its Implications for Future Research," *Journal of Marketing*, Fall 1985, vol. 49, pp. 41–50.

4. R C Lewis and B H Booms, "The Marketing Aspects of Service Quality," in *Emerging Perspectives on Service Marketing* ed. L L Berry (Chicago: American Marketing Association, 1983), pp. 99–104.

5. Lewis and Booms "The Marketing Aspects of Service Quality," See also V A Zeithaml, A Parasuraman, and L L Berry, *Delivering Quality Service* (New York, The Free Press, 1990), pp. 24–26; and L L Berry and A Parasuraman, *Marketing Services* (New York, The Free Press, 1991).

6. Zeithaml et al., *Delivering Quality Service*, pp. 25–26.

7. Maj-Britt Hedvall and Mikael Paltschik, "Intrinsic Service Quality Determinants for Pharmacy Customers, *International Journal of Service Industry Management* 2, no. 2, 1991, pp. 38–48.

8. E Babakus and G W Boller, "An Emprical Assessment of SERVQUAL," *Journal of Business Research*, 24, no. 3, May 1992, pp. 253–68; T Mersha and V Adlakha, "Attributes of Service Quality: The Consumers' Perspective," *International Journal of Service Industry Management* 3, no. 3, 1992, pp. 34–45; and M Bouman and Ton van der Wiele, "Measuring Service Quality in the Car Service industry: Building and Testing an Instrument," *International Journal of Service Industry Management* 3, no. 4, 1992, pp. 4–16.

9. A Parasuraman, L L Berry, and V A Zeithaml, "Refinement and Reassessment of the SERVQUAL Scale," *Journal of Retailing* 67, 1991, pp. 421–50.

10. J Wind, P E Green, D Shifflet, and M Scarbrough, "Courtyard by Marriott: Designing a Hotel Facility with Consumer-Based Marketing Models," *Interfaces* 19, no. 1, January–February 1989, pp. 25–47.

11. J Ryan, "Quality: A Job with Many Vacancies," *Quality Progress*, November 1990, p. 24.

12. "Domino's Pizza, Inc.," *Profiles in Quality* (Boston, MA: Allyn & Bacon, Bureau of Business Practice, 1991), p. 92.

13. Ibid., 91–92.

14. "First National Bank of Chicago," *Profiles in Quality* (Boston, MA: Allyn & Bacon, Bureau of Business Practice, 1991), p. 18–19.

Chapter 11   Service/Quality Measurement, Control and Analysis

1. J R Evans and W M Lindsay, *The Management and Control of Quality* (St. Paul, MN: West Publishing, 1989); J M Juran and F M Gryna, *Quality Planning and Analysis*, (New York: McGraw-Hill, 1980); A C Rosander, *Applications of Quality Control in the Service Industries* (New York: Marcel Dekker, Inc., and Milwaukee, WI: ASQC Quality Press, 1985); and H Gitlow, S Gitlow, A Oppenheim, and R Oppenheim, *Tools and Methods for the Improvement of Quality* (Homewood, IL: Richard D. Irwin, 1989).

2. James H Harrington, *Business Process Improvement* (New York: McGraw-Hill, 1991).

3. Lynn G Shostack, "Designing Services That Deliver," *Harvard Business Review*, January–February 1984, pp. 133–39; Lynn G Shostack, "Service Positioning Through Structural Change," *Journal of Marketing*, January 1987, pp. 34–43; Lynn G Shostack, "The Sins of Alfred Sloan," paper presented at *The Quality in Services Symposium (QUIS II)*, GTE Executive Development Center, Norwalk, CT, July 8–11, 1990; and Lynn G Shostack and J Kingman-Brundage, "How to Design a Service," *The American Marketing Association*

Handbook of Marketing for the Service Industries (New York: AMACOM, a division of the American Marketing Association, 1991), pp. 243–61.

4. C A Aubrey and P K Felkins, *Teamwork: Involving People in Quality and Productivity Improvement* (Milwaukee, WI: Quality Press, 1988); and O L Crocker, S Charney, and J S L Chiu, *Quality Circles*, New American Library (New York: Methuen Publications, 1984).

5. R W Hall, *Queuing Methods* (Englewood Cliffs, NJ: Prentice Hall, 1991).

6. D A Dillman, *Mail and Telephone Surveys: The Total Design Method* (New York: John Wiley & Sons, 1978).

7. Ibid.

8. Robert C Camp, *Benchmarking: The Search for Industry Best Practices that Lead to Superior Performance* (Milwaukee, WI: ASQC Quality Press, 1989).

9. Ibid., p. 10.

10. Ibid., p. 12–13.

11. John A Miller, "Measuring Progress Through Benchmarking," *CMA Magazine*, vol. 66, no. 4 (May 1992), p. 37.

12. M Norman and B Stoker, *Data Envelopment Analysis: The Assessment of Performance* (New York: John Wiley & Sons, 1991).

13. D A Collier and J E Storbeck, "A Data Envelopment Analysis Approach to Benchmarking in the Telecommunications Industry" (under review), November 1992; J E Storbeck and D A Collier, "Using Data Envelopment Analysis to Assess Continuous Improvement" (in progress), October 1993; D A Collier and J E Storbeck, "Monitoring of Continuous Improvement Performance Using Data Envelopment Analysis," *1993 National Meeting and Proceedings of the Decision Sciences Institute*, November 21–23, 1992, Washington, DC.; J E Storbeck and D A Collier, "A New Approach to Benchmarking" Proceedings of the 48th Annual ASQC Quality Congress, May 24–26, 1994 (under review). Las Vegas, NV.

14. Storbeck and Collier, "Using Data Envelopment Analysis"; and Collier and Storbeck, "Monitoring of Continuous Improvement Performance."

15. *LISREL*, 4th ed., version VI (Mooresville, IN: Scientific Software, Inc., 1986); and R P McDonald, *Factor Analysis and Related Methods* (Hillsdale, NJ: Lawrence Erlbaum Associates, 1985).

16. K Dehnad, *Quality Control, Robust Design, and the Taguchi Method* (Pacific Grove, CA: Wadsworth and Brooks/Cole, 1989).

17. *Blueprints for Service Quality—The Federal Express Approach* (New York: American Management Association, 1991), p. 30.

18. T K Baker, "Heuristics for Overbooking and Allocating Hotel Rooms Across Customer Categories," Ph.D. Dissertation, The Ohio State University, Department of Management Sciences, Columbus, OH (forthcoming Spring 1994).

Chapter 12 Service/Quality Standards and Performance

1. "Parking Ticket Spat Costs Bank a Million," *The Columbus Dispatch*, Columbus, OH, February 2, 1989, p. D1.

2. J Campanella, ed. *Principles of Quality Costs*, 2nd ed. (Milwaukee, WI: ASQC Quality Press, 1990); H James Harrington, *The Quality/Profit Connection*, (Milwaukee: WI: ASQC American Quality Press, 1989); and A C Rosander, *The Quest for Quality in Services* (White Plains, NY: Quality Press, and Milwaukee, WI: Quality Resources, 1989).

3. L W Phillips, D R Chang, and R D Buzzell, "Product Quality, Cost Position and Business Performance: A Test of Key Hypotheses," *Journal of Marketing* 47, Spring 1983, pp. 26–43; F F Reichheld and W E Sasser, Jr., "Zero Defections: Quality Comes to Services," *Harvard Business Review*, September–October 1990, pp. 105–11; and A V Roth and M Van der Velde, *World-Class Banking—Benchmarking the Strategies of Retail Banking Leaders*, Bank Administration Institute, The Center for Banking Excellence, 1992.

4. A V Freigenbaum, *Total Quality Control* (New York: McGraw-Hill, 1961), pp. 85–106.

5. P B Crosby, *Quality Is Free* (New York: NAL Penguin, 1979), pp. 15–16.

6. J M Groocock, *The Chain of Quality—Market Dominance Through Product Superiority* (New York: John Wiley & Sons, 1986), p. 254.

7. *Quality*, Newsletter #6 (Winter Park, FL: The Quality College, 1981), p. 2.

8. *American Competitiveness Study: Characteristics of Success*, no. 58059 (New York: Ernst & Young, 1990), pp. 1–53.

9. Ibid., p. 40.

10. The source of this quote is an anonymous reviewer for this book who works for a major US accounting and consulting firm.

11. "Customer Satisfaction Standards—Service and Sales Standards," a card given to customers by Ford Motor Company dealerships stating the mission statement and standards of performance for sales and service. Ford Motor Company Dearborn, MI, 1992.

12. D A Dillman, *Mail and Telephone Surveys: The Total Design Method* (New York: John Wiley & Sons, 1978).

13. "No. 1—And Trying Harder," *Business Week*, October 25, 1991, p. 24.

14. Detailed explanations of process capability can be found, for example, in *Managing for World-Class Quality*, ed. E S Shecter, (New York: Marcel Dekker, Inc.; and Milwaukee, WI: ASQC Quality Press, 1992), pp. 97–119; and J J Pignatiello, Jr., and J S Ramburg, "Process Capability Indices: Just Say "No!" *Proceedings of the 1993 ASQC Quality Congress*, 47th Annual Quality Congress, Boston, MA, May 24–26, 1993, pp. 92–104.

15. *Managing for World-Class Quality*, ed. E S Shecter, p. 108.

16. "Going for the Glory," *Business Week*, October 25, 1991, p. 60.

Chapter 13 A Service Management Approach to Implementation

1. "Quality: A Job with Many Vacancies," *Quality Progress*, 23, no. 11 (November 1990), pp. 23–26.
2. Ibid., p. 23.
3. Ibid., p. 25.
4. *International Quality Study—Banking Industry Report*, A joint project of the American Quality Foundation and Ernst & Young, Cleveland, OH, 1992, p. 42.
5. "Beyond May I Help You?" *Business Week*, October 25, 1991, p. 100.
6. Philip B Crosby, *Quality Is Free* (New York: McGraw-Hill, 1979); W Edward Deming, *Quality, Productivity, and Competitive Position* (Cambridge, MA: Massachusetts Institute of Technology, Center for Advanced Engineering Study, 1982); and J M Juran, *Juran on Planning for Quality* (New York: The Free Press, 1988).
7. The implementation guidelines defined here are a major revision of the ideas contained in the article "The Customer Service and Quality Challenge," by David A. Collier, *The Service Industries Journal*, vol. 7, no. 1, January 1987. Reprinted in D A Collier, *Service Management: Operating Decisions* (Englewood Cliffs, NJ: Prentice Hall, 1987). Also reprinted in *Managing Service Quality— An IFS Executive Briefing*, ed. Graham Clark (Kempston, Bedford, UK: IFS Executive Briefing Series, IFS Ltd., 1990).
8. K Bemowski, "Closing the Gap," *Quality Progress*, November 1990, pp. 17.
9. *International Quality Study—The Definitive Study of the Best International Quality Management Practices*, joint project of the American Quality Foundation and Ernst & Young, Cleveland, OH, 1991, p. 15.
10. Ibid., p. 17.
11. For example, see D L McLaurin and S Bell, "Open Communication Lines Before Attempting Total Quality," *Quality Progress*, June 1991, pp. 25–28; and G H Labovitz and Y S Chang, "Learn from the Best," *Quality Progress*, May 1990, pp. 81–85.
12. *Best Practices Report—The International Quality Study*, a Joint Project of Ernst & Young and the American Quality Foundation, 1600 Huntington Building, Cleveland, OH, 1992.

Chapter 14 Introduction to Interlinking

1. D A Collier, "The Customer Service and Quality Challenge," *The Service Industries Journal*, 7, no. 1, January 1987. Reprinted in D A Collier, *Service Management: Operating Decisions* (Englewood Cliffs, NJ: Prentice Hall, 1987). Also reprinted in *Managing Service Quality—An IFS Executive Briefing*,

ed. Graham Clark (Kempston, Bedford, UK: IFS Executive Briefing Series, IFS Ltd., 1990). Also see D A Collier, "Evaluating Marketing and Operations Service Quality Information—A Preliminary Report," Chapter 10 in *Service Quality—Multidisciplinary and Multinational Perspectives*, ed. S W Brown, E Gummesson, B Edvardsson, and B Gusavsson (Lexington, MA: D.C. Heath, 1991), pp. 143–56; D A Collier, "Measuring and Managing Service Quality," chap. 10 in *Service Management Effectiveness*, ed. D E Bowen, R D Chase, and T G Cummings (San Francisco: Jossey-Bass, 1990), pp. 234–65; D A Collier, "A Service Quality Process Map for Credit Card Processing," *Decision Sciences* 22, no. 2, Spring 1991, pp. 406–20; and D A Collier, "Interlinking Internal and External Performance," *Proceedings of the 1993 ASQC Quality Congress*, 47th Annual Quality Congress, Boston, MA, May 24–26, 1993.

2. J D Gibbons, *Nonparametric Methods for Quantitative Analysis* (New York: Holt, Rinehart & Winston, 1976).

3. *LISREL*, 4th ed., version VI (Mooresville, IN: Scientific Software, Inc., 1986).

4. P E Green and Y Wind, "New Way to Measure Consumer's Judgments," *Harvard Business Review* 53, July–August 1975, pp. 107–17; and R K Teas and W L Dellva, "Conjoint Measurement of Consumers' Preferences for Multiattribute Financial Services," *Journal of Bank Research* 16, pp. 99–112.

5. *SAS/ETS User's Guide*, version 5 (Cary, NC: SAS Institute Inc., SAS Circle, 1985).

6. R P McDonald, *Factor Analysis and Related Methods* (Hillsdale, NJ: Lawrence Erlbaum Associates, 1985).

7. K Dehnad, *Quality Control, Robust Design, and the Taguchi Method* (Pacific Grove, CA: Wadesworth & Brooks/Cole, Advanced Books & Software, 1989).

8. *1993 Award Criteria*, Malcolm Baldrige National Quality Award (Gaithersburg, MD: National Institute of Standards and Technology, 1993), p. 19.

9. C Gronroos, "A Service Quality Model and Its Marketing Implications," In *Managing Service Quality—An IFS Executive Briefing*, ed. Graham Clark (Kempston, Bedford, UK: IFS Executive Briefing Series, IFS Ltd., 1990), pp. 13–18.

10. "Chipping Away at No. 1: Long-Distance Competitors Find More Footholds," *The Columbus Dispatch*, Columbus, OH July 3, 1988, p. G1.

Chapter 15   Interlinking: Service/Quality Process Maps

1. *American Banker 1986 Survey*, "How Consumer America Views the Changing Financial Services Industry," *American Banker Magazine*, 1986, p. 6.

2. A V Roth and M van der Velde, *The Future of Retail Banking Delivery Systems* (Rolling Meadows, IL: Bank Administration Institute, 1988), p. xix.

3. D A Collier, "Evaluating Marketing and Operations Service Quality Information," paper presented at the *Quality in Services Symposium 1*, University of

Karlstad, Karlstad, Sweden, August 14–17, 1988. A revised version of this paper "Evaluating Marketing and Operations Service Quality Information—A Preliminary Report," was published as Chapter 10 of *Service Quality—Multidisciplinary and Multinational Perspectives*, ed. S W Brown, E Gummesson, B Edvardsson, and B Gusavsson (Lexington, MA: D C Heath, 1991), pp. 143–56. Also see D A Collier, "Service Quality Process Maps: The Power of Sensitivity Analysis," *Proceedings of the National Decision Science Institute*, New Orleans, November 20–22, 1989; D A Collier, "Measuring and Managing Service Quality," chap. 10 in *Service Management Effectiveness: An Inter-Disciplinary, Perspective*, ed. D E Bowen, R B Chase, and T G Cummings (San Francisco: Jossey-Bass, 1990), pp. 234–65; D A Collier, "Telephone Repair Service Performance," Paper presented at the *Quality in Services Symposium II*, GTE Executive Development Center, Norwalk, CT, July 8–11, 1990; and D A Collier, "A Service Quality Process Map for Credit Card Processing," *Decision Sciences*, vol. 22, no. 2, Spring 1991, pp. 406–20.

4. Roth and van der Velde, *The Future of Retail Banking*; and W E Sasser, Jr., and F F Reichheld, "Zero Defections: Quality Comes to Services," *Harvard Business Review*, September–October 1990, pp. 105–11.

5. Collier, "A Service Quality Process Map." Also see K G Joreskog and D Sorborn, *LISREL*, 4th ed., version VI (Mooresville, IN: Scientific Software, Inc., January 1986); and J S Long, *Covariance Structure Models: An Introduction to LISREL*, 4th printing (Beverly Hills, CA: Sage Publications, 1987).

Chapter 16   Service Encounter Management

1. C L Johnson, "1,000 Hours to Market," *A Summary of Proceedings at the Sixth Biennial W. Arthur Cullman Symposium* on "Manufacturing Excellence: Strategies for the 21st Century," The Ohio State University, College of Business, Columbus, OH, May 20, 1992, p. 16.

2. "Dinosaurs? IBM, Sears, and GM," *Fortune*, May 3, 1993, pp. 36–42.

3. "Extending Life Raises Hopes, Fears," *The Columbus Dispatch*, Columbus, OH, February 2, 1992, p. 6E.

4. "Beyond May I Help You?," *Business Week*, October 25, 1991, p. 102.

5. *International Quality Study—Banking Industry Report* (Cleveland, OH: Ernst & Young and the American Quality Foundation, 1992), p. 36.

6. *International Quality Study—The Definitive Study of the Best International Quality Management Practices* (Cleveland, OH: Ernst & Young and the American Quality Foundation, 1991), p. 26.

7. H J Harrington, "Closing Remarks," a Summary of Proceedings at the Sixth Biennial W. Arthur Cullman Symposium on "Manufacturing Excellence: Strategies for the 21st Century," The Ohio State University, College of Business, Columbus, OH, May 20, 1992, p. 26.

8. "Beyond May I Help You?," *Business Week*, October 25, 1991, p. 100.

9. "Shoe Buyers Move to Nike Town," *The Columbus Dispatch*, Columbus, OH, August 1, 1991, p. 2B.

10. "A Report of The Total Quality Leadership Steering Committee and Working Councils," The Procter & Gamble Company, Cincinnati, OH, November 1992.

11. "Readin', Writin', and Reform," *Business Week*, October 25, 1991, p. 142.

12. *ON Q*, vol. VII, no. 5 (May 1992), p. 1–2 (official ASQC newsletter).

13. "Industrial Policy," *Business Week*, April 6, 1992, pp. 70–76.

14. "Services Under Siege—The Restructuring Imperative," *Harvard Business Review*, September–October 1991, pp. 82–91.

15. "Less Buying Power a Problem: Thurow," *The Columbus Dispatch*, Columbus, OH, January 19, 1993, p. D1.

Index